Tiger In The Attic

To Mrs. Wood
with very best wishes
Christmas 1994

A.R. Sylvester

Tiger In The Attic

A. R. Sylvester

The Pentland Press Limited
Edinburgh • Cambridge • Durham

To Chas & George

First published in 1994 by
The Pentland Press Ltd.
1 Hutton Close
South Church
Bishop Auckland
Durham

ISBN 1 85821 232 4

Typeset by CBS, Felixstowe, Suffolk
Printed and bound by Antony Rowe Ltd., Chippenham

Contents

HOME FROM HOME

I suppose the outcome was inevitable really. It couldn't have been easy for a man on his own to raise children in the early thirties – or any other time come to that – what with the recession and everything of those times. And so it was that, some time before my Mother died, I was placed in the care of the local authority. Children's Homes, that is. My two brothers – both older than me – shared this fate, but apart from a short period at the outset we seldom saw each other. George, my elder by almost three years, was placed next door, whilst Chas, nearly five years my senior, was put in with me. Shortly afterwards Chas was moved to a third 'Home', leaving us all separated. I don't recall seeing either of them very much, until the outbreak of war in 1939.

The 'Homes' were tall urban villas whose rooms were large, with very high ceilings and wainscoting practically up to your knees. I'm not sure of my age at that time but this is my very earliest clear recollection, so I would guess about four or five. Our Home was mixed – girls sleeping quarters at the front of the house – boys at the back, with the room occupied by our 'House Mother' in between, as was the bathroom and W.C. We numbered about eighteen in total I think, yet all the girls fitted comfortably into one room, all the boys into another. Our room had two rows of beds, one down each side. Although these homes were run on very strict lines, with harsh discipline and painful punishment, they were impeccably clean – a condition to which we ourselves largely contributed – as we each had our allotted chores. And woe betide anyone who fell below standard.

The floor of our room shone like glass from constant polishing, and I loved it when we had to take down the long curtains for their periodic cleaning. I think we had three windows, and us boys would take a curtain each, fold it from side to side till it measured seven or eight inches in width, then lay it on the floor. Standing on it about two feet from the end, we then lifted that end up, thus forming a scooter. Up and down we whizzed, in the gangway between the beds. No wonder that floor gleamed. It was naughty, I know, but this sport took some of the sting out of the polishing. And the curtains were going off for cleaning anyway.

Chores covered everything but washing and cooking. The local laundry would

1

have taken care of the former, though I can't be sure now as to whether the clothes were ironed – they seemed a bit rough on your skin sometimes – but I expect they were really. All the vegetables were prepared by us, but I think that's as far as we went with food. The housework was all down to us though, boys and girls all scrubbing, scouring and polishing side by side. We each had our own specific jobs, though now and again we were swapped about a bit.

I did silver-polishing, which I quite liked, and oddly enough there seemed to be a fair amount of it, including all the very best cutlery, which wasn't of course used by the inmates. Then there was grate-cleaning and re-laying. This was a cold, knuckle-knocking job which I didn't much like, although I loved the smell of the coal and the lovely chopped wood.

First off there was the ash to shovel out from yesterday's fire and take out to the dustbin in the back garden. Then – having swept thoroughly all round the grate and hearth – all the front had to be black-leaded, and this was when my knuckles used to go through it! The brush was a nice shape, oval, with a handle coming up off the back, and I can't imagine now how that handle didn't protect my knuckles more than it did. Perhaps I was a bit clumsy at that young age. But the end result was very gratifying for not only did the grate look good, it smelt good too.

Then came the laying up – with newspaper and kindling wood, the former lightly crumpled, the wood laid criss-cross on top like layers of lattice-work. Next the coal, though only a modest amount at this stage so as not to weigh down too heavily and close all the air passages in the kindling.

By this time of course my hands were quite cold, for there was no other form of heating in the house, so it was a moment of great pleasure when I struck the match and put it to the paper. The wood flared and crackled as the flame spread quickly through it, and the sensation of warmth was instant as I knelt up close. I'd linger thus for a while – somewhat mesmerised – then realise that the big old coal scuttle needed filling up from the coal shed out back. So I'd be all cold again as I struggled back in with it! A polish up of the fender with 'Brasso' or somesuch and that was the job 'jobbed' – short of adding more coal once the first few lumps had taken. I think I would probably have enjoyed this daily job more had it not been quite so early in the morning – or so cold – for as I say, I really did love all the smells attached to it. Except perhaps, the ash.

By contrast, the conditions under which I did the silver-polishing were quite cosy. This wasn't done every day of course, rather once a week – or once every month perhaps. I did this sitting at the big table in the front room, where, if it was winter time, I would already have lit the fire much earlier. So it was both warm and comfortable doing this job.

As I say, there seemed to be a remarkable amount of silver – for an establishment of that sort – although I suppose most of the cheaper materials we might have used today would have been developed *since* those times. This was again a most gratifying job, seeing the beautiful deep shine of each finished article, further enhanced by the reflected flicker from the lovely warm hearth. Then there was the fun side of it – my own 'Hall of Mirrors'. I'd chuckle as I looked at my distorted reflection – especially in some of the spoons!

I also lifted rugs and mats and took them out into the back garden, where I threw them over the clothes line and beat them. It also fell to me to clean the outside lavatory, and – the job I liked least of all , shoe cleaning. I came to really loathe that job, well parts of it anyway, yet I think I was stuck with it for the whole of the time I was there.

Each afternoon on returning from school, everyone left their shoes, or boots in the kitchen. These I had to clean in readiness for the next day. I didn't mind the actual cleaning of them really, in fact I *adored* the smell of the Cherry-Blossom and Nugget boot polish. And I soon learned how to get a really good shine on them – never forgetting the in-step of course – before they were inspected by 'Mother'. No – the part I hated was having to make the decision as to their state of repair. Out of about eighteen pairs there weren't many days when I didn't find some in need of attention. And I truly did live in dread of the next bit, for I then had to go all the way up into the attic to fetch repaired replacements, and what a frightening place that was!

You never actually had your *own* shoes, the thing to do was to get down early each morning and find two that felt reasonably comfortable, especially if you'd had to hobble all the previous day. So each day began with a muted kind of tumult in the kitchen as we all fought it out. When you found a pair that seemed to fit quite well it was wise to put your mark on them for next time. Even then you needed to mark them both, as they seldom stayed in pairs. Some kids must have had pretty odd feet, for the last one down was often confronted by two boots – or shoes – of different sizes. 'Last come – worst served'. Although I can't actually recall anyone being left with two of the same side – either both left or both right! If you lost the pair you'd marked – even for one day – their shape had been altered by someone else's feet and they were never quite the same. Heaven would be to go off to school with both feet comfortable. But none of these tussles would, of course, be within earshot of 'Mother'.

That attic was reached by a second flight of stairs, which led up from the first floor landing. There was a door at the top of those stairs, and as I stood at the foot, looking up into the murky gloom, my imagination would run wild, filling me with absolute dread. I was my own worst enemy I suppose, for I should have boldly marched straight up those stairs and got on with it. But I used to stand there thinking about it, convinced I could hear all kinds of awful sounds coming from beyond that door. But there was no skipping it, that was my job and I had to do it. But I had many a nightmare about that room I can tell you. I really had to brace myself to climb those stairs and open that door.

In keeping with the rest of the house, it was a very large room, but poorly lit. And to a mite like me – 'five eighths of bugger all' as they say – extremely spooky. I can't remember now what else may have been kept up there, but all the repaired boots and shoes were arranged, in their various sizes, on a long tall wooden rack, which ran right down the centre. The ceiling seemed to slope in all directions and because of the very dim lighting, there appeared to be little cave-like nooks and crannies everywhere, all dark and sinister. As I moved along the rack, looking for the boots or shoes I'd come up for, my shadow passed across these fearful places and I was certain I could see things moving. Eyes glinting too! Wild animals I was sure – ghosts too, probably.

I remember reading – or more likely having read to me at that time – a jungle story. In this story the author came upon a small tent, deep in the interior, which appeared to be deserted. He moved cautiously toward the tent, having heard that a man-eating tiger had recently been spotted in the area, or signs of it at least. Outside the tent, in the long grass, he stumbled over something which turned out to be the body of a man, who had obviously been attacked and killed by this tiger. In my young imagination, a body was just a torso – no head, no limbs. And I visualised this huge, striped, sabre-toothed creature slinking stealthily through the undergrowth, licking smugly at its jowls, its stomach bulging with the head, legs and arms of its victim. It made a terrifying picture in my mind, which featured regularly in my nightmares. So whenever I saw a movement in the shadows – up there in that attic – I fully expected to be leapt upon by this fearsome tiger, and eaten alive!

Quite often the size-marking on the footwear would become obscure with wear, making selection difficult. I would measure the distance to the door, mentally of course, then with one last, cautious look at those evil shadows, grab quickly at the shoes, and with heart pounding furiously, hurl myself toward the door. Once safely through it I'd rush pell-mell down the two flights of stairs that led back to civilisation, and safety! I really did get worked up over this business and would be all-of-a-tremble by the time I made it back to the kitchen. Only to find that in my haste I'd sometimes grabbed the wrong size, or picked boots instead of shoes. Can you possibly imagine my terror as I had to go all the way back up again to change them? I can't believe now that I did it. But I did.

Washing up, drying up and putting away. Not a popular chore normally, but when 'Mother' had guests to dinner – well – that was quite different. This of course was when that silver that I loved polishing came out. The scraps they left on their plates were often very tasty – bacon rinds for example – and empty baked potato jackets. Perhaps a few peas or runner beans. Then there were suddenly lots of willing hands, and what scuffles took place! Scraps for scraps I suppose you might say.

So much for chores. There was one particular day in the year when, first thing in the morning, the whole place was absolutely awash with excitement. The promise of that day was such that old animosities were dropped, enemies became friends, and you could have hugged anyone. Even 'Mother'! It was the annual holiday.

We didn't go out much normally, just a visit to the local recreation ground some Saturday afternoons. This was in a very orderly manner, marching in two's and in the charge of the eldest girl. Girls always held positions of responsibility in such circumstances – as the age of senior girls was always much higher than that of the boys – for when boys reached about eleven or twelve they were moved on to an all boys home, as in the case of brother Chas. This would have been for obvious reasons – though these weren't clear to me at the time, being so young – but I do know we very much resented being bossed around by girls!! We must have broken ranks now and again though as I remember making daisy chains and things, (remember, I was only a tot!) and checking our liking for butter by holding buttercups under our smooth chins. And I was fascinated by the colour of the pink clover. We always attracted quizzical, sometimes sneering looks and taunts from the 'normal' kids as we maintained our well-disciplined order. That's the way kids are, and always will be I guess.

But on this day there was nothing like that. The excitement was there the minute you opened your eyes, but began to intensify with the issue of new clothing. I can't remember what the girls had, but us boys had new tunic shirts, new trousers, (which were always short-legged, even senior boys wore short trousers) new socks, and, something which we never wore at any other time – plimsolls. I don't know what happened to them once the holiday was over – perhaps we wore them out – but I can remember the wonderful smell of them now, especially once they'd had lots of sand and seaweed in them. As soon as we put them on we all wanted to run everywhere. And another once-a-year item was the belt. Normally we all wore braces, which went through loops in your underpants before going onto the buttons of your trouser waistband. It was all buttons then of course, no zips. But now – joy of joys – for the next two weeks every boy could strut around with his own belt. They were the simple, elasticated type, three coloured bands and a snake fastener. There was also a slide on them for adjustment. This really was living........ Weren't we just the cat's whiskers!

Those shirts by the way were of a fairly coarse, grey material, and boy, did they itch! They were terrible at first really, but such was the joy of everything else that you soon accepted that discomfort. The end justified the means. So once we'd swapped these new clothes about until all were reasonably suited, we washed, made our beds, dressed ourselves in these grand new (if itchy) clothes, and went down to breakfast.

As we descended the stairs, there in the hall stood a huge wicker hamper, which I expect was a laundry basket really. The lid was up, waiting for the last few items to be packed, and it was like an Aladdin's Cave. Amongst other things there were striped swimming costumes and plain ones, (albeit with legs down to your knees and broad shoulder straps) short-sleeved coloured shirts – that did *not* itch, off-white sun hats with a floppy brim all round – which us little ones had to wear on the beach and kids nowadays wouldn't be seen dead in, and most exciting of all – buckets and spades.

Those two final items still bore the magical smells of last year's holiday and stirred you up almost to fever pitch. By today's standards the buckets were quite heavy, being of sturdy metal construction. Not a bit of plastic anywhere. They were gaily painted – all in different colours – with animals, flowers, and scenes of happy children at play. And because of their construction, they had seams, and here of course was where those wonderful smells were trapped. One sniff and you were practically on the beach. The spades too were quite sturdy, most of them being made from a single piece of wood, with a D shaped handle. I remember a few though, whose main part was made of metal, with just the shaft and T shaped handle made from wood. These certainly sliced into the sand better.

After breakfast we cleared away and washed up as usual – then it all began. A charabanc arrived, the hamper was strapped down and loaded, followed by all us kids, each of us striving to position ourselves up front, though it didn't matter that much really – just as long as we were going. We arrived at the railway station and were transferred onto a super, green-painted steam train whose sides proudly bore the words, in gold lettering if I remember correctly, '*SOUTHERN RAILWAY*'. Other charabancs were arriving at the same time as ours, and each disgorged cargoes of similarly dressed and excited children from other homes, boys all scratching at their shirts. I used to keep my eyes open for my two brothers but didn't usually see them until we were there, at the camp.

I very much enjoyed the journey on the charabanc as this was about the only time we travelled anywhere that wasn't on foot. The train journey was even better. Our House-Mother always carried a jar of boiled sweets on this occasion, to be shared out amongst us on the journey, and this was a treat in itself. We were allowed to move about a little on the journey and I was always fascinated by the names of the little stations we passed through. We were only going to Dymchurch, but it seemed to us as though we were on safari in Africa. The feel of the wind and the smell of the smoke from the engine as you put your head out of the window was wonderful. And I loved all the hoardings advertising Oxydol, Rinso, Craven A, Bisto, Park Drive etc. And of course, those lovely little machines that gave you a whole bar of Nestle's Milk Chocolate for one penny were extremely inviting, not that we had any money at the time. These machines were to be found on most station platforms. And who remembers 'Kolynos' toothpaste – or did that come a little later?

The camp itself was made up of several largish dormitories, with stone floors. The washing facilities, if I remember correctly, were in separate buildings of similar construction – brick walls and stone floors. I don't recall us having hot water, but I'm sure we must have had. We slept on camp beds, the old-fashioned kind with two wooden side rails supporting a piece of canvas, on folding legs. One row down each side of the dormitory.

Last thing at night – probably about 9 p.m. – cake and cocoa were brought round to us all. In bed! This really was a treat, but I'm afraid we abused it on one occasion. It was always lovely rich fruit cake and each of us received a sizeable slab with our mug of delicious cocoa. One night somebody discovered that if you lightly broke up the cake in your mouth, shaped your lips a little wider than you would to whistle, then blew – you could really pepper your neighbour. He of course retaliated, and in no time at all the whole dormitory was a mass of flying cake pellets, with everyone joining in. What a dreadful thing to do. But what fun!

We did that only once though, for had we dared to repeat the performance, this privilege would most certainly have been withdrawn. We had no sheets on the beds, just blankets, and no matter how hard you tried, you just couldn't help getting sand in the bed. And what with the cake crumbs – all rather uncomfortable. But heavenly – and we loved it.

At meal times several tables were butted together, end to end along the length of the dining hall, making perhaps half a dozen very long ones. At normal meal-times, back at the home, we simply *said* Grace before starting, but here we sang it. And what a wonderful sound that was. Scores and scores of voices singing 'We thank thee Lord for this our food'. This was to the tune that normally accompanies the words 'All people that on earth do dwell'. Terrific!

Our days were spent on the beach, quite free, but ever under a watchful eye. I know it has been said so many times in recent years, but the summers really *did* seem to have been always good then. I certainly don't recall ever having to do something else simply because it was raining, not on those occasions anyway. Lovely warm sun and blue skies all the day long.

A regular feature during our stay was the sand-modelling competition, which always aroused lots of interest amongst us. These models ranged between small, conventional sand castles and some really large, elaborate efforts. Train-engines, aeroplanes, ships, animals etc., some upright, others in relief. Good use was made of the very wide variety of sea-shells – all so beautiful – and seaweed, and the whole thing seemed to stretch for miles. Prizes were awarded for those adjudged the best. Some took many hours to construct – but only a few minutes to dissolve when the tide came in. Then, yours was just as good as anyone else's.

I still have a small photograph of myself with my two brothers on the beach. Those costumes! Woollen, clinging, and right down to your knees. I've no idea who took it, but I'm very thankful that they did. I look at it now, and think of all the things that have happened since. We played the usual games – quoits, rounders, leapfrog etc., and had races along the lovely smooth sand. And it has to be said, whilst we thoroughly enjoyed all these beach activities, and the wonderful sense of freedom we all felt, we were always quite well behaved – given that there's always one! We had to seek permission from 'Mother' – or whoever might have been in charge – before embarking on anything else, such as popping to the loo or going for a swim. Or in the case of us little 'uns, a paddle.

I didn't much like the sea in those days, probably because I was washed up quite heavily against a well-encrusted groyne one day, which caused a good deal of severe scratching to my body. I had my arms and legs swathed in bandages for days, and I can still see faint scars even now. Neither did I care for jellyfish or crabs. Apart from that though, they were halcyon days. And I must say, I developed a very strong love of the sea some time later, as I shall no doubt mention further on. But *on* it rather than in it really.

We must each have been given a little spending money on arrival at the camp, though it wouldn't have been very much. It was up to you to spend it wisely, ensuring that every penny counted and that it lasted the whole two weeks. There was a small hut on a green, just off the beach. Here they sold ice-cream cornets and wafers, and ice-lollies in triangular cardboard sleeves, and the usual sweets of the day. Most popular I think were the 'Gobstoppers'. I think they were about a ha'penny each – and enormous! I used to lie on my back in the cool grass, with one of these in my mouth, watching those pretty little aeroplanes of the day – Tiger Moths, Gloster Gladiators etc., chugging across the clear blue skies. Miles Magister comes quite clearly to mind as well, although that was a monoplane and totally unable to equal the sheer beauty and grace of those gorgeous little biplanes. But this is just my opinion of course. I'd keep taking it out of my mouth – the gobstopper that is – to see what colour it was. One of those would last the whole afternoon, if you could resist the temptation to crunch. But taking it out too much really made your jaws ache – until you'd managed to suck it down a bit.

Strict though those Homes were, that holiday was wonderful. It made up for the rest of the hum-drum, well-disciplined year. And of course, I was able to see something of my brothers for a change. But, as with all good things, the end of the holiday came all too quickly, and although we still had the excitement of the train and charabanc journeys, this was tinged with sadness as normality drew ever nearer – with each turn of the wheels.

Bathtime in the Homes was always something of an ordeal, although it did have its lighter side. There was a row of numbered pegs along two walls of the bathroom, each child having his or her own. Mine was number six. On this peg hung your little drawstring bag containing face-flannel, toothbrush, and bright round tin of '*Gibbs Dentifrice*' *toothpaste*. A very pleasant flavour, which I can taste yet.

The girls went in first, whilst the boys lined up on the landing immediately outside. They all had to strip naked and stand beneath their respective pegs, whilst 'Mother' took them into the bath – two at a time – and bathed them. They then dried themselves, dressed, and resumed their positions under the pegs. I can't remember now but I'm sure the bath water must have been changed occasionally. The bathroom door was always left ajar, probably so that 'Mother' could hear what we boys were up to outside. And of course, this fact was always taken full advantage of as we all ogled and sniggered through the crack at those naked girls. When the last of them was finished, the positions were reversed – we all had to stand naked under our pegs whilst they stood on the landing, and got their own back through the crack. Occasionally this led to scuffles, as some of the older girls began to develop and resented the lack of privacy.

Bathtime was always preceded by another ritual which I don't think *any* of us enjoyed – boy or girl – least of all John Wakeman. Every night as regular as clockwork, that poor lad wet his bed. This was undoubtedly perpetuated by his fear of the punishment he knew would follow next night.

We were all herded into the bathroom, boys and girls alike, all fully clothed. We were made to stand and watch – in silence – as poor John had to strip naked and lay himself, visibly trembling, face down across the side of the bath. 'Mother' then gave his perfectly presented backside the benefit of the back of a long-handled hairbrush, and though he tried valiantly to 'take it like a man', he couldn't help crying out a bit now and again. She nevertheless continued stoically on until the punishment was completed. His poor buttocks were scarlet. He then joined the rest of us lads as we took up our position on the landing, and bathing commenced. He went to bed in terror that he might transgress again, and because of that – he did. And so it went on, night after night. I would think it probable that when the war came and he found himself in a new environment, the fear and the bedwetting went. I hope so.

Another ritual was Friday night 'medicine' time. The medicine chest was on the landing wall, opposite the bathroom door. We used to line up, all eighteen of us, in front of the cabinet and wait for 'Mother' to come and administer the doses. Some kids were able to take it, some even claimed to *like* it – I say claimed – for I'm sure that was just a touch of bravado. But others alas– just couldn't tackle it at all. So those that found it reasonably easy to take used to taunt the others mercilessly whilst we waited for the performance to begin.

There were two kinds of medicine. There was Syrup of Figs – which I for one didn't find at all unpleasant to take. And luckily I seemed mostly to be given that one, although I do remember having to take the other one on occasions. And this one was vile! Some didn't like the Syrup of Figs – I couldn't think why – but nobody *really* liked the other one. It was in a tall bottle with a straight cork and a label which bore the words 'House Mixture'. *We* all thought it should have shown the 'skull and crossbones' – or whatever the symbol was for deadly poison.

It was white, dry, and extremely bitter – at least to our young tongues. You edged slowly forward till it was your turn, and there you were – face to face with it. 'Mother' then gave you the spoon bearing your particular dose and ordered you to take it. If you just could not bring yourself to do it, you had to join another line and wait until phase one was completed.

These unfortunates were then taken in turn and laid on the floor, legs and arms securely pinned by others, ordered so to do. 'Mother' then pinched their noses with one hand – waited till their mouths gasped open for breath – then poured the stuff in with the other. They were held down until it was certain the dose had been fully swallowed, then released. It doesn't sound much now – well over half a century later – but it was rather unpleasant at the time, bearing in mind of course that some of us were still infants, and the eldest probably no more than twelve or thirteen. We were all school age, and in those days you left school at fourteen, unless of course you won a place at Grammar School.

Whether or not that stuff really had any effect on us physically I cannot now say. But what I *can* say – with absolute certainty – is that it definitely marred Fridays for several of us.

I have no significant memories with regard to the food we were given, so I'm sure it would have been adequate and quite wholesome really, despite our little squabbles over the washing up at times. But I was never a lover of meat, in practically any form. And in those days we still laboured under the delusion that animal fat was good for us, forming a sound lining to the stomach, thus repelling the ills of Winter's cold. So in addition to meat being placed before me at dinner time, which I disliked intensely, I was also faced with this fat, which I absolutely abhorred!

It was a lucky break for me then when I found myself placed next to a boy of about my own age named Eric Waterman. He was quite a plump fellow and I soon discovered why. When he saw me struggling with this meat and stuff he very kindly offered to help me out – fat and all. I don't know really which of us was the more grateful, but I came to like that little chap quite a lot. 'Mother' presided at the short table which was placed across the end of our long one, from where she had a commanding view of everybody. But she couldn't watch us all at once, so the transfer from my plate to Eric's wasn't too difficult. And as long as all plates were empty when they were taken from the dining room she was satisfied.

I remember ground rice coming up with some very dry lumps in it though, which I didn't like. But neither alas did Eric on my right, nor the child on my left. So I just had to lump that, and it was awful. I really don't know what I'd have done without good old Eric, (Old? I guess he was *all* of Six!) he could eat almost anything.

The doctor visited regularly – about once a month, I guess. This was a very similar business to the bathroom scene, as far as embarrassment went. Doctor took up position in the armchair to the right of the big fireplace in the sitting room, stethoscope joining his ears together, bag on the floor beside him. He always chose this chair, presumably because the window was behind him and the light fell upon you rather than in his eyes. No doubt he was as normal as any other doctor but to me he always appeared very big and very stern, and I lived in fear that he'd find something wrong with me and take me off somewhere. But he never did.

We all had to strip again, but this time we kept our underpants or knickers on. The girls' knickers were those thick navy blue things with elasticated leg-ends almost to their knees, and a pocket in one leg for their handkerchief. I guess our underpants looked just as awful, with their similar length legs, button-over front flap and loops for your braces to pass through. They were of a fleecy type of material in an off-white, beige kind of colour. Proper passion-killers the lot of them! Well – by today's standards anyway – although I have to admit to being one who very much preferred the world as it was then, to what it is now. Generally speaking that is, and with the possible exclusion of those knickers. But I only say possible.

In went all the girls, forming the usual line, with us boys waiting outside again in the hall. As ever the door was left ajar, so we indulged in the usual capers, peeping and sniggering. The doctor would check you all over, eyes, ears, throat, chest etc. Then came the crunch! With everyone looking on you had to lower your one vestige of modesty, whilst he checked out that particular area. I shall never forget the poor girl who'd slipped her chewing gum up her knicker leg on one of these occasions. Needless to say it had stuck quite fast to her skin, and she had to stand in full view of everybody whilst Doctor or 'Mother' prised it off. Didn't us lads giggle out there! Still – the girls had their turn afterwards, when we were inside.

Christmas was a wonderful time in the Homes. Not that we received very much in the way of presents or anything, some were luckier than others in that respect of course. No – it was the warmth, and the glitter of the tinsel in the flicker of the fire's flames, and the simple sounds of Christmas. The sitting room was always heavily decorated with great big paper-chains, about twice the diameter of a concertina, huge balls and bells, and the simple chains we'd made at school. We had a tree, which was decorated, though I don't recall any lights on it, and the whole scene was liberally draped with tinsel. Each time the door was opened or closed, everything shimmered. There was no central heating of course so the fire was always well stoked up. And with such high ceilings the effect was truly magical, especially when the light was turned off.

You awoke on Christmas morning to find a small, string type stocking at the foot of your bed. There wasn't much in it really, but we all treasured them. 'I've got a colouring book!' one would say excitedly; 'So have I – *and* a whistle!' 'Me too' squealed a third. A pink sugar mouse, an orange, and one or two other odds and ends completed the treasures, and you'd have thought we'd been given the Crown Jewels, we were that delighted.

We washed and dressed ourselves, made our beds, then – with a few last goes on those blow-out paper rollers with a squeaker inside and a feather at the tip, which we'd each found in our stockings, we'd troop expectantly down the stairs. Breakfast was always taken in the back room, next door to the kitchen. All there was in here was a long, stout deal table with a long wooden form along each side. We each had our own place on these forms and on this special morning your eyes would fall hopefully to the area immediately behind yours as you entered. For this was where your presents would be – had you received any. Nobody had that much really, just the odd item or so, due probably to the hard times. But behind my place would always be a round tin, of about six inches in diameter, filled with toffees. This was from my Dad. We didn't have sweets at any other time – other than the annual holiday – so imagine my delight. And toffees were my absolute favourite.

After breakfast we cleared away, washed up, and set about our normal chores. Then we had a lovely Christmas dinner, with scrumptious Christmas pudding afterwards, and what with the crackers and paper hats, life was suddenly quite wonderful. After dinner, tables were moved to the side and we were allowed to play, there in the sitting room, with the presents we'd received. Although I don't think I'd have played around with *mine* too much, I loved them so. We could also get the toys out of the toy-cupboard in the corner of the sitting room. Such things as the beautiful, colourful humming top, kaleidoscope, building bricks – which also provided the facility for making six different pictures – teddy bears, dolls, aeroplanes made mostly of tin, wooden engines etc. All pretty well-handled as you can imagine, yet the only time they normally came out I think was on a Sunday, which was also Parents' Visiting Day. Though not every parent came every Sunday, not by a long shot! There never seemed to be more than three or four at any one time, and some weekends none at all.

There were still several crystal sets around then, but music in those days was generally provided by either a wireless set or a wind up gramophone. I don't think we had either normally, but a gramophone was procured for this day and it was really wonderful to hear all the lovely carols coming out of that big horn. We had a few other records too – 'The Laughing Policeman' 'Ten Pretty Girls' 'Teddy Bears Picnic'. Not exactly 'Top of the Pops' to today's youngsters, but we loved them. Somebody always seemed to receive a xylophone, someone else a tin drum. But we all tolerated each other.

We went to church sometime over the Christmas period and it was beautiful. We always attended Sunday School, every week regularly, but I don't recall us going to church services normally. We had a party after tea – just amongst ourselves I think – and didn't we all enjoy it! There were balloons and games – musical chairs, blind man's buff and the like – then roasted chestnuts from in front of the fire. We went to bed tired out but oh, so happy. Christmas Day and our annual holiday at Dymchurch were the two highlights in an otherwise very dull, restricted year, and we all made the very most of them, and were truly thankful.

I'm sure the homes into which my brothers were placed were run on the same lines as the one I was in, although I have scant knowledge of their experiences. Except for the time Chas told me of the apple tree. His home was, as I've said, for boys only, and in the back garden was an apple tree. I don't know what variety it was but one year it yielded only a very sparse crop. Their 'House-mother' obviously had designs on these few apples herself, although such things were never available to the inmates. You couldn't just go and pick an apple from a tree without first asking, even if there were a *glut*. This rule applied to anything and everything. You never took anything without first gaining permission. And this was sought in a most polite, respectful manner. Especially at the meal table.

So you may well imagine how incensed their 'Mother' was when she came upon Chas and two accomplices one day, hiding in the coalshed, happily feasting upon one of these apples. They were immediately marched into the sitting room, and as punishment for their crime made to kneel in front of the fire with their hands outstretched before them – not in – but so close to the fire itself as to cause considerable pain. And they were not allowed to withdraw their hands until it was felt they had well and truly 'learned their lesson'. I shouldn't think they scrumped from *that* garden again! This is not of course, first hand knowledge, but I never, ever had reason to doubt my brother's integrity.

Little else stands out in my memory from that rather hum-drum period of my life. School was very much stricter than it appears to be today. *Very* much! You spoke only when spoken to, other than in your own time of course, and were encouraged to strive very hard toward success. But none of us are any the worse for it, of that I'm certain.

Then – just before my eighth birthday – the War came. And with it, though I didn't realise it immediately, my first short taste of freedom.

NORTHAMPTON

As an eight year-old, the coming of war didn't register that much until, that is, the end of the summer of 1939, when all us kids in the Homes had to go to school each day with a label on our coat-front and a kitbag – containing all our belongings – on our shoulder. Then, soon after Neville Chamberlain's utterance of those most fateful words, 'We are at war with Germany', we were marched off to the railway station and taken to Northampton. It was like journeying to the end of the earth to us, the furthest we'd ever been was Dymchurch.

I remember that as a rather long but very exciting day. No doubt children from normal homes would have viewed it all quite differently, indeed there were lots of tears and very much sadness. But to me it was the shedding of shackles, and finding out what the world was like beyond our school.

We were a rather large crowd, moving very slowly along the streets of Northampton and it's suburbs, gradually diminishing in size as the good local folk took us in, one here, two there and so on until – round about tea time – all had been found a billet. This was the first ordinary home I could ever remember being in, and it felt marvellous. Strange....... but marvellous. Chas once again had been put in with me, and George – as usual – was placed next door.

Chas and I were at Number 5 St. Edmund's Road, with a Mr & Mrs Rose, whilst George was at Number 3, with a Mr & Mrs Keene. The Roses were a very nice couple, who had no children of their own as I recall, but a lovely Collie dog called Jack. I can't remember anything about the Keenes now, I don't think I ever set foot in their house.

On arrival at Number 5 Chas and I were given some lovely bread and jam, and a big wedge of caraway seed cake each. We thoroughly enjoyed that, and directly afterwards we hung our kitbags on some pegs in the hall, then – joy of joys – we were allowed to go out. This really was sheer bliss, unscheduled and unaccompanied.

We collected brother George from next door, and the boy who had been put in with him, although ever after this we steered clear of that fellow, regarding him as 'a bit mental'. We set off to explore these strange new surroundings, and within a couple of minutes found ourselves in what the locals called 'The Meadow'. And it *was* just that, with lots of cow-pats laying in wait for us, and a super boating lake.

The boats were all tied up for the night and everyone had gone home. The weather had been fine that day as I recall, and the 'conkers' hung thick and heavy on the horse-chestnuts that abounded in that meadow. We had a *fine* time knocking them down.

Before we left for 'home' we went for another look at the lake, and I'm afraid I got a closer look than I'd bargained for. I fell in. Fortunately the water was quite shallow, but I got a pretty good wetting all the same. We set off, pockets bulging with conkers, and if Mrs Rose was cross with me for the state I was in, that dear lady didn't show it. We found our pyjamas in our still unemptied kitbags, and prepared for bed. And I must say, we were tickled pink at having to go to the bottom of the garden for the toilet. Mrs Rose gave us each another slab of seed cake and a lovely cup of cocoa. We'd never experienced such luxury as this – other than at Dymchurch – and we knew right there and then that we were going to really enjoy this war. We were given a lighted candle in an enamelled, saucer-shaped holder with a finger grip, and to the strains of 'Run Rabbit Run' from the wireless, we climbed the little staircase, escorted by the flickering shadows the candle made, to our room. It was a small room with one bed which we shared, and it was so homely it was like being in heaven – at least, what I imagined heaven to be like from our Sunday School teacher. What a thrilling and eventful day that had been! I wondered how brother George was faring next door. Was he as happy as we were? We quickly fell asleep, thoroughly tired out, and woke in the morning to find that Jack had chewed the bottoms out of both kitbags during the night, and all our things were in a heap on the floor.

This sudden paradise was slightly marred by having to go to school, though even this was better than we might have expected. We went to St. Edmund's School, which was very handy – just across the York Road. This was one of those small, grey, old-ish little single-storied schools that you saw everywhere in those days, before all those sleek, cold, characterless modern places appeared on the scene. Quaint is the word for it, warm and friendly – if a bit dusty. When I say 'warm' and 'cold', I am not necessarily referring to the temperature of course. They always seemed to have tall-ish arched windows, each formed from several small panes, with a pole close by for reaching the catch at the top. The bonus to us – and no doubt the local kids too – was that we could only attend on a half-time basis. There just wasn't room for us all at once. So one week we went to school mornings only, the next week afternoons, and so on. This was great, and continued to the time we left Northampton.

Yet still I played truant once! Brother George – eleven to my eight – led me on I have to say, and we struck out for the open country to keep out of sight. He *would* choose an afternoon when one of the classes was out on a nature walk! We rounded a bend and very nearly ran smack into them. I think we managed to avoid detection, at least I don't remember anything coming of it, but I never ever played truant again. Neither I think did George.

The Roses used to go to what I think must have been a Working Men's Club on a Saturday night. As far as I can remember it was called 'The Mounts'. They took me with them – Chas too I suppose, although I can't really remember him being there – and I loved it. There was Ginger Beer and Potato Crisps, hitherto unknown to us kids from the Homes. And listening to all those smashing songs of the day, played by live musicians up on the stage. It was great, and if this was war – long may it last! That's the way young minds work I suppose, not really seeing the tragedies, which was just as well I'm sure.

I'm not sure why, but Chas and I were moved from Mr & Mrs Rose's house after some time and became separated. All three of us were apart once again. We moved further away from the school, and my new billet was in Upper Thrift Street, with a Mr & Mrs Marchant. I shared a bed again with one or two other lads, I'm not sure if they were evacuees or the sons of the Marchants. I now had quite a long walk to and from school, and I had to pass the Rose's house. Both Chas and I were invited to call in on our way home every day, for a piece of that delicious seed cake which we'd both come to like so much.

We called one afternoon and received no answer. This was very unusual, so we took a peek through the letter box and were sickened to see poor old Jack the dog, lying dead in the passage. We learned later that he'd been run over by a coal lorry. This really saddened us for a long time, and for a while I loathed all coal lorries. He'd been a great pal to go walking and playing with in The Meadow.

It was in Northampton that I first experienced shops. These were exciting places, especially Woolworths. I can remember the smell of that place now, a mixture of sweets and the dusty wooden floor. Not that I'm suggesting the place was dirty I must add, it was just the smell that kind of flooring had – schools were exactly the same, and not offensive at all. In here they sold lots of things for sixpence (2½p) each, giving birth to the saying 'Tanner Woolworths'. We must have started getting a little pocket money from somewhere, for the three of us clubbed together and bought a pair of brand new roller skates – for sixpence! Of course, they were very flimsy and didn't run very well at all. One of them soon collapsed in fact, but we had fun with the other for a while – albeit darned hard work – till that too went. They were 'cheap and cheerful' really, but our very first possession.

After a few months our father re-married, and the Welfare Officer told us we would probably soon be having a *real* home – of our own. This prospect really thrilled us. Little did I know it would bring the worst four years of my life. But for now, it looked very promising and our Dad, who I didn't really know then, sent us a brand new pair of roller skates – EACH! And these were *real* skates, made in the U.S.A. They were called 'Union', and had ball-bearing wheels, self-guiders, and were fully adjustable. And didn't they go! Mind you, they were so much freer than the Woolworths ones and took some getting used to. There was so little traffic on the roads then (the 'Yanks' hadn't yet arrived), you could skate right down the middle of the road quite safely, though not on the main roads of course. Not far away was a park area called 'The Links'. It was quite hilly there and all the sloping paths were laid in lovely smooth tarmac. We had some super times there, with those terrific skates.

A memorable part of our stay with Mr & Mrs Rose was Friday evenings. They had what I think of as a semi-basement room, which was below ground level at the front, but you walked straight out into the garden from the back, at which end there was a window, with a sink beneath. There was a big-ish fireplace in here although I can't remember whether or not it was a kitchen range. Whichever, a galvanised bungalow bath was set in front of it, containing as much water as we were allowed to use then (although I think restrictions on bath water – four inches deep – came later) and in the warmth of the dancing flames, Mrs Rose bathed us.

I don't know why we didn't bath ourselves – probably because that good lady wanted to be sure we were done properly. Mind you, with *our* upbringing there was no need for her to have worried. All these years later the standards I set myself in all things are still very high, but with age, not always too easy to attain. And I know this is the same with my two brothers, although Chas, sadly, is no longer with us.

Sitting on a stool, tantalizingly close to us, were two lovely big green apples. One for each of us on completion of our bath. At the time we took them to be cooking apples, but although they were a bit sharp to the taste I'm sure now that they weren't. We loved them. *And* bath time. It was so much cosier than the very formal, disciplined business of bath time in the Homes. And there was no punishment to witness here either.

A smell I associate with that little house, which would have been typical of all of them I'm sure, was the musty kind of smell in that basement, also out in the garden. It was probably dampness, but I liked it. I also remember the smell of the 'caps' as we shot each other to bits with our cap guns on a Saturday morning. This was as we galloped away from the 'pictures', beating hell out of our own backsides after watching Roy Rogers or Tom Mix. We also thrilled to Flash Gordon and Buck Rogers in their space-ships, but they weren't so easy to emulate. And what about Pearl White? She was terrific, and played at the time by Betty Hutton I seem to remember.

There was a butcher's shop near us, just a little further up the road on the other side. Here the butcher did his own slaughtering and cutting up, and not really being aware of the plight of the poor animals that were taken there, we used to stand and watch when a cattle truck arrived and they were unloaded. Their eyes were wide with fear as they smelt what was coming, and they tried desperately to escape.

George and I were just leaving for school one day when a truck arrived. We mooched across to watch, and were horrified when one poor beast managed to break through the side barrier and get loose. It seemed to head straight for us, snorting like a dragon, and whichever way we turned, it followed. We tried dodging down a side street in an effort to shake it off, but still it was there. We were terrified. We must have gone quite a bit out of our way to school that day, but eventually we managed to shake the poor thing off. The butcher and his boy had set off in hot pursuit and finally caught it and drove it back. But they were given a good run for their money.

We weren't so keen to watch this event after that, for fear we mightn't get away with it next time. All I could see as I lay in bed that night, trying to get to sleep, were eye-whites and puffing nostrils. Phew!

I seem to recall a fairly substantial snowfall that winter. And didn't we enjoy it!.We'd never really played in the stuff before, other than a few snowballs to and from school, before our freedom. We made some beautiful slides on the footpaths up at The Links, and if you took a good run you could slide for miles. The slopes were just right. I wonder now though, how the poor local people managed to get about behind us. You don't think of such things at the time. Some of the local kids had toboggans and these provided even more fun. Then we used to roll up enormous snowballs, giving up only when they were too big to push any further. They were abandoned everywhere. If Hitler and his mob had landed just then I think we'd have had him. We went home each night with burning faces, and hands and feet that really, really ached from the cold. They took a long time to 'come to' – but the pain was well justified by the sheer pleasure of it all.

Winter eventually gave way to the Spring of 1940, and before the summer came we were suddenly snatched away from the paradise we'd revelled in for nearly eight months, and taken to my father's new home in Middlesex.

MIDDLESEX

The three of us boys stood expectantly at the front door of this fairly new, attractive, bow-windowed house with it's nice, sizeable front garden, neatly trimmed privet hedge and black wooden gate. It looked fine, and I couldn't believe this was to be our very own, real home.

The Welfare lady who'd brought us rang the doorbell, and a rather sharp-featured person answered. A few brief words were exchanged – there on the doorstep, then the Welfare lady bade us farewell and we were ushered inside. We had with us a bag of sweets that someone had kindly given us, and were quite disappointed when they were instantly taken from us. We were even more disappointed a day or two later – *very* much more – when our beautiful roller skates were also confiscated, never to be seen again.

After just a few days our dreams were shattered when it seemed as though a great black cloak fell upon us, and I feel it would be prudent to say as little as possible as to what went on beneath it. Suffice it to say that the moment we were able to, we all ran away. Chas was first, being the eldest he was a working lad by then. George was next, just after he'd started work, but being that much younger, I wasn't able to follow them for quite some time, and I took quite a bit more stick after their departure. *And* inherited even more chores than I already had. I was there four years in all, and at the ripe old age of twelve, I too made the break.

I thought life had been hard in the Homes – well it had really – but it had been almost a picnic by comparison. I must point out here that my father knew little of what went on there, in his absence. He knew things weren't right, but we daren't tell him anything for fear of reprisals. He'd re-married into a large family – all adults – and that house was quite full. He was well out-numbered, so we had to accept our fate in silence. He learned the truth in the end though, and I know he was very much saddened by it. He was a good-natured person, and extremely popular with the children round about. He used to give them rides of his heavy 'Roadster' cycle as he made his way, on foot, up the long hill to our house. They used to run to him at the foot of the hill where they knew he would dismount, calling 'Give us a ride Uncle Mac!' He never refused them even though he came home from work exhausted most nights. He'd lift them up onto the saddle, one at a time, then push away, stopping now and then to change over so that nobody was disappointed. And he had a huge black wooden box on his carrier, though I'm not too sure what was in it. But he'd cut people's hair for them in the lunch hour at work, and very often in the evenings he'd be mending shoes on his last out in the kitchenette. So I guess his box carried tools and equipment for these sidelines, neither of which of course, was his regular calling. Needless to say he cut hair and mended shoes for *our* household too.

I have many memories of that era, quite apart from those I choose not to mention. The '*Battle of Britain*' took place whilst I was there, also the '*Blitz*', and being right on the edge of London we became much more aware of the horrors of war. Bombs rained down on us relentlessly at times, and you wondered how long it would be before one found you.

Each morning, once the 'All Clear' had sounded, we all emerged for school with the same look on our faces. 'Who's copped it this time?' our expressions asked. I had about a 2¼ mile walk to school, so I had plenty of opportunity to see the results of 'Jerry's' ferocity. One morning, in the very early hours, a Children's Day Nursery had received a direct hit, just around the corner from us, and had been obliterated. What a good thing it had happened in the night, when it was empty.

When you arrived at school the first thing you did was to look around to see who was left. Every day saw more empty desks. Mind you, being only youngsters we became quite blasé about this after a while, being rather more interested in the hunt for shrapnel, and inquiring as to how many we'd shot down that night. I saw one youngster lying dead on the rubble of his home one morning. His eyes had been blown out, and one still lay on his cheek. I looked at him for a few moments, then continued the search for shrapnel.

I had mixed feelings toward school. I wasn't too keen on it in the early years, except for the fascinating stories that were read to us by the teachers. There were all the Bible stories of course, which were usually included in the morning Scripture Lesson every day, then there were the great children's classics such as 'The Water Babies' 'Black Beauty' 'Wind-in-the-Willows' 'Peter Pan' 'Robin Hood' 'Huckleberry Finn' etc. etc. Best of all though, as far as I was concerned, was 'King Solomon's Mines'. I was absolutely enthralled by this one. I wonder if the young ones have stories read to them in school nowadays? I do hope so, I've loved reading ever since.

I also liked art lessons, especially designing posters on the '*War Effort*'. We'd have '*Dig for Victory*' '*Wings for Victory*' '*Warship Week*' etc. I would have been spurred on I suppose by mine being pinned up on the classroom wall. I wasn't anything special on the academic side until just before the State Scholarship Examination, which we sat when we were eleven years old. My maths had begun to improve, and I had always been reasonable at English Grammar and its associated subjects – spelling, composition etc.

Just before the big exams, I remember struggling with a 'long-division'. I'd taken it out to 'Sir' for marking. His name was Mr Gruchy, and as you will no doubt have gathered, he was French – and a bit of a Tartar at that. It was him you went to when you'd been awarded punishment, and boy – could he cane! Anyway, he suddenly mellowed toward me on this occasion – after checking my work. He marked it incorrect, but said I was so close I should sit and go through it again. This I did – twice more – and was absolutely delighted when finally he gave me a 'tick'. From then on I never looked back, and quickly moved across to the right hand row of desks, where the 'brighter ones' sat. Now I was enjoying maths equally with English and Art, and by the time we sat the dreaded exams I passed fairly easily. It's amazing what a little encouragement can do. From then on I loved school, yet although I'd won a place at Grammar School, I was forced to leave at fourteen in order to earn my keep.

Those four years dragged by. I had some good friends at school, including the youngest of two brothers whose father played in Geraldo's band. But I was never allowed out to play with anybody. My only outings were daily shopping trips. There was a shopping area either side of our house and each was about a mile away. 'Parade' was the name they had then. And what queues I used to stand in. I could be four solid hours on a Saturday morning just collecting the essentials. All my school pals would be at the Saturday morning cinema, as I had been during those eight wonderful months in Northampton. Most mornings I had to run errands before setting off to school. Then I'd have to run as fast as I could the 2¼ miles – hoping against hope that I wouldn't get a 'Bad Conduct' mark for being late. Which was seldom possible. I became a pretty good runner though, which helped a lot in school athletics.

The road in which we lived was at least a mile long I seem to recall, with houses on both sides of its entire length. They were very nice houses, all with good sized gardens back and front. The road rose steadily for most of its length, and we lived near the top. The railway ran behind the houses on the side opposite us, and every night throughout the blitz, you could feel the house shake as the anti-aircraft guns which were positioned there, released seemingly thousands of shells into the droning swarm of Heinkels and things above, as they in turn hoped to dodge the shafts of the hunting searchlights. All very frightening really, but extremely exciting to us youngsters.

Throughout its length our road sported hardly one motor car. Nor in fact did any of the other residential roads thereabouts. Autocycles were very popular at that time, they were extremely cheap to run and could be housed quite comfortably in the garden shed. In any case, it was mainly only doctors, reps and wealthy traders who had cars in those days. Times were nothing like as affluent as they are now. But they were certainly very much happier – in spite of the war. Generally speaking, that is.

It was just as well there was this lack of cars on our road, for had it looked as it probably does today – parked bumper to bumper – where would they have put all those brick-built air raid shelters? These shelters were probably about 25 feet long by 8 feet wide, though this is now a guess of course, and were erected all down one side of our road. They would look something like railway coaches parked all along the kerb, about 25 feet apart. And there they stood, all through the war. Well, for the four years that I lived in that road anyway. Less of course, any that 'Jerry' might have found.

At the bottom of our road was Sudbury Town. That sounds a lot more than it was really – there was a small parade of shops on either side of the road, about sixteen in all I'd guess, a pub whose name I can't recall, and the 'Odeon' cinema. At the top of the road – about 150 yards beyond our house, the road ended and became a footpath, which ran through some allotments, finishing after about one mile at Sudbury Hill. I have no idea what it all looks like now, but when I left there in 1944 it was all very nice – and quite rural. At Sudbury Hill there were also shops, similar to Sudbury Town, but including Woolworths and the Co-op. There was also a railway station of some sort – 'Tube' I think. Here was where I spent nearly every Saturday morning, queuing at one shop then another, to get our weekly rations. As I've said, this always took the entire morning.

Though I've pledged not to enlarge too much on this part of my life, I will just recall one particular memory. I'd joined the first queue one morning – it was the greengrocer's – and as usual it stretched right up the road, across the fronts of all the neighbouring shops. There were queues everywhere and you had to hang on to your place. I'd steadily worked my way down my queue and was fairly near the front, when a hand fell upon my shoulder. I swung round to see my brother Chas, who'd run away some time previous. I hadn't seen him since he'd left and I was delighted to see him now. He was with some friends, including Doris, the daughter of the folks he was staying with.

The queue kept shuffling forward and I was trying to hold a conversation, then quite unwittingly, I stepped out of the queue as we chatted, and by the time I realised what had happened I couldn't get back in. I chatted a little longer, than bade my brother and his friends farewell and rejoined the queue – right at the back end. By the time I'd worked my way right down it again all they had left were a few King Edward potatoes. I took these – knowing I'd be for it when I got home – and crossed the road to my other ports of call. They were all either sold out or closed! God, I really *was* for it now. And rightly so I guess. I did manage to get a loaf of bread, and as I nervously retraced my steps through the allotments, without realising it I was picking away at the soft, un-crusted end of the loaf. By the time I got home it looked a bit of a mess. And I really did cop it too – but I'll not go into detail – suffice it to say that on a scale of 1 to 10, I copped at least a 9. And I don't exaggerate. This would have been about 1 p.m. and my father hadn't yet returned from work. When he did arrive he was simply told that I had been sent to bed for my misdemeanours, and there I stayed till Sunday morning.

As I say, my father knew little of what befell us in his absence, and of course, for my last two years there, both my brothers had gone, which left me sitting none to prettily.

I still see the humour in many of these incidents, even so. It's always easy in retrospect I guess. So perhaps just one more........

It was about a year later, and I was sitting at the dinner table, picking away at this stuff on my plate, which I knew I could never get down in a million years. I'd scorched the 2¼ miles home from school, knowing the journey didn't leave much time for eating a meal *and* washing all the dishes before tearing back for the afternoon session. If it was a meal I could manage easily, and not too big a wash up afterwards, I could just about make it. But not this day. For it was breast of lamb – one of the very worst as far as I was concerned. Cooked in an appetizing way, a meat lover may well find this meal very tasty. But I disliked meat intensely, and fat sickened me beyond words.

My back was to the mantelpiece, on which stood the clock, ticking away those precious seconds. Also behind me, in an armchair by the fireside, sat my tormentor, knitting. I daren't look round to see the time. I could just see this revolting lump of cold, fatty, nauseating stuff on my plate. And *no* way would I be leaving that table till my plate was empty. Tick-tock-tick-tock went the clock, clickety-clack, clickety-clack the needles. This must be the end. I was definitely in for a Bad Conduct mark today, for there was no avoiding being late back to school.

Our headmaster by the way, whose name was Willis, was a very strict disciplinarian and commanded absolute respect from everybody, including the staff too I shouldn't wonder. A bit more of which wouldn't go amiss today incidentally. He was also steeped in music, instructing the entire school in that subject. Consequently, the four School Houses were named after people famous in the world of music. We were strongly encouraged to take immense pride in the House into which we'd been placed when we first entered the school. My House was Davies, after Sir Henry Walford Davies, the British composer and 'Master of the King's Music'. You did all you could to see that your house came top each month, whereby you held the coveted shield. So of course, anyone doing things detrimental to the welfare of their House was looked upon none too kindly by their House-mates. Hence my fear of being late.

Anyway, back to the story. Suddenly – and without warning – my tormentor rose, went through into the hall, and closed the door. I couldn't believe my luck. I'd already worked out what I would do – given half a chance – and *here* it was! In the kitchenette, as it was called, a large kitchen cabinet stood against the wall. This free-standing cabinet was typical of its day – it had a retractable enamelled worktop – with cupboards above and below. It was quite tall, and cleared the floor by no more than two or three inches.

The instant that door closed, I grabbed my plate and shot into the kitchenette, scooping this revolting mess off with my hand as I went, and hurled it as hard as I could under the cabinet. I thought I heard it slap as it met the skirting board at the back. Phew – made it! I quickly made for the sink and the washing up, although I had resigned myself to being late for school – even if I *flew*. I heard the rattle of the door-knob as the dining room door re-opened, and instinctively sensed trouble.

This entire sequence of events by the way, had taken about five seconds – if that. And I think I might well have been home and dry – but for one thing. I hadn't noticed *him* as I'd hurled it under the cabinet. But now – for all to see – was Stinker the cat, clawing feverishly at the gap, as he tried desperately to reach the stuff. I swung a quick foot at him, hoping to put him off, but he was having none of it. Scratch scratch, *miaow miaow*. Of course, the game was up. Betrayed by a damned cat! In retrospect however, I'm sure this must have been a craftily conceived plan. And I fell for it!

I tried to look unconcerned as I set into the washing up, but *I'd* been rumbled all right. The cat was fought off – no longer an ally for the moment – that heavy cabinet eased away from the wall, and there it was, all covered in fluff now. I fully expected to be force-fed it – just as it was – but it was my lucky day, I just got a good hiding instead. Brother George was still living there at the time, and he'd gone back to school without his coat. And now it was raining hard. So the coat was thrown out onto the coke-heap – just outside the back door – to further vent the wrath of my adversary.

I disliked cats for many many years after that, although I would never harm *any* animal. I now have a sneaking admiration for them in fact – cats, that is – and have a great respect for all animals.

I suppose meat lovers would find it hard to understand, but I used to live in absolute dread of the stuff. It had a way of disrupting my already rather turbulent existence even further. I used to have to sit and try to eat tripe, an excellent name for the stuff, which looked like white leather but tasted considerably worse. I would bravely manage a few bits – and believe me – this isn't self-congratulatory, for I was retching the whole time. But I could never manage it, and finished up being force-fed. How I managed to keep it down I've never been able to fathom, though of course, taking it this way, I swallowed rather than chewed it. Ugh. I've often said I would live all my life again, just as it was, but I really think the forced-feeding might prove to be my stumbling block. I don't know – in all honesty – how I allowed that to happen to me, but I'm none the worse for it now.

After the unsuccessful business with the kitchen cabinet, I had to try and think of something else in a hurry, for that was a very determined person I was up against. Fortunately – it wasn't long in coming. You learn to be pretty resourceful under certain circumstances, and I feel I developed that particular attribute quite young. And have it yet I'm glad to say.

The new plan was fairly simple really, though rather messy. But one has to get one's priorities in order doesn't one, and in this instance mess was of a rather secondary consideration. I used to cut the meat into smallish chunks, then push it to the side of the plate, away from gravy and the like, to dry off a bit. I'd develop a bit of a sniff, necessitating the use of my handkerchief, and as I took it away from my nose, I'd cloak one or two chunks as I returned it to my pocket. Here I'd shake it free, as gently as I could, which wasn't too easy as you can imagine. Another sniff or two and out came the hanky again, for the next scoop. Four or five such passes would see it all transferred successfully from plate to pocket. To this day, I can't think how I got away with that, for the condition of my trouser pockets must have been *unspeakable*. Also my socks. I was still wearing short trousers, as we did then almost up until we started work. When my pockets couldn't quite cope with the job, I tucked some down inside the top of my socks. I'd have to move through the washing up a bit gingerly then – praying the cat was elsewhere – before going out through the back door. I'd whistle nonchalantly as I walked casually down the back garden path, all the time feeling the moisture oozing through my pockets and on to my legs. Once through the gate and out of sight, I couldn't get at it quick enough.

There were several dogs in the area, as indeed there are anywhere else, and on my initial trip the first one I met had a real feast. I left him gulping it down as I set about my 2¼ mile dash. He couldn't believe his luck I fancy, and appeared regularly after that, each day accompanied by more of his pals. Word soon gets round. It wasn't long before they were virtually queuing up outside our back gate every day. I had to go some distance then – with all these dogs leaping excitedly at my trouser pockets – before I could start spreading it far and wide, so as not to draw too much attention. I don't know what people must have thought, I must have borne some resemblance to the Pied Piper I guess, with all these pooches scurrying along behind me. But I got away with it.

Once a week we had to have our laxative. I thought I'd left all that behind me in the Homes. I suppose the stuff we were given here wasn't bad really, it was just the thought of it. Sometimes we had 'Brooklax' – sometimes 'Exlax' – though they seemed identical to me. Both were in the form of slim squares of dark chocolate, a good disguise really, but no matter how I tried to convince myself that it was merely chocolate, I just couldn't make it. Psychological I'm sure, after the trauma of Friday nights in the Homes.

We were given this on a Sunday at breakfast time, and disposing of it was simplicity itself. Slipped once again under the top of my sock, or in summertime down the rolled-up sleeves of my shirt, I could wait a little while, then stroll out into the back garden and slip it quietly through the slots of the drain grating. For a time we were switched onto something else, called Brimstone & Treacle, but I don't think this lasted very long. Perhaps it was discovered that we liked it better than the Brooklax! I really can't remember much about that one now.

After both Chas and George had gone, the time really did drag. Not being allowed out I had few diversions, other than looking after my two young half-sisters – doing my chores, weeding the vegetable garden for my father, and all that blasted shopping. Yet somehow I seemed to settle to this routine, and as I've already said, I managed to do quite well at school – though this has amazed me ever since. For I really was unhappy there and was only ever a short step away from another hiding.

The bombing lessened in our area, and moved more to the centre of London, as if *they* weren't getting enough already. The part of Middlesex in which I was living was still, as I've said earlier, quite rural in places then. In fact Horsenden Hill and all the surrounding fields were only a spit away from our house, although I think Northolt Aerodrome was fairly close by too, and that would obviously have been a choice target for Jerry.

But I was bored, though I hasten to point out that boredom wasn't the common complaint it appears to be amongst today's youngsters. We could be quite content with a set of 'fivestones' – or a home-made cotton reel 'tank'. Then there were matchstick guns, which we made from an empty matchbox, three elastic bands and a small, flat piece of wood – rather like a present-day lolly stick. And with a couple of metal puzzles – which were two intertwined pieces of bent and twisted steel rod that you had to separate, a magnet, and one of those things the size of a small powder compact where you had to manoeuvre some tiny steel balls into their sockets, you could amuse yourself for hours on end. And *all* these things could be carried in your trouser pockets! Mind you, anything carried in *my* trouser pockets would have smelt pretty awful I should think.

I was remembering those few months of freedom in Northampton, and the company of my two brothers. That had been a wonderful time, and I was ready for more. Yet it would be ages before I was old enough to start work, which was the situation with both Chas and George when *they'd* left. But I'd certainly had more than enough of my present existence, and became quite restless.

LONDON

And so, one Saturday morning early in 1944, I popped my one or two simple belongings into a small brown paper carrier bag, slipped through the gate at the bottom of the back garden, and left my father's house for ever. I was twelve. I knew where my school pal Terry lived – the one whose father played in Geraldo's band – so I called on him and he, being far more worldly than I at that time, escorted me to London where, after a bit of searching we found the place to which my brothers had gone.

Chas had gone first, to my great sorrow *and* envy, but he soon ran into difficulty over food. The people he'd gone to – friends of my parents before my mother died – were really great. But with the best will and kindest hearts in the world, dear Ma and Pop – as we fondly called them – just couldn't find enough food for everybody. So Chas was forced to approach our Dad with a view to obtaining his Ration Book. Dad was willing of course, but there was solid opposition from other quarters. So poor Chas was forced to come back, and things became very much worse than before. He'd had another little taste of freedom, and losing it so soon was just too much for him to bear. He was very soon off again, and this time he applied through the courts I believe, for his Ration Book. To his great delight his application was successful. I think actually our Dad had managed to swing it for him. And he it was too who ensured that our Ration books were accessible to both George and myself, when our turn came. He knew of our plans to 'escape', and though he didn't want to lose us again, he knew we'd be much better off.

I seem to remember George going just after Christmas. He was now a working lad and without warning, he disappeared for the whole of Christmas. He returned after a few days – a very much bolder George than I'd known before – and announced that he too was clearing off. A bit of a scuffle followed, or maybe it was just heated words – I can't be sure now. Either way the outcome was the same. George left and went to join Chas with Ma and Pop. And with him went his Ration Book!

So, one of those items in my small carrier bag was my passport to survival – my own Ration Book. You couldn't possibly become fat on your wartime rations, but you'd have surely starved without them. Unless, of course, you had connections with the 'Black Market' – which we did not.

Ma and Pop rented a strange sort of place in the High Street, just two doors away from 'The Savoy' cinema on the corner. What a grand name – but what a crummy little place. It was no match for all the other really plush, sumptuous looking cinemas that abounded at the time. We called it 'The Bug Hutch' or 'Flea Pit'. And we were right. It was a shame really, for when I first saw it I thought how very handy it could be. I went once – to the Saturday morning kid's cinema – but never again! Mind you, I regret to say it but I think it might be regarded as quite passable in today's world. Standards, like morality and common decency have, alas, declined considerably. But again, this is *my* opinion, but one that I know would be reinforced by countless others of my generation.

The landlord of Ma and Pop's place was a barber, and he had most of the ground floor for his shop and storeroom. All we had on that level was a kind of basement – bare brick walls and stone floor. Ma used to do all the washing down there so it was referred to, naturally, as the Wash-house. But it later doubled as our 'Gym', when dear Chas obtained from somewhere a super punchball. The ball was mounted on a stout steel stem, with a coil in it for flexibility. The base was a very heavy cast-iron plate of about 24 inch diameter. Each time you punched the ball hard – which incidentally was leather with an inflatable bladder inside, just like the footballs we had then – it used to tilt the base, which then returned with a resounding clang. I don't know how that poor barber managed, especially with the shaving, which lots of men had done at the Barber's shop in those days. We used to have sessions lasting hours on end. Scrape scrape; CLANG CLANG! Scrape scrape; CLANG CLANG! And he was quite an elderly man too, but I don't remember him saying anything much about it. There must have been blood everywhere, rather reminiscent of Mr Sweeney Todd! I never went to him, just in case, choosing to have my hair cut by a barber just up the road near the snooker hall.

The rest of the accommodation was spread over three floors, although two of them were separated by only four stairs. The top floor of course, was an attic. Out back was a very small walled garden and the loo. Ma and Pop kept chickens out there, (in the garden – not the loo) having reared them from day-old chicks, and they really looked after them well. We did quite well for eggs, and for some reason not known to me today's eggs aren't a patch on them. Although I must say, they do seem to have improved a little in more recent times. I loved collecting the eggs from the nest-boxes, they were beautiful and warm with a smell all their own. And although we kept taking them each day, those dear old hens bore no malice. They just kept laying more. They certainly did *their* 'bit'.

The chicks were reared in an incubator on the front room table, heated by one light bulb. The sight and sound of those perky, pretty little yellow balls of fluff really fascinated me, and I was quite desolated when occasionally one poor little soul couldn't make it. But the bulk of them won through and I used to watch them daily as the grew first into sturdy pullets, then fine hens with lovely big red combs. I've liked chickens ever since. Again, one smell made a lasting impression upon me, and that was the 'mash' that Ma cooked for them each day.

We had a nice black dog named Prince. He was about labrador size, with jet-black curly fur all over, except for one small white patch on his chest. He and I soon became great pals.

Ma and Pop signed some papers and became my 'Legal Guardians'. I enrolled at a nearby school and got myself an enormous paper round. I obtained a bike from somewhere and spent 2¼ hours before, and 1½ hours after school each day delivering papers. Fridays and Saturdays were extra big days, for there was the local weekly rag to deliver as well, *and* I had a leather shoulder bag for collecting all the cash. I collected plenty too, for that was the way most folk paid for their papers then. It wouldn't do in today's world though, with all the 'muggers', some of whom I'm sad to say, could be as much as three or four years younger than I was then. And I was only twelve. Truly lamentable. The job was a bit of a struggle, and for my effort I was paid twelve and sixpence (62½p) per week, which I handed to Ma toward my keep. My father and brothers may well have contributed to this as well, I'm not sure about that. But I *am* sure dear Ma would have given me back a bob or two for myself.

The bombing was still very heavy, and so was my paper bag, but I was free again and very happy for it. I soon made friends at school and 'played out' with them when I had time. Ma and Pop cared for us all very well, although it was just about this time that Chas joined the Royal Navy. In spite of the blitz I was enjoying life very much. Doris – Ma and Pop's seventeen year-old daughter – used to go to the cinema quite a bit with a girl friend, and she began taking me along. There were some really good films showing then, backed up by great cartoons and features such as 'Stranger than Fiction', which I always found most interesting. And of course, there were the newsreels full of the war, Pathe Gazette and Gaumont British.

The best night was Friday night at the Granada. The cinema was always packed to capacity and after the first full-length feature film there was a long interval, at the start of which a great electric organ – complete with organist – rose from just in front of the screen, playing all the good old songs. The words were up on the screen, with a 'ping-pong' ball hopping from one to the next, telling you which to sing. The bombs kept falling and the anti-aircraft guns kept booming, and everyone sang their heart out, like one big happy family. It was smashing. After a good long sing-song the organ sank slowly back again, playing till it was right out of sight, and the M.C.

came on stage to set the next treat going. This was an amateur talent contest and there was never a shortage of contestants. Some of them were pretty awful, but there were some really good turns as well. The whole thing was most entertaining and everybody seemed to thoroughly enjoy it. Anyone could go up and have a go, and the winner, judged by the volume of applause at the end, always received a prize. Then it was the main feature film, rounding off a great evening.

Doris was a really nice person, and took me to see several shows and plays. I can only remember 'Arsenic and Old Lace' now, and somebody I shall never forget, Dorothy Squires, at the Metropolitan in Edgware Road. She had us all absolutely spellbound, and without a microphone! I really was enjoying this war, odd as that may sound, but then – we never knew whose name might be on the next bomb, so why not? I think most of us had that 'live for today' outlook.

We slept in the attic, Ma managing to fix the three of us up with a bed each, one of which was a camp bed like those we'd had at the Dymchurch holiday camp. This room had a dormer window and steeply sloping ceiling, which created shadows. But these shadows weren't hiding fearful tigers, like those in the children's home of a few years back. Of course, I was that much older now, and my horizons were broadening a bit as well.

Some mornings, after my brothers had gone and I lay in that room alone in the early light, that ceiling would take on a magical aspect. I used to see pictures – actual moving pictures! There was usually a shop, with bullseye bow windows, and people of Dickensian appearance all milling about. And there were animals too. The pictures didn't vary much but they were always fascinating. I cannot explain it but they were always so clear and realistic that I'd swear I did actually see them. But with hindsight, I guess it was no more than childish imaginativeness.

I began to settle quite happily to my new life. The only rub was that I could not go swimming straight after school with my pals. I had to report to the paper shop for my evening stint. Still – it was small price to pay for regaining my freedom. And there was always the punchball anyway. Poor old barber!

I'd been at my new home about six months when Pop had a letter from an old army pal. He was a Yorkshireman named Edwin Martin, and he lived on the outskirts of Leeds. I think they were ward-mates when Pop was recovering in hospital after being buried alive for three days under rubble. They'd kept in touch and now Edwin was writing to say that if Pop had any youngsters he'd like to get away from the blitz – which really was something to live through day after day, night after night – they would be more than welcome up there. The question was put to me, and although I was very happy just then, with Ma and Pop, my two brothers, (although I think Chas was serving in the Far East by then) Doris, Prince, and the chickens and everything, it sounded like an opportunity too good to miss.

I must just include another of the joys of living with Ma and Pop. They had a piano in the front room, along with the chicks, and we used to have some super sing-songs round it. Especially when Chas came home on leave, looking real handsome in his sailor's uniform. The songs I remember us singing most were 'Together' (We strolled the lanes) 'Always' (I'll be loving you) and 'Let the rest of the world go by'. I still get a lump in my throat whenever I hear them. Happy days'.

So one day, still in 1944 but having aged a bit – to 12½ – I was taken to King's Cross station by Doris, and her husband-to-be Bob – who had just joined the R.A.F. – and put on a train bound for Leeds. The whole station was packed with people, mostly uniformed servicemen and women, en route to their various destinations. I found the whole noisy, shrill and steamy scene quite fascinating. And when you got up close to those magnificent steam engines, each proudly bearing it's initials G.W.R. – L.N.E.R. – L.M.S. etc., they were like mountains.

I boarded my train and found myself in that little corridor at the end of the carriage, arms in front of me, hands under my chin, squashed against the wall. Fortunately I was right by the door so I did have the advantage of the window. And in spite of the discomfort over such a longish journey, I really did enjoy the excitement and hub-bub of it all. The only thing I was not too happy about were the sandwiches Ma had very thoughtfully packed for me, and which I had slipped inside my jacket. After the first leg of the journey I began to feel hungry, but of course, in the crush of tightly packed bodies, I was unable to get at them. They were unrecognizable when I finally reached my destination, several hours later, and finished up in the litter basket on Leeds City Station.

YORKSHIRE

I arrived at Leeds station in the early evening after a truly exhilarating journey, in spite of the very cramped conditions. Half a century later I find I cannot really remember any of the stations we passed through although Grantham seems to come to mind for some reason. Perhaps I had to change there, I don't know. In today's world, London to Leeds is no distance at all, practically local in fact, but then – well – I could have been on the Orient Express!

A lot of the stations we went through and the locomotives I saw on the journey seemed much larger than those of the Southern Railway trips to Dymchurch before the war. And much more grimy and dull. But there was so much life and activity, and changes of scenery! And of course there was the chatter of my fellow travellers, so light-hearted and seemingly untroubled by the horrors of war. But what were they *really* feeling inside? And where exactly *was* I going? What would I find at the end of my journey, and where would I sleep tonight? A complete void as far as I was concerned, but I said I'd go – and now I was almost there.

I left the train and showed somebody the address I was seeking, written on a small piece of paper. I've thought since, what a good job it was that I didn't lose that screwed up scrap, for I couldn't have contacted anybody. I knew the address from which I'd come of course, but Ma and Pop weren't on the telephone, who *was* in those days? But I hadn't lost it, and after a few 'ee lad's and 'bah goom's I found myself on a really wonderful vehicle – a Yorkshire tram. It had hard, wooden-slatted seats, with similar backs that swung across so that you could sit facing either way – grand for when you had more than one travelling companion. She lurched her way along the track, and I loved it. This was much more exciting than the London trolley buses, so smooth and quiet.

I paid my ha'penny fare, and was put off further along the way, and on to another tram, exactly like the first one. I paid my fare, again a ha'penny I think, and watched the grimy but impressive buildings of the city give way to the less spectacular ones of the suburbs. When we'd almost run out of buildings, a hand fell upon my shoulder and the broad Yorkshire voice of the conductor said, 'sithee lad, this stop's thine' and I stepped down most reluctantly from that magnificent vehicle. It was just beginning to get dusk, in spite of the 'double-summer-time' we enjoyed then when the clocks were advanced the usual hour in Spring, then another hour some weeks later – giving us daylight till about 11 p.m. I watched and listened in wonder as the tram moved off and into the distance. I looked forward to having lots and lots of rides on *those* beautiful things.

Well – this was it then – I was a Northerner. I'd simply to find Greyhound Street, which turned out to be pretty close anyway, and as I humped my big, rather old and battered suitcase towards it, I was struck by the houses. No matter how long each street was there seemed to be no gaps between them anywhere. And no gardens either. And all the roads – other than some of the main roads – were cobbled, with quaint gas lighting. Real George Formby stuff, although he of course hailed from Lancashire, as did Gracie Fields, who also did much to keep our spirits up in those trying times.

I found the house I wanted and knuckled the door. A dog barked, then the door opened revealing a rather plump, bespectacled, kindly looking lady in a pinafore. Eyeing my suitcase she said 'Ee – thah moost be t'little lad from Loondon, coom in loov, thah's had a long journey'. I climbed the beautifully coated steps and found myself in a small but homely little room. It smelt of food, and of people living close together in cramped conditions. And there was the dog, a spritely little wire-haired terrier whose name eludes me now. I don't mean to suggest it was unpleasant in any way, on the contrary, it was a warm, homely kind of smell.

I had indeed had a long journey and was dying to spend a penny, at which request I was handed a large key and told to walk back up the street a little way, and look for a black-painted wooden door in a brick wall. So there were in fact, breaks between the houses here and there, although they were joined by this brick wall. The door opened on to a smallish walled area, paved in dark grey, well-worn flagstones, in the middle of which was a row of four brick-built lavatories, backing a row of four 'middens'. Heaven *only* knew what a midden was, but right now the other facility was of far greater importance. I found the one that the key fitted – which it turned out we shared with another family – and re-locked the door on leaving. I was tickled pink by this experience, but one thing I will say – those lavatories were spotless.

I made my way back to the house, feeling all the time that I was being watched. Apparently they didn't normally see folk from so far away – I think I was the first 'Sootherner' most of them had ever seen – and they'd awaited my arrival with great excitement. I was given food and drink, and made to feel most welcome.

Mr and Mrs Martin, the latter being the lady who'd opened the door to me on my arrival, had three married daughters, all of whom lived close by. One of them, Edith, lived right opposite in Greyhound Terrace, and her three children, Joyce, Valerie and Keith, aged eight, six, and about three respectively, had been waiting for me all day.

They now came over and eyed me in wonder. I don't know what they'd been expecting to see, but I was just the same as them! Except for the accent of course.

Everybody was so friendly, though I had some difficulty understanding them at first, their dialect was so strong. But I'd had a long, magical day, and the food and warmth and excited chatter were making me tired now, so when I was asked if I was ready for bed, I was quick to say yes.

I shared a bed with Raymond, the Martin's only son. He was fifteen and a working lad, and the difference in our ages – though only 2½ years – showed. I think he was rather disappointed that I wasn't more his size, someone to have a good wrestle with. We never became close, but we got along. Just as well – sharing a bed and all! I was a little surprised at this sleeping arrangement, even more so when I saw another double bed on the other side of the room. The room itself would have been no more than about twelve feet square. This bed was the one used by Mr and Mrs Martin themselves. Yes – all four of us slept in the one room. Which was quite understandable really, for it was the *only* room upstairs.

Those little houses were literally 'one up and one down', although there was a coal-cellar below ground, which was filled through a round manhole in the flagstone pavement outside. They were also back to back, which meant, of course, that three walls of each room were shared with other families. No wonder the loos and middens were up the road – the latter of course being the place where household waste was put, awaiting collection.

On a fairly recent coach-trip to Scotland, we passed through that part of Yorkshire, and the driver – who originated from those parts himself – went slightly out of his way so that he could point out the only remaining 'back-to-back' houses. It was a short row, and everyone looked on incredulously, including himself. 'To think,' he mused, 'people actually used to *live* in those!' And these, I noticed, had small gardens, in which I spotted dustbins. And I would suspect also that they had their own loos, even if they *were* outside! So I value very highly my first-hand experience of all those years ago, for I'm sure the majority of Yorkshire folk today have never lived in a one up, one down 'back-to-back'!

The streets themselves were where the washing was strung across from side to side, line-props wedged in the cobbles of the road, clothes billowing and flapping like ship's sails. Hardly any traffic used these streets anyway, the milkman and coalman were about the only suppliers who called frequently and *they* each had a horse and cart. I can't actually remember the middens being emptied, though I can't think why, for they must have been emptied many times over during the two years I was there – overall. And many of the men had an allotment – sometimes quite some distance away – so the horse-manure never went begging. And the kids of course, used the streets as playgrounds.

So it was very generous of Mr and Mrs Martin – very generous indeed – to offer to share their restricted facilities with a complete stranger. People were like that in those days though, maybe not very sophisticated by present-day standards, but so warm, friendly and generous.

The living room contained a dining table and some dining chairs, and one rocking chair. And I think that was it. There wasn't room for much more in any case, although – wait a moment! I have in fact forgotten the sideboard. There was a big, shiny black kitchen range where all the food was cooked – with the exception of bread – and to one side of this was a white china sink, fed by one solitary tap. Which was of course, cold! All washing, shaving etc. was carried out in this room, with nowhere else for people to go so that you were left with a little privacy, although I think there was a curtain to pull across. And the lighting was provided by gas mantles, although I think most folk had an oil lamp as well. Candles too were still very widely used.

But I took to this way of life instantly and was very quickly accepted as one of theirs. I came to like the food too, especially Yorkshire Pudding, Spice-Loaf, and Bakehouse Bread. This isn't to say that northern food was better than southern food; it's just that some was different, as in fact would be the case right across the country.

I was straight away enrolled at school, which couldn't have been closer. Our house was fifth from the end of the street, and the school railings ran across that end, blocking it off. The pavement outside our front door ended slap-bang at the school gate, a distance of about twenty paces. T'was a good job I enjoyed going to school, for I'd have found it difficult playing truant I should think, being that close.

We were allowed to play in the school yard out of hours, which was very useful for me, right on my doorstep. Mind you, the occasional window got broken, especially when we became over-zealous with those super 'flying' tops. Whip and top was all the rage then, had been for quite some years I should think, for they were simple enough, and well within everyone's reach. There were various types of top, mushrooms, bullets, spinners – although I expect they'll be differently named from county to county. But these flyers were strongly fancied by those lusty lads, and great fun, till of course, you heard that tinkle of glass.

The girls skipped and played hopscotch as well, and did french knitting and 'cat's cradle'. All simple and inexpensive pastimes, yet everyone was happy. For French knitting you needed one empty cotton reel and four panel pins. The pins were tapped a little way into one end of the reel, forming a square around the hole. Wool was then passed around the outside of the pins, and as you passed each pin on the second turn, you lifted the first turn up past the second, then over and off the pin, letting it settle on the inside. You kept going round like this, pulling the work down through the hole by the tail that you'd left when casting on. Any oddments of wool would do, and the work came though as a braided cord, about a quarter inch thick. This was wound round and stitched into flat pads, forming colourful mats to be used as teapot stands and the like. No doubt many other useful things were made from it too, but I can't remember now, after all, it was a girls' pastime really.

The cat's cradle was made from a piece of cord about 35 – 40 inches long, whose ends you joined to form a loop. Two people took part, the first placing it round her hands as you would a hank of wool when holding it up for somebody to wind into a ball. An extra turn was then taken around each palm, then the second person would lift it off and onto her own hands in such a way as to alter its shape. It was then transferred from one to the other, each time changing shape until the end was finally achieved.

Each of these pastimes cost practically nothing at all – could be carried around in a pocket – could be done over and over again, and in any situation. And by necessity the latter brought two people close together, with a common aim. And of course, each provided excellent exercise for the fingers and the mind. How different from today, when so many children sit in front of a screen, in their own little world, taking in endless drivel. And at what cost? Our forefathers had practically nothing, but they certainly knew how to derive maximum pleasure from it, benefit too.

All the women shared one particular pastime – the making of 'Clip Rugs'. You never saw woven carpets anywhere, or mats, other than in upper-class homes of course – and cinemas. Just these traditional and very cleverly patterned rugs, made from some sort of sack-cloth backing, and scrap material – such as skirts or trousers – cut into strips about four inches long if I remember correctly. The strips were poked through the sacking, then back up again somehow so that both ends were uppermost. Different colours were introduced in such order as to finish up with a perfectly symmetrical pattern. I myself spent a few hours at this – in short snatches – just for the sake of it. But not enough it seems, to recall the procedure in more detail.

Most living rooms had one of these rugs, wall to wall, and they certainly made it warm and cosy. *And* quiet. Which was just as well in view of the closeness of your neighbours – *on three sides*! Yet I certainly can't recall any sounds coming through those walls, hard as I think back. Fortunately, none of today's high-powered music systems were around then, otherwise the situation might have been very much different. All we had then was the good old wireless, although Raymond did have a piano accordion, and Edith across the road a piano, upon which Joyce did an hour's practice every day. Oh yes, the harmonica was quite a popular instrument then as well, and I think there was the odd banjo about. But people were much closer then, and I'm sure much more considerate towards each other.

Most of the menfolk, between the ages of about eighteen and the late forties, were away fighting the war, so the women were left largely to themselves. So when the day's work was done they used to pop into each others' houses for a 'cal'. I don't know the origin of this word, or whether I've spelt it correctly, but it rhymes with pal. This is when they would sit together, either knitting or rug-making, and generally having a jolly good chin-wag, which I think was the *real* meaning of the word. And swooning around the wireless as Donald Peers woo-ed them with 'In a shady nook' and the like.

They were less inhibited than the southern women – in certain respects. They would sit breast-feeding their young in full view of whoever happened to be in the room, without a qualm. Unless it was just me; perhaps they felt that at the tender age of twelve I was too young for them to worry about. But I'd never seen that part of a woman up until then – apart from those sniggering peeps through the crack in the bathroom door at the older girls in the Home. But that was different. This was so open and it embarrassed me. I'd be sitting there listening to the conversation, or the wireless, then suddenly and quite without warning they'd undo a button or two and whammo! – there it was. I didn't know where to look. Well, to start with that is, for I *jolly* soon got used to it!

As dusk fell the women would start calling in their youngsters who were playing out. They could be in their own street or any other in the area. So the custom was to stand on the doorstep and 'holler' the child's name. This would be in two syllables, and on two notes – either end of an octave. 'Val-REE' – 'Alf-EE' – 'Kei-EETH'. So from dusk onwards the air used to ring with these calls, other than in high-summer of course, when it was light until about 11 p.m.

This also used to happen on a Sunday morning, just before dinner time. But we were all anticipating this particular call – eagerly awaiting it in fact – and were never far away. So one call was usually enough. It was when the first batch of Yorkshire Puddings had been made, ready for dinner. On the kitchen range, stacked high on one or two plates, were these thin, pancake-shaped puddings. They varied in size – but never in taste – and were absolutely delicious. Custom was that the kids all had one before they actually came in for dinner. A kind of foretaste. Off we skipped, grinning broadly at each other as we happily gorged ourselves, other kids tumbling through doorways doing the same.

At dinner time proper the Yorkshire Pudding was always a separate course – served first – and came in a lovely gravy, with onions. You could keep going back for more, until they were all gone. And go they always did, for whatever food *might* be left over – never was it Yorkshire puddings. I for one could have filled myself up with them – and nowt else. The main course followed, usually a simple meat-and-two-veg meal, but I can't recall having a pudding, or sweet as some call it. Perhaps we did occasionally, but there was never a lot of money about then.

I mentioned earlier 'Spice Loaf' and 'Bakehouse Bread'. These two items compared equally with Yorkshire pudding for deliciousness. The Spice Loaf was the equivalent of Christmas cake – Yorkshire style – but there was no icing or decoration on it of any kind. Just a beautiful mixture of fruit and spices. It would be sliced like bread, and eaten with cheese. I couldn't imagine it at first, especially as I wasn't all that keen on cheese at that age. I hasten to add though, that I have since developed quite a partiality for it. But when I tried it – on my first Yorkshire Christmas – I loved it instantly. The women would make their own mixture, fill anything from one to say five loaf-shaped baking tins, then at the appropriate time pop them across to the 'bakehouse'. They must have put some form of identification on them I guess, for when they were collected later. I'm not sure why they didn't bake them themselves, but that bakehouse was used daily by everybody anyway, and the baker was a very popular fellow, very popular indeed.

Which brings me to the bread. Each morning, quite early, one member from each household trekked across the York Road to the bakehouse, a single-storied building of no particular character, which stood alone on a seemingly waste piece of ground, just beyond the end of our road. Most were sleepy-eyed children – not long out of bed – but I always wakened fully to the wonderful smell that greeted your approach. You said how many you'd come for, then were handed that number – straight from the oven almost. They were round, again pancake-shaped, and something up to about two inches in thickness, if my memory serves me correctly. And there was a small hole in the middle, though I never did find out why.

Back home with it you were each torn off a hunk, which you split with your fingers, using a knife merely to lay on the 'butter', which, as they were always eaten before they'd cooled down too much, melted right in. The overall flavour and texture were quite superb. Used dry, the bread was also great for mopping up the juice from your egg, bacon and tomato breakfast on Sunday – if you were lucky!

Other than those three specialities food was much the same as I'd known in the south. I said 'butter' by the way, because being wartime, the women used to mix our meagre rations up somehow, to make things go further. I don't know what they mixed it with but they called it 'best butter'. As opposed to margarine I guess.

Mr Martin – whom I called Grandad – was one of those who had an allotment. It seemed a long way away at the time but was perhaps no more than a mile or two. He had a big wooden box on wheels, with a pair of wooden shafts, much like a roadsweeper's handcart. This he'd fill with horse-manure, which as I've said, was quite abundant. Young Keith – his only grandson at the time, was set on top of this, then with the dog on one side and me on the other, off we'd set. It was a nice trip, for we always saw lots of tramcars, showing various destinations. They were all foreign to me at first of course, Gipton, Harehills, Roundhay, though I did get to all these places at a later date. I suppose I ought really to say that Keith would have been sitting on a cover of some sort, not directly on the manure!

Nearly every chap on these allotments kept pigeons – which I strongly suspect was the *real* interest behind it all, though of course the produce was very welcome too. So instead of a mere garden shed, they had something a bit bigger, which doubled as a pigeon loft. The first thing then – on arrival – was to release the birds for their exercise. I must say, I found their sleek appearance, lovely colouring and gentle coo-ing most attractive, and I loved watching them swoop to and fro in perfect formation. We'd jigger about a bit with the allotment, in between watching them, but they were without doubt the main attraction. At length, when it was nearly time for us to be leaving, Mr Martin began a gentle whistling, through cupped hands, calling them home. They continued circling a while, still in beautiful formation but coming closer and closer, till eventually they landed, and strutted jerkily back into their quarters. He did whatever he had to do for them, then off we all trudged home. A most enjoyable experience for me, and one that I repeated many times.

It wasn't long before I moved in with Edith and her children across the road. Doug, Edith's husband, was away at the war, and theirs was one of three houses that had a second bedroom, and immediately beneath it a separate little kitchen. They were still back-to-back but each had, to the front, a small walled garden. There were scores and scores of houses in the area, all in unbroken rows, but these three were the only ones with these extra facilities. They stood in a short row on their own, ours being at the end where the loo area was. Beyond this was the school yard. So we were quite conveniently placed – and – we had our own loo, the other two families sharing the second one.

In the main bedroom there were two double beds, with a single bed in the small second bedroom, which was where Keith slept. I shall never forget their kindness in giving me this small room and bed all to myself, whilst they all squeezed into the other room.

I became a kind of big brother to Joyce, Valerie and Keith, called Mrs Miller 'Mam' as they all did, and in no time at all lost my southern accent completely. I was speaking as broad Yorkshire as any of them. This happened quite naturally, and after a while I couldn't believe I hadn't always spoken this way. Places and people were not at all as cosmopolitan as they are now, so I was completely surrounded by this strong Yorkshire accent all the time, both at home and at school.

With no bathrooms and very restricted toilet facilities, much use was made of the 'Public Slipper Baths'. I'm not exactly sure what a slipper bath was, but every Saturday morning I used to go across for my weekly bath. Need it or not! The place was quite close to us, no more than about a hundred yards I'd say, and also housed a full-size indoor swimming 'bath'. So for tuppence (less than 1p) I was handed a clean, but very hard towel, a small slab of soap, and a ticket, and had a bath all to myself.

After passing through the turnstile you took your place on a long wooden form, alongside all the others who were waiting their turn. Women and girls of course had their own area, separated from ours. It was quite damp in there naturally, wet stone floors and white tiles everywhere, all running in water. A bit scary at first to a little 'un like me. When your turn came the attendant went in ahead of you to clean up after the previous user, then he'd start the water running and come out and let you in. The main thing I remember about it all now is how cold it always was. There were no ceilings to the cubicles, which were quite big, and gaps of about six inches at the bottom of the walls. In fact, with little effort anyone could look in on you, either above or below the walls. The water seemed always to be cold, or very nearly so, and you stood on a duckboard to dry yourself off. Talk about goose-pimples! I was always mighty glad to get my clothes back on I can tell you. But once over that little discomfort I always felt nice and refreshed.

During your bath you'd hear several budding Carusos, all airing their voices at the same time – and *all* singing different songs. And of course, no sooner had you shut yourself in your cubicle than those still waiting outside began chivvying you up so that they could get in. You'd hand in your towel on your way out, then probably go off to play football with your pals, getting all nicely muddied up again!

I used the swimming bath occasionally at first, but after catching impetigo, I gave that up in case that was where I'd picked it up. It was in the summer that I caught it. Mrs Miller took me to Leeds Infirmary where I was treated, and swathed in bandages for weeks. It seemed like weeks anyway. It had started in my ear, and still wearing short trousers I had soon transferred it to my knees, as well as all over my hands. So I was bandaged everywhere, head, hands, knees – I must have looked like Jim Brady the *Invisible Man*. I was very relieved indeed to see the back of that episode. It may well have come from some source other than the swimming baths, but I wasn't going to chance a second helping! The only thing in its favour was that I didn't have to go to school. But in truth, I liked school anyway.

School was much as it had been elsewhere, with nothing standing out significantly. Except that is, being invited to write for the 'Boy's Own' magazine. I had always liked composition, and regularly received pretty good marks for my work. But I felt this would intrude into my fun with the lads, as indeed my paper round had done earlier. So I declined the invitation, but have wondered ever since how things might have turned out had I accepted.

Television was a long way off then, nobody had even heard the word. Well, not in *our* world anyway. So the item which provided the main topic of conversation amongst the kids – apart from sport and the 'pictures' – was the comic. As I've said, nobody had much in those times, but somehow we all managed to lay our hands on those. So popular were they that squabbles would break out between brothers and sisters as to who should have first read. I clearly remember popping across the road when it was my turn, and curling up in 'Grandad's' rocking chair, so that I should enjoy my read to the full.

The 'Dandy' and 'Beano' were the most popular I think, though I can remember enjoying also the 'Knockout' and 'Film Fun'. For the very young there was 'Chips Own' – or was it 'Chicks Own'? – with Tiger Tim and all his animal friends. Then later, us older boys would go on to the 'Hotspur', 'Rover', 'Wizard' and the like. But these were pretty well all text, no comic strips. But I'm sure that overall, by far the most popular were the 'Beano' and 'Dandy'.

The characters were marvellous. There was Lord Snooty and his pals, Korky the Cat, Keyhole Kate, Doubting Thomas, Freddie the fearless Fly, Desperate Dan – forever stuffing himself with enormous 'Cow Pies'. These are the first that come to mind, but I'll never forget 'Our Ernie'. I can't remember which comic he featured in, it was either the 'Beano' or the 'Dandy', and he always appeared at the very end. The first frame showed him setting off from home in the morning for school. He'd never get very far before he became caught up in the most fantastic adventures – outer space and *everything*. (And we knew practically nothing about space then). But the final frame always saw him walking nonchalantly through the back doorway – home from school – dressed as ever in his school cap, short trousers, socks down to his ankles and satchel slung casually across his shoulder. And the final caption never varied either as he calmly inquired, 'What's for tea Ma?'

Yes, comics – in my opinion – not only gave tremendous pleasure in the reading and swapping, but brought us all together as well.

One of the first questions put to me when I was introduced to some of the local kids the day after my arrival was, 'Cat-light or Proddy-dog?' I was flummoxed. What they were actually trying to discover was whether I was a Roman Catholic or a Protestant. Quite honestly I had to stop and think, for in the south the question had never really arisen. I gave my answer, but it made not the slightest difference to our relationship with each other. Yet it had seemed necessary to know – much as on 'Boat Race Day' with 'Oxford or Cambridge?' Just a formality probably. The

question never arose after that in any way, shape or form. If ever there were
disagreements between people, I don't recall religion coming into it. We all lived
and played together quite harmoniously, whatever our beliefs.

Our street was quite short compared to most of them, due to the school wall
cutting right across one end. At the other end was the main York Road, where we
went for our daily bread, and our weekly bath, and where those wonderful, fascinating
trams ran at regular intervals. They used to stop at the end of the street, so we could
hear them building up speed and clanging their bells as they pulled away. I used to
lie in bed listening to them coming and going, till I fell asleep. *Wonderful.*

The street next to ours was also short, for the same reason – the school. Then there
was a long road called Saville Green, whose surface was the exception to the rule in
that it was Tarmacadam and quite smooth. From the York Road end it sloped
downhill all the way, coming to an end at a largish piece of waste ground known
locally as 'The Hollow'. There were turnings to either side of this road throughout its
length – all cobbled and with gas-lighting – in which were more back-to-back, one-
up-and-downers. In fact the whole area comprised this type of dwelling as I say.

One of our favourite sports was to place a piece of board, about nine by twelve
inches, or more likely and old 'Rupert Bear' annual (very popular then) on a roller
skate at the top end of the road, sit on it, then with hands gripping the sides of this
seat for steering, and knees tight up under your chin so as to get your heels on – off
you'd go.

It became a 'chicken-run' amongst us lads of course. As you gained speed, so the
sensitivity of the steering increased and you could start to wobble quite a bit. Then
you might either fall off, or lose your nerve and chicken out by turning into one of the
cobbled side streets, which wasn't really much better. The object was to stay the
whole course, finally making for the last turning on the right, on the corner of which
was the local 'Bookie's' house. I reckon we must have been doing 30 – 40 miles an
hour by the time we'd reached that point, so the landing was always a bone-shaking,
painful business, as you spilled off onto the cobbles or hit the kerbstone in front of
the Bookies's and were tossed onto the flagstones.

But you'd made it – and felt justifiably proud. You'd pick up your skate, tuck
your book under your arm and – grinning – though inwardly wincing, limp back up
to the top again. As I've said, there was little or no traffic on these side roads, so the
only danger you were really confronted with was your own 'bad-driving', or timidity.
Lack of bottle in today's language. We'd have several runs to a session, giving up
only when the champion of the day had been established, or when everyone was so
bruised and bloodied as to make going on sheer lunacy. But the former was usually
the case. A most enjoyable, if painful pastime, and generally inexpensive. I can't say

totally inexpensive, for your clothes could sometimes get ripped up a bit.

Near the bottom of Saville Green was the 'Chippie', one of the three places of significance in the area. The other two were the previously mentioned 'Bookie', and 'The Glassie'. The latter was the local pub, and was really just one, or maybe two of the houses converted for the purpose. It's proper name was 'The Glass and Bottle' I think, but I never heard it called anything other than 'The Glassie', (rhyming with lassie). These three establishments were heavily frequented every single day, so I'm sure the proprietors must have made a pretty good living.

The only one I used was the Chippie. In those days fish and chips was an extremely tasty, yet quite inexpensive meal. I don't suggest it isn't still just as tasty today, but my goodness, it's anything but cheap now. Even allowing for inflation. For about fourpence or fivepence (about 2p) you could really fill yourself up. They also made 'Potato Cakes', which I particularly liked. I think they were slices of potato, probably about 2½" in diameter by about ½" thick, deep-fried in the normal batter. They were really scrumptious. When us lads were really hard up – which was quite frequently – we used to ask for a ha'porth of crackling. They'd run their scoop through the frying oil, or fat – whatever it was – collecting all the little bits of batter that had become separated in the frying. If you were lucky with your timing you'd get a big bagful. I don't suppose it was very good for us, being so fatty, but we sure did enjoy it and it helped satisfy our hunger.

When we had fish and chips as a main meal, we had lots of bread and butter with it, and a pot of lovely hot sweet tea. When I say pot, I don't mean teapot. I mean mug, in the southern vernacular. Everyone, at least every male, had a large mug, usually white and with a capacity of a pint, or very near. And it was always called a 'pot'. I very soon got used to this idea too.

The Bookie as I say, was a very busy chap, especially as he did a normal day's work as well – or so I believe. There wasn't much for the menfolk to do after work, by comparison with today that is, mostly looking after their pigeons and allotments – those that had them. Other than that it seemed, it was mostly the Glassie. I guess they just hoped to win enough from the Bookie to be able to treat their wives and youngsters occasionally or have a jolly good drink with their pals. Women used the pub as well, but I'm sure the clientèle was predominantly male. I had a couple of flutters at the Bookie's later, after I'd started work. But I had no luck and soon wrote this off as a futile pastime. Unless of course you were the Bookie. But The Glassie I *never* used, for I'd left Yorkshire before I'd really reached that age.

'The Hollow' covered probably no more than an acre or two, and it was quite rough ground. Grass struggled sparsely here and there, but it was a good place for the kids to play, although they mostly preferred the streets or school yard. But us lads found it ideal for football or generally 'laiking' about on – laik being the local word for play – though again, I'm not sure of the spelling. Occasionally, though not very often, I seem to remember The Hollow being used as a place to settle arguments, that had perhaps been raised in the Glassie nearby.

Whitsuntide was a big occasion in those parts at that time, and not only for the obvious religious reasons. This was the time when all the kids had new clothes. At Whit-weekend itself we all went strutting about in these smart new clothes, comparing ourselves with each other. It mattered little if your shoes maybe pinched a bit at first – as they invariably did in those days – we all felt quite grand. I never discovered the origins of this particular practice, and don't know if it still persists. Instead of having an Easter parade, we had a Whitsun Parade.

Quite often, on a fine Sunday afternoon in summer, we – like lots of other families – took a tram ride to Roundhay Park. I don't remember much about that particular place, but I do know that I very much enjoyed going there, with my 'family'. I have a feeling there was a nice lake there, but I could be wrong about that. I also seem to remember a bandstand, where those wonderful brass or silver bands gave us free entertainment. What super music that was – I *loved* it – and do yet. And of course, the tram ride home absolutely rounded off a right 'gradely' afternoon. Well for me it most certainly did.

I also remember Mr and Mrs Miller taking us all to see Kirkstall Abbey. And I felt so lucky, enjoying such a good life and with such nice people. At Christmas they took us to see a pantomime. I can't remember which one it was, but what a treat! As Christmas approached, we kids were encouraged to save whatever pocket money we may have come by to buy our Christmas 'Spice'. I wondered at first what this Spice was, but soon discovered it was Yorkshire for sweets. Us four, that is, Joyce, Valerie, Keith and myself all managed somehow to receive identical amounts when Christmas actually came, even though I'm sure we hadn't all saved the same sum. I suspect their parents had a hand in that of course. I can remember even now, watching that panto and eating a delicious Mars Bar – savouring every morsel.

We were taken to the 'pictures' occasionally as well. This was to see the kind of films appropriate to our tender years – 'Snow White and the Seven Dwarfs' – 'Wizard of Oz' etc. I thoroughly enjoyed these trips, and the films. But I must say, the whole scene was quite tame after those Friday nights at the Granada in London, with the sing-songs, talent contests, and bombs dropping all around us!

I liked football a lot in those days, though I regret to say I have little interest in the game now. It's a different game altogether, lots of play-acting and tantrums. And absolutely ridiculous earnings, although I think I should substitute the word 'rewards' for earnings, for in my opinion nobody actually 'earns' that kind of money, whatever their walk of life. Again, that's my opinion, but I'm sure it's one that'll be shared by many. There is so much suffering and deprivation in the world today, some of us do what we can to help, but others turn their heads. But I digress...

In those days I think the players regarded football as a job as well as a sport, and the professionals earned a wage that wasn't that much more than people in ordinary jobs earned. In the late forties when I used to go to Highbury as a regular supporter of Arsenal, top players such as Logie and Lewis earned only about twelve pounds per week, or so I've always believed. Here in Yorkshire, we went to Elland Road one week to watch Leeds United playing football, and Headingly the next to watch Rugby League.

I must have played the game quite well myself I guess, for I was in the school team. I generally played at Right Half. We had no facilities for football at our school of course, placed as it was, so our matches were often played on a Saturday morning on a park somewhere. We walked home after the game, all muddied up and still wearing our boots and strip. The old style football boots didn't lend themselves too well to walking long distances on hard ground. In fact they really made your feet hurt. But we were that proud – especially if we'd won. We had to pass a baker's shop on the way home from the park we mostly played on, and always called in to buy a cake each. I always had an almond slice – they were gorgeous, and at least twice the size they are today. Or does my memory play tricks? No – they *were* twice the size.

We had no facilities at our school for woodwork either. So when that lesson came up we had to go to another school some distance away. We each had to provide our own apron – a proper carpenter's apron with kangaroo pouch, slanting breast pocket and everything! I very much enjoyed these lessons for I love working with wood, especially by hand, as we were. And for twelve-year-olds we made some pretty good things – table lamps, letter racks etc. The best bit though, was walking home afterwards. As with the football strip, we kept our aprons on, and weren't we the cat's whiskers again! Proper little show-offs the lot of us!

Mr Clegg, the woodwork master, was a very strict man, unlike his namesake on the very popular television series 'Last of the Summer Wine', which has been showing for some years now. If he caught you not paying attention to his instruction, he'd throw a mallet at you. We mostly paid attention.

I have a couple more memories of those times which I hold very dear. The first, and clearest, is of the 'Knocker-Upper'. I don't know whether it was because people couldn't afford alarm clocks, or whether it was purely traditional, but this person came up and down the streets with a long pole. He'd start very early, probably about 4 a.m. – though this is now a guess – tapping on the bedroom windows and calling out the time. 'Coom on, Alfie lad – it's nigh haff past fower'. Then on a bit – 'Haff past fower Jackie!' 'Ayoop ower Annie, it's five and twenty oop!' Some of the streets were quite long, yet somehow everyone was called at the pre-arranged time. I think there must have been more than one Knocker-Upper.

Soon after, you'd begin to hear front doors being pulled shut, and footsteps *hurrying* across the cobbles as folk made their way to work. For it wouldn't do to be late, this was much frowned upon and could easily cost you your job. I soon got used to this early morning clamour, and like everyone else who wasn't being called, learned to sleep through it.

Then there was the Lamp-lighter. As I've said earlier, street lighting was by quaint little gas lamps – of the sort George Formby used to 'lean against'! The lamp, lighter carried a short ladder if I remember correctly, which he rested against the short cross-bar just under the lamp itself. This he mounted, then he opened one side of the glass case and lit the gas. Then on to the next, and the next, till every lamp was lit. Some time later he must have come back round again to extinguish them all I guess, but time has clouded the memory on that part of it, I'm afraid.

The light given off by these lamps was somewhat dim I think, but the pleasure they gave us kids was great. A piece of rope thrown over the cross-bar provided endless fun, for girls and boys alike. In retrospect, I cannot remember whether those lamps were lit during the war years, although I suspect not. They certainly wouldn't have been down *south*. I rather fancy they were in 1947 though, when I returned to Leeds after the war, which I shall come to later.

As I write, I cannot for the life of me remember why, but after about a year I left this life and all my friends behind, when I returned to London, and Ma and Pop. So vague is this part now that I can't even remember whether I was happy or sad. I would most certainly have been very happy at the thought of seeing Ma and Pop again, but equally, I would have been very sad at leaving Leeds. But was it for a sad reason? I just cannot remember now. I can't even recall the train journey back – yet the journey up had thrilled me to bits.

BACK TO LONDON

I pretty well picked up where I'd left off at Ma and Pop's. It was now 1945 and I was in my fourteenth year. Chas was in the Far East with the Royal Navy, and I believe George had gone to live at his pal's house about a mile away. If he hadn't gone then he went shortly afterwards. But Prince was still there, so too were the chicks and chickens. And so of course, was Doris, engaged now to Bob, who was in the Royal Air Force. If I remember correctly he was stationed at Colchester, and I think he managed to get week-end leave pretty regularly, but I could be wrong there.

The barber still did his barbering below, and the 'Bug-hutch' was still going strong on the corner. I think the air-raids may have eased off a bit since I had left, but we now had the added hazard of the 'Buzz Bomb', (V1).

I returned to the school I'd left the year before when I'd gone to Leeds, but it wasn't long before another school at nearby Neasden received a direct hit and was too badly damaged to be usable. Our school was the nearest, I suppose, so once again it was part-time schooling whilst the bombed-out kids shared ours. Mind you, we had a few very close shaves ourselves. I remember having lessons in the school air-raid shelter one day. We heard the approach of a Buzz-bomb, and looked at each other apprehensively as we listened to that awful, harsh drone of its motor – and waited.

For anybody who didn't experience those times, the V1 looked very much like a small monoplane, of the normally manned type. But it's tone was absolutely unmistakable. It was a very sinister sound, which even the hardiest of us couldn't help regarding with a certain amount of fear. But it wasn't so much the *sound* of it that you dreaded. In fact, all the time you could hear it you were relatively safe. It was when the motor suddenly, and very abruptly cut out that your pulse quickened. For at that point the thing began its descent, and unless you could actually see it, you had no idea where it was going to hit. But you knew for certain that it *was* coming, and I shall never forget that awful feeling during those few seconds of deadly silence before the explosion. Were these our last moments?

On this particular day the motor cut when we could tell it was within striking distance of us. 'Down!' yelled our teacher, which was the signal for everyone to lie flat on the ground, face down. I threw myself forward rather quickly – and rather

49

carelessly – for my nose made pretty firm contact with the concrete floor. The doodlebug (it's common name) passed over us, but it must have only just missed us,for we clearly felt the blast of the explosion, and when we emerged after the 'All Clear' had sounded, we could see just how close the stricken houses were.

Anyone seeing my bloody nose could have been forgiven for thinking that it was our school that had actually copped it! And I must say, I regard myself as very lucky really, for with the exception of the one year that I spent in Yorkshire and the eight months in Northampton, I'd spent my entire war in London. And the worst I experienced was blast damage to doors and windows. And I don't think much had happened during those first eight months anyway, on the Home Front that is.

Mind you, as an avid collector of shrapnel, as indeed were most youngsters, it's a wonder we didn't lose a hand here and there. For Jerry started dropping things that I'm sure were named 'Butterfly Bombs' – but again – I could be wrong about the name. These despicable bombs would be in the form of things that were very eye-catching to children – a small toy, a brooch, maybe a fountain pen. They lay inert, but extremely inviting, as bait to a doomed animal. As soon as they were touched – *Bang*! Fortunately we were well warned about these booby traps, and all the other dangers that abounded during the war, which must have minimised the injuries to some degree. For although we were quite young, we certainly took such things seriously, although we never *ever* let it get us down. Even in the worst of the blitz – and the doodlebug menace – morale was extremely high amongst us all, young and old alike. But of course, this could be quite badly dented at times for some, as loved ones and dear ones were lost.

Thinking back, I guess these Butterfly Bombs might well have been placed rather than dropped, for the enemy – as we were constantly warned – mixed freely amongst us.

As 1945 progressed, excitement began to mount. We knew the end of the war was in sight – right had again triumphed over evil. And we looked forward eagerly to the better times that would follow. In some ways this was indeed quite true. No more bombing on the home front, and the assurance that absent, but still living loved ones would soon be returning from the war front itself. But in many ways things weren't much better, to the contrary in fact. But we didn't know this then, and after all the rigours and deprivations, couldn't wait for it. The threat of the V2 loomed, but how much *that* actually affected us I can't say, for I never saw one, nor did I have any experience of them that I can recall.

As victory in Europe became more imminent, there was lots of bustle as preparations were made for the celebrations we'd all dreamed of for 5½ years. On VE night itself there were street parties all over London. Everywhere else too I'm sure. Tables were butted end to end in the centre of each road, throughout its entire length – excluding the main roads of course – to form one enormously long one. Chairs were put to them and they were laid with table-cloths and all sorts of goodies, carefully saved from everybody's rations. There were cakes and jellies and paper hats and crackers, and every youngster had his or her fill. And there was bunting and the like stretching from one lamp-post to the next, zig-zagging across the street as it went. And streamers flew everywhere. And needless to say, the good old Union Jack – as we wrongly refer to the Union Flag – hung everywhere.

There was music later, and as kids laughed and cried, as they always do at large gatherings, grown-ups danced and drank and kissed and laughed their way all through the night. What an experience! And what a mess the next morning! But everybody – yes *everybody* buckled to, as we did then, and in no time at all those streets were all clean and tidy again, though how everyone managed to sort out their own furniture, tablecloths, crockery and cutlery I can't imagine.

The same happened on VJ night (victory over Japan) in the middle of August, just a few weeks short of six years since the war had started. But although this definitely marked the end of the war, I can't be sure that the excitement matched that of VE night. And yet, thinking back, there were bonfires the length and breadth of the British Isles, and apparently most major cities were 'painted red' – London most *certainly* was. So it probably did.

Peace was something of an anti-climax at first, well to me personally at least. There was lots of talk and planning for the future, but I missed all the action and excitement of the war. Barrage balloons came down, sandbags were removed, shelters and Operations Centres became suddenly defunct and the nights were disturbingly quiet. Rationing continued just the same so no relief was felt there. And I imagined all our troops and airmen wandering aimlessly about, their mission completed. The *Navy* would be busy for some time yet though, fetching everybody home.

I finished school at the end of that year, even though I had won a Scholarship place at Grammar School and should have stayed on two or three years longer, as I would have loved to have done. But I was now fourteen and legally entitled to take up full-time employment. And under the circumstances it seemed only fair that I should earn my keep as soon as possible.

In the meantime, Ma and Pop had taken me about with them quite a bit. The place we went to mostly was the Railwaymen's Club at Wembley Park. This was always at week-ends. I don't know what their connection with the railway could have been. I don't think Pop had ever been employed thereon, but I do know he had several friends who were engine drivers and the like. Some of them had allotments, and I went along with them now and again. But no pigeons! And once I was treated to a ride on the London Underground – in the driver's cab. This was quite unofficial, of course, but what a fascinating and noisy experience that was. I think really I would have much preferred a journey on the footplate of one of those massive yet beautiful steam engines. But alas, this was not to be.

Once or twice I went to the dog-racing with Ma and Pop at the White City Stadium – then we'd have the occasional trip to Cookham in Berkshire, for a day out in the country. I loved that, for I am most surely a countryman at heart. Pop also took me to Petticoat Lane once or twice on a Sunday morning, and Club Row. All new and fascinating things to me. Then there was the fair at Hampstead heath – that was *marvellous*.

I came to really enjoy these trips to Wembley Park. It was a low and very pleasant building, on the edge of a large and very attractive sportsground. Further along from the club itself was a smart and spacious pavilion, and behind the club was the house occupied by the Club Steward and his family. The whole lot belonged to the Railway. There was a very well kept cricket pitch, with a running track all round it, and in the pavilion was equipment to do with other sports and athletic pursuits.

It was a wide and open situation with plenty of trees all around. The inside of the club was very smart and comfortable, and of course, we were still in the days when good dance music was provided by equally good bands. It was mostly families that went there so I made the odd friend or two. Then the Steward and his family suddenly left and replacements came. And, this was to have quite an impact on me for the next year or so.

Mr and Mrs Elsey – the new Stewards – were nice people, and they had two sons. Bernard was about my age, Roy a year or two older, and quite tall and slim. Bernard and I were still at school – just – and Roy was working for an Insurance Company, I think. Their arrival opened up a whole new scene to me. Being part of the management they had access to the pavilion, and use of the grounds. So after the week-end cricket matches were over, we used to stage our own athletic events. Shot-putting, running, throwing the javelin etc, although I think the javelin we used was home-made.

We had fun in the pavilion too, especially after dark. There was another boy who came to the club with his parents. He was a wimp, and we didn't really want his company but he clung to us like a limpet. So after dark we'd let him follow us into the pavilion, which was unlit and quite spooky, then frighten the life out of him in the hope that he wouldn't bother us again. But he always did. Occasionally we'd watch the cricket in the afternoon, but mostly we went off to some other event. I'd never packed such a variety of interesting things into my life before and this was a very thrilling period for me, very thrilling indeed.

Saturday afternoon began the week's cycle of events. When Arsenal were playing at home the three of us would go to Highbury and give our support. The game was good then, hard but fair, and football hooligans had not yet evolved, thank goodness. There was a rivalry between opposing supporters of course, but friendly, and in the true spirit of the game. You could stand shoulder to shoulder without any fear whatsoever. Hard to imagine today!

When the 'Gunners' were playing away, we'd either watch the 'B' team or go to Herne Hill to watch Reg Harris and his contemporaries on the cycle race-track. Or we might go to Cricklewood Roller Skating Rink and roll the afternoon away. Then it was back to Roy and Bernard's for tea, which always finished with a Lyon's Individual Fruit Pie each – to which I became very partial. Then we'd be off down the road a little way to watch Ice Hockey at Wembley Pool. I quite enjoyed watching this sport I suppose, but in no way could I match the enthusiasm of my two companions. It wasn't really my game, very fast but clumsy.

Sunday afternoon we whiled away at something or other, then off we'd go to Wembley Pool again, for an evening's ice skating. I really enjoyed this, once the initial embarrassment was behind me. This I had to endure at the start of every session, and it went on for a good many months too. The trouble was we didn't have skates of our own – few people did – and had to hire them when we got there. The first time, all three of us queued up round at the men's side, but when I said what shoe size *I* took, it was one size below the smallest they issued at that counter. So I had to go and queue up round the other side – with the women and girls!

To see the female leg very much above shin-level was quite rare then, except at the pictures of course, but now – I was surrounded by them – right up to and even including a bit of the bottom! They wore the teeniest skirts on the ice, which was fine when you were all out there together. But here, I was on my own amongst them. They soon sensed my unease and brother – did they exploit it! Once I knew the boots I'd been issued were the right fit I tore round to the men's side and finished putting them on there. Was I glad when I'd grown that little bit and needed the next size – for which I could queue up with my taller pals.

I don't recall doing much in the evenings at the beginning of the week. Now and again I'd go to the cinema by myself, sometimes I'd stay in with Ma and Pop, listening to the wireless. I loved the wireless, and even now, if I had to choose between radio and television, I know which I'd go for.

There was 'The Happidrome', and Carol Levis with his talented 'discoveries'. And Big Bill Campbell, passing the 'applejack' around the camp fire in between giving out with some good old country music. There were some darned good comedians around at the time too, and excellent drama. And of course, the music of the day was absolutely fantastic – Artie Shaw, Tommy Dorsey, Glen Miller, Benny Goodman, Duke Ellington. And the *singers*! What a tremendous era to have been around in. And no way could I leave out Django Reinhardt, who with Stephane Grappelly, founded the unsurpassable 'Hot Club de France'. Ser-*mashing*!

Then it was Thursday. And for us three it was, without doubt, the highlight of the whole week. For on that night we went to Wembley Stadium to watch Speedway racing. The most thrilling and exciting of all sports – for me at any rate. We idolised the entire Wembley Lions team, led by Bill Kitchen the captain, who was more than ably backed up by Tommy Price, Bronco Wilson, and others whose names are beyond my recall just now. The 'Lions' were champions at the time, although West Ham and Manchester's Belle Vue were quite their equals, always providing tremendous opposition. The Stadium was always packed to capacity and the atmosphere was terrific. Speedway Racing was one sport which appealed to men, women and children alike, and was well attended by whole families. And again, there was never any trouble. Off the track at least.

We saw poor old Bronco Wilson run into serious trouble one night though. He was a big, gawky rider with a rather clumsy looking style. Hence the nickname. Riders came under two categories, regarding style. They were either 'Foot-forward' or 'Foot-trailing'. The former was by far the more sedate, but the foot-trailers caught the imagination rather more, as it looked quite dangerous. It certainly was for our hero anyway.

Up went the starting gate, and the four riders hurtled forth as fast as they could, each striving to gain the advantage on the first bend. Bronco went *so* hard at it he was going too fast to take the bend, and he shot straight on and into the crash-barrier. And that – unless my memory fails me – was the end of Bronco. He'd thrilled us all plenty whilst he'd lived though, and had certainly lived up to his nickname. We really did miss him, he was a real character.

Win or lose, we'd go home after these meetings thoroughly satisfied, and as happy as sandboys. But not on that particular night.

On Friday nights we finished the week off with another session of ice skating. I feel I may have omitted one or two things from this chronicle of events, but it really was a whirlwind of a time for me. After the 'Home' and the following four miserable years, it was like a dream.

As I've said, I left school at the end of 1945, and January 1946 saw me take the first of many different jobs that were to follow over the next few decades. When you left school in those days you were sent to the 'Juvenile Employment Exchange' to seek work. Having tried to ascertain what aptitudes you may have, the clerk would decide on the type of job to send you after. I was very keen on art and maths, and practically *anything* that involved writing. So I was sent to a smallish building firm, where I was taken on as a Carpenter's Improver. *Very* relevant! The work was mostly bomb-damage repairs and not all that interesting, even though I was quite keen on woodwork, and have been ever since.

Builders in those days employed all their own tradesmen, as well as labourers, whereas today it's pretty well all sub-contract. We had our own Carpenters' Hut, which must have measured about fifteen by ten feet, and was quite well equipped. There was a nice stove, with it's chimney angling up through the roof. This was great, for it was January as I say and the winters were jolly cold then. There were two joiners' benches and they had plenty of hand tools. The smell of the sawdust and wood-shavings was divine.

The two chippies were named Fred and Jock. Fred was really ancient, at least he seemed so to me at a mere fourteen. He was bent and quite frail looking, with a shaky hand and a permanent 'dew-drop' on the end of his hook nose. Jock was probably about thirty-ish, and a sturdy red-headed Scotsman from Inverness. They were good fellows and treated me well, and I say this in spite of the fact that one of the first tasks they set me was the 'ripping' of great lengths of 4" x 2" – right down the middle – to form 2" x 2". This was used to make a great stack of trestles. They marked right down the centre with a pencil line – on both sides – then as I progressed, frequently checked the underside to ensure that I was sawing 'square'. Length followed length, and I don't know how long I was kept on that exercise, it seemed like weeks but was probably no more than a few days. I know my arm was jolly stiff at the end of it whatever! But, it was an invaluable lesson, and one from which I have profited many times since.

We made and fitted dozens and dozens of weather boards to the front and back doors of local council houses. We also made many wooden draining boards, which we fitted in their kitchens. Fred and Jock each had what would be a normal carpenter's tool kit, but several of their tools were quite new to my eye. We hadn't seen Rabbit (Rebate) planes at school, nor yet Ploughs and the like, and I found them quite fascinating. I should think carpentry was a little more interesting then, inasmuch as a lot more style and character seemed to be fashioned into things.

For instance, when we were called upon to replace something as everyday as skirting boards shall we say, much time would be spent getting the shape of the moulding exactly right. Architraves and bannisters too were more ornate than the majority of those of the present day, and required great skill in the fashioning, which again, was done by hand in our workshop. Although I loved the smell of the interior of that shed, there was one exception. I wasn't at all keen on the smell of the glue we used, which would bubble away on the gas ring occasionally.

Tea-breaks were super, the morning one particularly. A whistle was blown to announce its arrival, whereupon we'd drop tools and make a dash for the Tea Hut. The tea was poured into your mug from a two-gallon galvanised bucket and was lovely and hot and quite sweet. Bread rolls had been fetched by the 'Tea Boy' – to your order – and went down beautifully with this brew. You ordered either soft or crusty rolls, plain buttered or cheese-filled, so everyone's taste was satisfied.

I never had tea from a bucket at any other time, other than when I was in the British Army at a later date. But it was common practice then, it seems; at least it was on building sites. I don't suppose there are any 'tea boys' today, everyone probably taking flasks. But it was a very pleasant interlude in the day's work, and you ran into some very interesting and amusing characters as you sat in the Tea Hut, all yarning and joking over their tea and rolls.

I began to build up a tool-kit of my own. Fred and Jock had lots of tools in each of their kits, and very kindly fixed me up with a good many, including a plough, *and* a 'rabbit' plane! And each week I religiously bought at least one more item, so it wasn't long before I possessed a pretty respectable kit. I quite settled to this life, and was all set to be a carpenter when – wham! The firm went bust or something. Whatever it was, I was out on my ear along with Fred, Jock and all the others. And after only six months.

There is one fact worth noting I feel, before I move on from there. In the light of today's 'Holiday Entitlement' – anything from three to about eight weeks per annum – I can't help remembering how meagre it was then, in the building trade at least. We received just one week! And only then because we bought it in advance. Each week when you received your pay, you would find under the heading 'Deductions' the item Holiday Stamp. I can't be sure now as to exactly how it was worked out, but it would make sense if each stamp had been to the value of one fifty-second of a basic week's pay. When holiday time came around – which was usually at the Management's choosing – the stamps were no doubt converted to cash, and that was what you received as holiday pay. *Very* generous!

I quickly set off in search of another job. I could ill afford not to be earning, and not just for the need to pay Ma and Pop for my keep either. There was also the 'Tally Man'. Which was of course, the more popular name for a Credit Salesman. I earned only about twenty-five shillings per week then – at fourteen – and couldn't afford to buy clothes outright. So I paid him something like a couple of bob a week and kept myself quite smart and respectable. I wasn't able to quickly come by a job the same as the one I'd just lost, but was sent by the Juvenile Employment Exchange to a firm by the name of Hickman's. The name of the firm that I'd just been forced to leave by the way, was Callow and Wright.

Hickman's turned out to be a large-ish factory on the North Circular Road, between Staples Corner and Neasden. I went there in the summer of 1946, and took out an Indentured Apprenticeship in wood-machining. The duration of such an apprenticeship in those days was seven years.

The chaps I worked with were an average bunch really, much as you'd find in any similar establishment. Many of them were still fairly fresh from seeing service on the front, so there were lots of stories to enliven the tea-breaks. I'd keenly followed the progress of the war right from the very start. I'd learned the Morse Code off by heart, and was almost as good at Semaphore. Then there was Aircraft Recognition – ours *and* theirs – and suchlike. Most of the youngsters shared this interest in those times. And like many another, I filled a huge scrapbook, which I dearly wish I'd kept. But these first-hand accounts – straight from the horse's mouth so to speak – were quite fascinating, though I suspect our goggle-eyed attention drew a few embellishments.

There was one particular thing that all these chaps had in common, and I planned to steer well clear of that if I possibly could. This was 'diminishing digits'! You should have seen their hands, some of them were awful. Worst of all I think was old George on the circular saw. I should think he'd been at it longer than anyone else. In fact I should think he was fast approaching retirement. He had no whole fingers at all – nor thumbs! Little more in fact, than a couple of bunches of stumps. Yet he managed to feed the work through all right, and was always cheerful. He'd have done better to have gone in for crookery I should think, for they could never have had him on finger-prints!

In the one year or so that I was there, I witnessed two incidents of that nature. There was a very tiny man named Les. He was under five feet tall and weighed probably less than seven stone. Yet I saw that quite minimal weight reduced even further one day. He worked the band saw, though how he reached the work-table I cannot think. He was sawing away on this occasion, chatting as he worked to one of the other chaps who stood alongside watching, when suddenly he stopped, and,without a sound, collapsed in a heap on the floor. He'd sawn off his thumb, and it wasn't till he saw it lying there on the work-table, right next to his workpiece, that he realised what he'd done!

On such occasions it fell to us boys to clean up afterwards, once the casualty had been whipped off to hospital and the hub-bub had begun to die down. Of course, micro-surgery had not yet evolved, so all severed digits were dumped – unceremoniously – into the waste bin.

A similar fate befell Alan on one of the planers later on. He was a very quiet, softly spoken and pale-faced man. He suddenly stepped out of character on this day though and bellowed out loudly. He'd just planed the tops off all the fingers on one hand. I didn't think it was possible for him to look any paler than he normally did, but just before he passed out I'm sure he found a couple more shades. After he'd been taken off to hospital, two of us lads had the usual clean-up job. But this time, the blood and flesh etc. had spattered all over the finished work that was stacked alongside his machine. So we had quite a scraping job on our hands as well.

Three smells come instantly to mind whenever I think back to that job. The not at all pleasant smell of the glue as it bubbled in pots on Bunsen Burners down in the Joiner's end of the factory. The beautiful smell of pine as the timber was sawn, moulded, planed and mortised by us wood machinists in our half. And if I reach a hundred I shall never forget the deliciously gorgeous smell that came out of Kemp's Biscuit factory as I walked past each morning on my way to work. And I expect the lucky devils who actually worked inside there never gave it a second thought. It really was dee-vine!

As far as I remember there was little or no heating in the works other than in the Mens' Room, as it would now be called. This room was something like fifteen feet square at a guess, and in the middle stood a coke-burning brazier. This was more for the purpose of preventing the water freezing in the pipes than for the comfort of the workforce. In the depth of winter – *especially* that of 1946/7 – chaps would have to go up there pretty regularly throughout the day, to put a bit of life back into their fingers – or stumps – for our hands were in constant contact with the cold steel of the machinery. But, you had to beware of over-staying in there, for the atmosphere was thick with killer fumes from the coke. We used to come out choking and spluttering, and grimacing at the horrible taste that it left on your tongue. But at least our fingers were nimble enough to grapple with the work again. For a little while. *That* winter certainly went into the record books.

It was in that winter that the stretch of water that lay behind our firm, which was, and probably still is known as *The Welsh Harp*, froze absolutely solid. These waters were said to be extremely dangerous normally, having claimed the lives of several not-too-expert swimmers. Yet I, and two other apprentices walked fearlessly across from bank to bank many times over that winter. Mind you, we crept very cautiously the first time over, our hearts in our mouths as we inched our way. Every now and again we gave the ice a bit of a stomp to test its strength, gradually gaining confidence, till finally, we fashioned some branches and found something resembling a puck, then every dinner hour was thoroughly enjoyed playing ice hockey, right through till the thaw eventually came. How the poor wildlife suffered though, every day we had to clear dead moorhens from our pitch, frozen solid, before we could start.

I think there were three apprentices in our end of the factory -which was known as

The Mill – and half a dozen in the joiners' end. They were all two or three years older than us scrawny 14/15 year olds, and generally that much bigger and stronger. So of course, they used to taunt us and try to intimidate us quite a bit, especially when they were in a bunch. One of them, Malcolm Edgington, was particularly unsavoury. He had those prominent eye-teeth, and when he sneered at us – as he mostly did – they gave him a truly evil, detestable appearance.

One day, as we were 'clocking in' after the dinner break, he stuck out a foot and sent me sprawling. I rose, quite incensed, and hurled myself at him instinctively. We'd barely closed with each other when we were yanked apart by the foreman of his section. 'If you've something to settle' he growled, 'do it in your *own* time, not the firm's.'

Any fight – or initiation ceremony – (more of which later) was a Company Occasion, to be attended by all and looked forward to with great anticipation. So this fight was staged for dinner-break the following day, and word quickly went round. Edgington continued to leer at me for the rest of that day, egged on by his mates, and I must say, I slept none too easily that night.

Morning came, eventually, and in spite of my apprehension I knew I had to go in and face him. All the chaps in the Mill rallied round, trying to inspire me with a little confidence. I'd have felt better if I could have struck whilst the iron was *hot*, and not had all this nerve-wracking wait. My anger had long since subsided and I was in no mood for a fight now. Not that fighting was ever my scene anyway.

I looked around for Edgington, to see if I could assess his mood, but I couldn't see him. The eight o'clock hooter sounded and I knuckled down to the morning's work.

Suddenly I was aware of murmurings – and I couldn't believe my ears. He hadn't turned up! He'd chickened out. What a let-off. My relief however, was short-lived, for everyone was so looking forward to the coming spectacle that they now began to complain at the prospect of being denied it. Ned Spicer, the foreman who'd set it all up, came to me and said – 'What are you going to do about it? You'll have to have a fight with *some*body – after all, everyone's been *told* now!'

I couldn't believe it. In my book I'd won by default – with him failing to show up – but, I wasn't getting off that easily. 'What about your mate Don? Have a fight with him – just to keep 'em all happy'. Well, this was utterly ridiculous, Don and I worked side by side all day and were really good pals. As it happened, we were perfectly matched physically – same height, same age and weight, same scrawny build. We also shared the same interests – and neither of us was interested in *this* stupid proposal. As the morning wore on however, the pressure became so intense that we finally agreed to have a go, just friendly like.

Neither of us fancied dinner-time coming, but come it did, and we squared up to each other – in front of the crowd – and started jabbing a bit. I think Don felt as daft about it all as I did, up to that point. Then suddenly, he landed a punch that felt unnecessarily hard to me. 'Right' I thought, 'two can play at that game' and I promptly returned the compliment. From then on there was no holding us, we really laid into each other, fists whipping to and fro like pistons. We held nothing back, and the more he hurt me the harder I went back at him. As the fight progressed we seemed to become more and more vicious, each giving our utmost to the hatred we'd suddenly found for each other.

The crowd *loved* it and urged us on excitedly. It was so ridiculous, neither of us was aggressive by nature, yet here we were! Goodness only knows which of us would have folded first – had not the 'back to work' hooter intervened. Even then we had to be dragged apart, dripping blood and fists still flailing, much to everyone's reluctance – including our own. They all cheered and clapped us heartily, patting our backs and saying that was the best scrap they'd ever seen. I should think it was! We were the toast of the whole firm – including the joiners – for a good many weeks. Even Edgington's pals warmed to us, having dropped *him* for his cowardice.

Don and I cleaned ourselves up – in silence – then got back to work, equally bruised and swollen. We kept looking at each other as we worked, but nary a word nor a smile passed between us. This situation prevailed for some days till suddenly – pain mostly behind us and swelling subsiding – we burst out laughing, shook hands, and became firmer buddies than ever.

Edgington didn't sneer after that, and I knew I'd have beaten him on the day. He was nothing on his own. Some time later I waylaid him as he came in through the big shuttered entrance one dinner hour. I quickly brought him down, then applied the 'scissors' and 'half-Nelson' simultaneously. Didn't he squeal! I must say, I felt quite sorry for him after that, having exposed him for what he really was. But not half as sorry as I was for myself on a later occasion.

My pal Don left. His parents moved from that area and he couldn't make the journey from his new address. And youngsters stayed at home until they were married in those days. Well mostly that is. So a new apprentice was taken on in his place. I'd been there several months by now, and I became as pally as it was possible to with David, the new kid. He was a very surly character who never smiled, and seemed always to have a chip on his shoulder. He and I used to stroll around outside the firm some dinner hours, or go down to the Welsh Harp to skim stones. Anything for a break from the workplace.

Then one day word reached our ears of a forthcoming '*initiation ceremony*', in which we were to feature a mite too prominently for our liking. We didn't let on that we'd heard anything, but we made darned sure we were through that door the instant the dinner hooter sounded. We made ourselves scarce, even walking in steady rain till the very last minute, returning just in time to resume work. Neither of us wore a watch – they were a luxury in those days – and even if you *did* have one you certainly wouldn't wear it for work. We somehow managed to judge the time pretty accurately anyway.

Then of course, one day the inevitable happened. We got careless and came back far too early. And our fate was sealed. They'd seen us coming and lay in wait. As we rounded the doorpost the whole pack of Joinery Apprentices pounced. I was on the side nearest to them and stood no chance. But David managed to give them the slip, so they gave up on him and settled for me. It was 'orrible. They were six big, strong lads, and restrained me with little effort, carrying me struggling and protesting – like a sacrificial offering – to the joiners' shop.

I was laid on the floor in a hastily prepared clearing between the benches, arms and legs very securely pinned. Touches of medicine time in the children's home! People were sitting and standing all around – grinning expectantly – and I was horrified to see amongst them Ellen Bradbrook, the girl of my dreams. She was a pretty fifteen year-old blonde who worked in one of the offices. I was relieved to see that she wasn't smiling, in fact she looked almost as embarrassed as I felt. I'd had my eye on her for some time as she ran errands through the workshop, and was desperately trying to pluck up the courage to ask her out. I'd not yet spoken to her, but I was sure she'd sensed my intentions. There'd be no chance now. Not after this.

I smelt the approaching glue, then shuddered as I felt it being applied to that most private part of my body. I was terrified. Not so much of the ordeal *itself*, which was bad enough, but of what would happen when I got home that night. The wood-shavings and sawdust quickly followed, then I was released. The fact that most apprentices were subjected to this kind of treatment was little comfort to me as I lay there, with everybody gawping on.

Amidst much cheering I dashed off to the men's room to see how bad it was. That morning I had borrowed brother Chas' football shirt, completely unbeknown to him. It was neatly folded in his drawer – ready for the Saturday match – and I couldn't see the harm in wearing it, just the one day. He was now back in Civvy Street – a very keen footballer – and pretty good at it too. And now this! My fears were well-founded, for the glue, which came off me – eventually – had set on the shirt and wouldn't be budged.

I went back to start work, sore from the scrubbing and resigned to my brother's wrath that evening, to find that David had been cornered. He looked really wild and clutched a very heavy piece of equipment, swearing he'd let them have it if they came one step closer. They figured there was still just time to 'do' him, and being undeterred by his threat, moved in for the kill. But David was as good as his word, and hurled it at them. It was so heavy it landed only at his feet – and shattered! David wasn't there long after that, a matter of minutes if I remember rightly.

He'd been there long enough to take me in though. And *I've* always regarded myself as pretty shrewd. He said he had a bike for sale. It sounded a very good bike, it had a darned good name anyway. It was a Rudge Whitworth. It had 3 speed gearing, which the majority of roadsters didn't at that time, and hub/dyno lighting, also quite uncommon I believe. And according to him it was in tip-top condition throughout. I felt I could do with another bike, I can't remember now what became of the one I used on my paper round. And this seemed too good to miss. He lived too far away for me to go over and see it, so I had to take his word.

I forget what price he was asking but it was far more money than *I* had right then. 'Haven't you anything else –' suggested David '– that you can give me instead of money?' No, I hadn't. Except – wait a minute – what about all my carpentry tools? I didn't need *them* now, as a wood machinist. So the bargain was struck and I began taking them in on the bus each day, one or two at a time. When I suggested that I must have brought enough to equal the bike's value, he assured me the bike was well above average. So I took more.

He finally had to concede, which was just as well for he'd had the *lot* by then, plough, rebate plane and all. He agreed to bring the bike in the next day. Over the next few days there were various reasons as to why he couldn't fetch it just yet, and just as I was beginning to feel they were becoming too lame to be plausible, this initiation business came about. Which he'd managed to dodge anyway.

We never saw David again – nor did I see any bike! I did hear shortly afterwards though that the police were trying to trace him. A right character was David. And a right mug *I'd* been. There never had been any bike of course, and he'd obviously sold all my tools. Ah well, we live and learn.

So I'd lost my pal Don, which I very much regretted, and now I'd lost the company of David, which I did not regret in the least. But something was coming which I was to regret more than anything just then. Indeed, it was quite devastating. The Elseys gave up their position as stewards of the club at Wembley Park and moved right away from the area. And with them went my two pals, Roy and Bernard!

I was fully accepted at work now – following the recent ceremony – and was quite happy with my job. But my days too were numbered. Suddenly I'd lost all my friends – even the dreadful David – in practically one fell swoop. And I couldn't help thinking of all those I'd left up in Yorkshire.

BACK TO YORKSHIRE

So here I was again, stepping down from the tram at the end of Greyhound Terrace. It hadn't changed at all in the two to three years that I'd been away, just as grey and grimy looking. But my heart began to beat that bit faster. I'd already written to Mam (Mrs Miller) of course, and she'd very kindly consented to my return. Gosh it was good to ride on those beautiful trams again, and they'd lost none of their magic.

Doug (Mr Miller) was now demobbed and living at home, as were all the others who'd been away at the war last time I was here . Those that had come through that is. And of course, one other thing had changed – my accent had reverted. And most of my old pals had, like me, become working lads. Well, I was hoping to return to that status pretty quickly anyway.

I settled in again – in the small second bedroom – and immediately felt happy, and as much at home as I was with Ma and Pop in London. And again, I was so grateful to them for squeezing me in, after all, there were more of us now and we were all that bit older. Not to mention bigger.

First things first; I must get a job. There was a firm almost identical to the one I'd just left, about four hundred yards away – just along the York Road. They were Storefitters like Hickman's. What a bit of luck – and so conveniently placed. I'd brought my Indentures along with me, and thus armed, went confidently along to this place. But I was to be disappointed, for they needed no more apprentices at that time, which was quite a blow as you can imagine. But I swallowed my disappointment and went along to the Juvenile Employment Exchange in the City of Leeds and enlisted their help. After flicking through the files for a minute or two the clerk withdrew a card and handed it to me, giving me a few brief directions for finding the address thereon.

I can't remember the name of this firm, but I think it was on the outskirts of the city. I eventually found it, and got the job. It wasn't quite what I'd been doing at Hickman's, but it was the nearest they could offer. It was in fact, a cooperage. Not very large but delightfully quaint. I guess a dozen or so were employed there, and the machinery and equipment was very old – even then. (1946/7)

Today's Health and Safety people would have had a ball with the poorly guarded machinery and suchlike. There were some overhead shafts, bearing pulleys of various sizes, with belts coming down to drive the different machines. You had to pick your way pretty carefully past these slapping belts which were, as I say, very poorly – if at all – guarded. And the machines themselves seemed to be slotted in all higgledy-piggledy – if I remember rightly. The floor was wooden and on two very slightly different levels, with a single step between levels. I don't know how long the firm had been in existence, but that step was so time-worn it could almost have been trodden by William the Conqueror I should think. Just up my street – the whole thing.

I have little or no recollection of the techniques of the business now, but I know I found it all very interesting. I liked the rumble of the machinery and the slap slap of the driving belts, and the smell was gorgeous. I mainly took the work off the machines as the craftsmen fed it through, assembled the ends of the casks, and generally made myself useful. Most jobs have some disadvantages of course, and the main one here was that the air was constantly laden with wood-dust.

The part of the job that I enjoyed most was going to the goods station to fetch the wood from which the staves were made. These being the side timbers of the casks. The firm's transport was a huge horse-drawn wagon, something after the fashion of a brewers' dray, I think. And the horse was a fine big dapple grey. I used to sit up there on that wooden seat, alongside Bill the wagoner, and it felt really grand. Horses were still fairly widely used then, drawing milk-carts, coal-carts and the like, and of course – rag and bone carts – of the Steptoe & Son type. But as we clip-clopped our way into the city, at a nice leisurely pace, I felt like a settler heading west, sitting so high on ours!

On arrival Bill and I would load up the wagon whilst the horse – whose name I can't recall now – waited patiently between the shafts. Once loaded we'd settle him with his nosebag – the horse that is – then, the part I looked forward to most of all, make our way upstairs to the canteen. Here we'd have a big pot of lovely hot sweet tea apiece, and some delicious, thickly cut dripping toast, still hot from the toasting. Bah goom that was gorgeous. The chatter from all the other wagoners was always humorous and good-natured, and I had my leg pulled quite a bit, being just a young shaver, or 'nobbut a lad' – as they'd have said. It all felt really marvellous and I loved it.

When we'd had our fill, we climbed back on to the wagon and began the steady plod back to the cooperage. There was a fair-sized yard out back, and here we unloaded and stacked the timber for later use. Yes, I really loved those trips – which always took the entire afternoon.

These timbers were machined to shape and size, then placed in the steam kilns in order to obtain the curve as the hoops were driven on. As I've said, my recollection of the methods and techniques is quite vague now, but I do know that I liked it there.

I'd picked up my old friendships, and life generally was quite varied and enjoyable. The cinema was still a regular favourite, but now and again we'd have an evening at the 'City of Varieties' music hall in Leeds. This establishment has since become quite famous, having featured in a regular television series in latter years. But then – well it wasn't quite so smart as it appeared on the small screen. But smart enough, and super entertainment. Really super.

We never had much money in those days – who did? – so we always went up in 'The Gods', the cheapest part. It was as you'd imagine, quite high, and ran down each side of the theatre, as far as I remember. If you happened to finish up at the very end – nearest the stage – the height and rather acute angle impeded your view quite a bit. But it didn't seem to lessen our enjoyment.

Quite often, on a Saturday afternoon, we'd go into the city to watch the all-in wrestling. I've no doubt a good bit of sham was employed by the exponents, it *must* have been – or there'd have been a good many fatalities – from the things they appeared to be doing to each other. But I suppose I was somewhat gullible, not having watched any wrestling before, and I took it all in. I used to come away feeling quite sick, after all the eye-gouging, finger splitting and suchlike. Then we'd be off to the pictures for the evening, or maybe the 'Verts' – which was the local term for the City of Varieties – and I felt good again.

I remember us lads going to see the great Al Jolson. Well, he was great to us, and everyone else in those times I fancy. I think the film was 'The Jolson Story', and it was packed with great songs. We learned them all instantly, word for word, as you do at that age. Then, on those nights when we couldn't afford to go anywhere, we'd laik around for a while, then go down to the Chippie and spend what few coppers we could muster between us. Eating our chips and crackling we'd make our way up to the top of Saville Green, where it met the main York Road. Here we'd stand – for maybe an hour or two – singing these and other great songs of the day. We'd harmonise a bit, have a good laugh or two in between numbers, and thoroughly enjoy ourselves. The houses finished a bit short of the end of Saville Green so we didn't really disturb anyone. After a good old sing-song we'd all make our way happily, and peacefully home. Nobody had thoughts of vandalism – we didn't know the word then – or violence. And yet these were all strong, spirited, lusty young lads. It makes you wonder.

I started smoking as soon as I returned to Leeds. I was a working lad now, and all my pals smoked anyway. And of course, it was the height of sophistication to smoke. All the adverts in the papers, and on the hoardings that were everywhere, and on the cinema screen during the interval, made that *perfectly* clear. How little we all knew about it then. I really enjoyed smoking for something like thirty-five years, but it is with a much greater enjoyment, and satisfaction, that I can claim to have been a non-smoker for nigh on thirteen years now. And I am, thankfully, none the worse for all those years of stupidity, as far as I know. When I think back, those film sets must have been awful places, especially for the few non-smokers. The stars seemed always to be in a fog, with practically all of them smoking non-stop.

It was 1946/7 and cigarettes were still extremely hard to come by, most of them being under the counter, for special or regular customers only. Sometimes, if you were lucky, you may find a shop where they had a few popular brands standing loose in a spirit glass behind the counter. These were for general sale, to anybody, but they didn't appear very often. And even when you did click, you'd seldom get more than one. Two at the very most. There were several strange brands on the shelves though, and these were available to all. Names we'd never heard of before. Star – Robin – Turf are some that come to mind, but there were others too. And what about those Turkish cigarettes? I remember smoking Pashas – they were flat instead of round – and highly scented. At least they were to my nostrils. But they were all we could get so we smoked 'em! Blooming *awful* some of them were.

I began to worry a little about all the dust I was working in at the cooperage. We received neither masks nor milk – to prevent or counteract the danger – and on the advice of one or two older folk, I decided to seek an alternative. I would be very sorry to leave the place though, and particularly sad never to be riding shot-gun on the wagon again.

But leave I did and I next found myself working in a place where they made furniture. I think it was all bedroom furniture, albeit in the utility style, as most things still were. The name of this firm was Gough's, and it was somewhere in Leeds.

They employed a good number of deaf and dumb people here, in addition to us more fortunate ones, so I soon learned quite a bit of deaf and dumb sign-language. This was as much from necessity as simple desire, for we had to communicate with each other. And some of those chaps were real wags, with a really keen sense of humour – even without hearing and speech. They very soon taught me to swear in sign-language, and that's a fact. But in moderation I should add.

My job initially was rubbing down. The furniture was actually built downstairs, then passed to the floor above for staining, lacquer-spraying and french-polishing. I remember nothing of the downstairs, for I was set to work upstairs and that's where I stayed. For a while at least.

So when the items came up to us they were stained first, which or course raised the grain. So I had to smooth it down all over with very fine sand-paper, before passing it across for lacquer-spraying. From there it went to the french polishers, who made it shine like glass by rubbing it with a little pad, which was dipped from time to time in methylated spirit I believe, using tiny circular movements – practically non-stop all day. It was a bit boring at first, all day just rubbing down. Wardrobes, dressing tables, chest of drawers, tallboys. But I stuck to the task, for as I say, they were a decent bunch of chaps and the humour was good.

There were two regular sprayers, whose names were Vic and Alf. And they made a really *great* singing duo. Each had a good voice, and they harmonised most of the time. It was really beautiful. Their favourite – and mine – was 'Now is the Hour'.

After a while I was put on spraying. But not – I hasten to add – on the external surfaces like Vic and Alf. The insides were never stained of course, but were sealed with a clear lacquer, so a few little errors in the spraying were of far less consequence here than they would have been on the outside. I quite enjoyed doing this part of the job, but I wasn't too keen on what it was doing to me. Although there was an extractor fan at the back of the spray-booth, it was rendered totally ineffective when you were spraying *in*sides, as your workpiece screened it off. The spray dust simply bounced straight back at me and I was getting lacquered just as much as – if not more than – the blooming furniture itself. So after a while, I decided that this too was not for me.

Job number five was nothing to do with furniture. Or barrels. In fact wood didn't come into it at all. I don't know how I came to make the change – liking wood so much – but I now found myself in engineering. It was a bit strange at first, but it wasn't long in capturing my interest. All my life I've loved a challenge, as far back as that, it seems. But I missed the lovely smell of wood being worked.

The firm, which specialised in complete engine reconditioning, was called Power Units Engineering Ltd, and was no more than a decent walk away from home. Just the other side of The Hollow in fact, in Torre Road. It was on two levels again, with all the machinery and test beds on the ground floor, and all the fitters' benches on the floor above. I was put to work upstairs first, with the fitters.

I spent many hours a day just scraping the main bearings in the engine blocks, which had been 're-metalled' to build them back up after many miles – or years – of wear. The crankshafts were ground downstairs on some quite big machines, then a perfect fit had to be achieved between the two. They were assembled together, using 'mechanic's blue', which showed the high-spots when they were dismantled again. These high-spots were then very carefully removed with a bearing scraper, the parts reassembled – again using blue – then dismantled again and scraped as necessary. This process was repeated as many times as were needed to remove all high-spots, and achieve a perfect fit on every bearing.

The connecting rods – commonly called con-rods – were also re-metalled and went through the same process on the crankshaft 'journals'. Various other tricky operations were carried out upstairs, culminating in the final reassembly of the complete engine, after all the machining had been done downstairs. It was then transferred below again, mounted on a test-bed, set in motion and finely tuned, then returned to the customer, normally a garage.

There were a good many fitters and machinists there, and always plenty going on. The fitter with whom I was first placed had a good voice, and fancied himself as a bit of an opera singer I think. All day long he'd sing – '*Tiny ball, tiny ball; with a gentle rapping and a gentle tapping of that fascinating thing; tiny ball on end of string*'. Occasionally he'd sing something else like '*Hear my song – Violetta*' for example, but always return to '*Tiny ball*'! I enjoyed working with him.

After some time upstairs I was placed down below, with a couple of chaps who did all the Cylinder-boring. I liked this part of the job, which was again, quite high precision, and soon became quite an expert. But a part of the job that I liked as much as any was going into the centre of the city to fetch parts. My vehicle was one of those big, heavy old trade bicycles that you saw everywhere then. There was a plate beneath the crossbar bearing the firm's name and services offered, and a great basket in front in a framework above the very small front wheel. Almost like a penny-farthing in reverse!

I'd struggle back from the city with the basket full of new pistons, liners, con-rods, gudgeon-pins, oil pumps and various other items. It was a fair distance from the firm so they always ensured that I had a full load, so as to obtain maximum value from the trip. It was very hard on the legs, having no gears either, and I am occasionally reminded of this when I see the advertisement on television for Hovis bread. But sadly, I didn't have the benefit of Dvorak's beautiful symphony accompanying me! But it made a nice change to get out, and find my way around. And overall, I was quite happy there.

Us lads continued with our leisure pursuits, going to watch football, rugger or all-in wrestling in the afternoons, cinema and music hall in the evenings. And we kept harmonising at the top of Saville Green, and eating our chips and our crackling. We roamed about a bit at week-ends occasionally, taking a bus into Otley or Pontefract, Tadcaster or Wetherby, or one of several other villages, although there wasn't really very much to do once you'd got there. Sometimes we'd just go exploring the surrounding countryside, which I particularly liked, simply to see what we might see.

We once had a very narrow escape from an angry bull. We were strolling leisurely across this meadow, when we suddenly noticed him. We were some way from the gate and not wishing to appear scared, we continued at our leisurely pace, though I'm pretty sure we all lengthened our stride a fair bit. Suddenly Alfie Varley swung round and yelled – 'Bloody 'ell, the booger's coomin' – let's 'erry oop and get to t'gate!' We began to run but he took up the chase, and as we quickened our pace, so did he, and we finished up going flat out for that gate. We all arrived at once of course, and I still can't fathom how we all cleared it before he reached us. But we did – just! We all looked at each other, puffing and panting and marvelling at our luck. 'Sod this' – said Jackie Broadhead – 'Ah'm gooin' 'ome – oo's coomin'? It doesn't sound much now, reading it back, but that old bull fair put the wind up us all I can tell you. He was *hef-ty*.

Three of us decided to camp out on Ilkley Moor. Someone had procured a smallish tent from somewhere and had erected it on The Hollow. We'd all looked at it, prodded it, walked round it, crawled inside it. But it didn't do much for us and we were just about to write it off when somebody dared us to go camping in it. 'What, in that thing!' we sneered, and started to walk off. 'Ah reckon they're scared' taunted one of the lasses, which was enough for us of course.

It packed down quite small, enabling us to take it on the bus fairly easily, and boldly we set off, the younger kids watching us in awe, and – we thought – admiration, as we made our way to the bus stop. We had of course first cleared it with parents or what have you. We boarded the bus, and tried to impress the other passengers with our light-hearted chatter about camping on the Moor. 'What brave, courageous lads' they'd be thinking. Daft boogers more like! For all we'd taken with us was one blanket between the three of us, a bag of jam sandwiches and a bottle of Dandelion and Burdock.

We penetrated the moor a fair bit, before erecting our tent by a small brook. Now what? There was nothing whatever to do in that wide open bleakness, so we decided to eat some of our sandwiches, and drink some of our drink. We'd nothing to make a fire with and it began to get a bit chilly. But our morale was high, and we chatted a bit and tried to laugh.

But it got colder, so we ate more sandwiches and drank more Dandelion and Burdock. Then suddenly, it was all gone. It wasn't yet dark, but we decided it would be a good idea to bed down for the night, after all, we didn't know what we might be getting up to tomorrow. And at least it would be warmer.

We lay side by side in that tiny tent, our one blanket stretched across the three of us. We yarned for a while, and cracked a few jokes, then bade each other goodnight. It got colder and colder as the night deepened, and we turned up our collars, tucked our trousers into the tops of our socks, put our shoes back on, and fought over the blanket. But still we couldn't get warm. We must have dozed off eventually however

– from sheer exhaustion I should think – for we were woken with a start at 4 a.m. when a sheep poked its head through the flap and bleated at us. Scared us half to death it did – not knowing what it was for a few seconds.

We shoo-ed it off, then discovered how cold and stiff we all were. No food. No drink. Nothing to make a fire with. What a state we were in! We ran and jumped about a bit in an effort to get warm, then washed ourselves in the brook. And was that water cold! We shivered as we discussed our situation, but were unanimous in our decision. 'To hell with courageousness and camping – let's sod off home!' So we packed up that tent again, trudged back to civilisation, and, starving hungry and somewhat disillusioned, caught the first bus home. We took a bit of ribbing when we got back of course, but no way could we have faced another night on Ilkley Moor. Not as ill-equipped as *we'd* been at least.

We were getting to be about sixteen years old now. And girls were beginning to take an interest in us. Or was it us in them? Either way, things were beginning to change a bit, and we were all shaving quite regularly, need it or not. My pal Jackie had a sister named Iris, who was about a year older than me. She was a very nice lass, warm and homely and the possessor of a really lovely smile. We started walking out occasionally, and it was nice. It was completely innocent, I didn't even kiss her on our first few dates, although she was indeed, a very kissable lass.

Then I noticed another lass – Joyce – who was sixteen and still at grammar school, looking at me a bit strangely. She was blonde, and just as sweet and lovely as Iris, who was a brunette. And I was equally sweet on the pair of them. Then, just as things looked as if they might get a little awkward, I had a letter from my brother Chas. He was getting married and wanted me to go down to London for the wedding.

I took a train down, and it was great to see Chas again. And to meet Stella, my Sister-in-law to be. I think I had seen her before, at the club at Wembley Park when Chas was home on leave once. They were dancing at the time, and I remember thinking how much Stella – a black-haired beauty – reminded me of the lovely film star Hedy Lamarr. Stella's younger sister Betty was making it a double wedding by marrying Bill, her sweetheart of many years I think.

It was a good, memorable day and ended with Chas having a long and earnest chat with me. The upshot of which was my being persuaded to return south again, to be near my brothers.

The next day, Chas took me to see my Aunt Grace and Uncle Charles, who lived not too far from Stella's parents' home, which was where the newly-weds would be starting their married life. Uncle Charles was my Dad's only brother, and they had a son, Tony, who was a year younger than me. I'd not met them before that I could recall, but after a chat with Chas, they asked me if I'd like to go and stay with them.

The thought of leaving all my good friends in Yorkshire again saddened me immensely, but Chas was so convincing that I agreed. After all, I'd had only shortish snatches of my brothers' company this far through life.

So I returned to Yorkshire to say my farewells and tender my resignation at work. The excitement of it all was very much tinged with the sadness of losing my friends again, especially on the day of departure. I walked across to the tram-stop, humping my now very battered but faithful old suitcase, and there, waiting to see me off, were both Iris *and* Joyce! Iris gave me a packet of 5 Woodbine cigarettes – I can't remember any parting gift from Joyce. I kissed them both goodbye, and have seen neither of them since. Nor in fact, have I seen any other of my good Yorkshire friends, nearly fifty years later. With one exception – which I shall mention later.

When I left Yorkshire the first time, I couldn't recall why. I have a similar mental blank now when I try to think why I moved in with my Aunt and Uncle, when I left the second time. Why didn't I move back in with Ma and Pop, where I'd been so happy? They were barely a mile away. There must obviously have been a perfectly good reason, but right now – I haven't the foggiest idea what it was.

LONDON AGAIN

Aunt Grace and Uncle Charles lived in a rather nondescript, but adequate house. It was typical of the day and was one of a long line of many. There were identical dwellings to either side of them, and on the opposite side of the road. All the other roads in the area sported houses of the same, or very similar style. There was a tiny front garden to it – no more than about four feet in depth, with a low brick wall and privet hedge bounding the pavement. They each had a back garden in which – if you'll forgive the dreadful expression – you could have just about 'swung a cat'.

Most of the houses were owned by the local council I believe, in any event very few of the occupiers would have been owners – and were shared by two families, one upstairs and one down. No division had been made structurally – there was just the one front door – so you either stuck to all rooms downstairs, or climbed the wide but open staircase to those above. Originally, they would have been individual properties of fairly substantial proportions.

So the entrance hall, as far as the foot of the stairs, was communal. Quite a friendly arrangement – if you were on good terms with your neighbour. Which happily we were. And that was just as well really, for that communal stretch of passage was right alongside the two bedrooms of the lower section. They were never referred to – or even thought of as flats, probably because they weren't – just largish houses. And there wasn't even an 'A' after the number, to distinguish between the occupants – *we* were number 242, and so were the folks above. When the postman delivered, each trusted the other to take only their own mail. This arrangement kept you in fairly close contact with each other, so it was much nicer if you *were* on friendly terms.

People generally were on much better terms with each other than they seem to be today anyway, though of course, this again is a purely personal observation, but nevertheless, one which would be held I'm sure by most other folk who shared those times. And of course, the war wasn't very long over then – late forties – and that wonderful communal spirit that had seen us all through still largely prevailed.

Television began to appear in normal homes at the end of that decade, though it would have been around for some time amongst the more opulent. We acquired one from somewhere, it had a tiny nine-inch screen, and was of course black and white, as they all were then. And it broke down – *frequently* – as indeed did everyone else's! You'd just be enjoying 'Café Continental' or 'What's my line?' when *click*, you were left with a screen full of snow. Or else the picture would keep rolling over, making it hard to concentrate. Then perhaps it might shrink, or stretch, or quiver, or flicker, whereupon you'd have to juggle with all the knobs – Line-hold, Frame-hold, Vertical-hold, Contrast, Brilliance etc. Which was quite a battle at times, and you earned your enjoyment of it.

Friends or neighbours who didn't yet have a set of their own would often be invited round for an evening's viewing, making a kind of party of it. Then, if it broke down completely, we'd fall back on the good old playing cards and enjoy ourselves just as much with Rummy, Newmarket, Cribbage etc. And the wireless of course was still a source of excellent entertainment. Nowadays it's mostly non-stop 'pop' music – though I fear the word music may be grossly misapplied here – or those interminable chat-shows, which seem mostly to be platforms from which budding, or even established authors plug their work.

Radio, then, in the forties, and for the next decade or two, was extremely entertaining. It brought us high-calibre comedy shows such as ITMA, The Goonshow, Much-binding-in-the-Marsh, Charlie Chester, Ray's a Laugh, Hancock's Half-hour, to name a few. Thrills and suspense came from such sources as Paul Temple and Valentine Dyall – 'The man in black'. And what about 'Dick Barton – Special Agent'? The signature tune of that programme was 'The Devil's Gallop' and seemed to match perfectly the excitement provided by Dick, Jock and Snowy. Other pleasant programmes were Housewives' Choice, Down Your Way, Desert Island Discs, Semprini at the piano, Johnny Morris with his super stories. And the standard of the Drama and Variety sections was still very high. None of the violence or vulgarity that makes up so much of today's television. Well, that's my opinion again.

I shared Cousin Tony's room, another single bed having been put in there for me, and I stayed there for close on two years. I lost no time in getting a job, and was able to continue my Engineering Apprenticeship (Auto) which I was very pleased about. My new place of work was a garage, situated about 1½ miles away. I came by a very old push-bike, which I stripped and overhauled, then used for the journey.

Grey's Garage – as my new work place was called – was another place I very much enjoyed working at. We did practically everything there including complete engine overhauls, body repair work, and spraying. We had a contract with the General Post Office whereby we spray-painted all their new vehicles, as they acquired them. The vans would come to us brand new and clad only in primer. We then applied undercoat and topcoat in our spray-shop upstairs, then took them elsewhere for the sign-writing. What with that job and *general* body repair work, I sometimes spent days at a time just rubbing down between coats and feathering the edges on the repair jobs. Rather reminiscent of Gough's and all that bedroom furniture. But to see the sparkling end-product was very rewarding.

I watched our Works Manager one day, as he was setting up and reboring an engine block. He was the only one entrusted with this particular part of the business ,and I could see he wasn't too happy at it. I'd just been doing nothing but reboring and sleeving – all day and every day for the past six months or so in Yorkshire. And with an identical tool, the Van Norman Boring Bar. So of course, although I was nobbut a scrawny sixteen year-old, I was fully confident in my ability and offered my help.

He was a gentlemanly type of person in his late fifties/early sixties, and he gladly stepped aside whilst I completed the job, applying the special finish I'd been taught up north. He was very impressed and fetched Mr Grey, the boss. He in turned called his son – the *young* Mr Grey – who had been a captain in the army during the war, down from his office. I was asked if I would take on the reboring of Mr Grey junior's 1934 Austin 10/4 saloon, and I naturally agreed. Why not? There wasn't all that much to it – once you'd been properly trained – which as it happened, none of them had!

I finished the job and left the block standing on the workshop floor – 'Power Units' style, that is, with a piece of white paper beneath to reflect up through the bores, and the micrometer set and laid on top, for final approval. They were so complimentary it was embarrassing, and I almost wished I'd kept my mouth shut in the first place.

Up until then they'd fought shy of reboring, only doing the occasional one they'd been unable to avoid. Now, they mounted something of an advertising campaign and the work came rolling in! Still, I didn't mind at all really, and I thoroughly enjoyed all the other work as well. We stripped everything down ourselves in those days – no exchange/replacements as is today's way, which made it much more interesting.

This was the late forties, and there were still a great many American cars over here from the war. I guess a lot of the 'Yanks' must have sold them off before returning to the U.S.A., opting to buy new ones rather than have all the hassle of shipping them back. And weren't they super? Their streamlined sumptuousness and beautiful suspension really grabbed me. I couldn't wait to try them out, after the work on them was finished. There were Buicks, Cadillacs, Chryslers, Dodges, Hudsons, Packards, Pontiacs, Studebakers, and others I can't recall just now. Proper Al Capone and John Dillinger stuff – just like we were seeing on the movies right then. I thought they were terrific – I really did.

Not that I didn't like all our own cars of those days, although our saloons were mostly that bit smaller and rather more sedate. And certainly not as swish as those beauts. But our sports cars were great, especially the Jaguars, Triumphs, Bentleys etc. About the biggest car I ever drove there – though not on the road – was a Lagonda. She was an open-tourer sports job in black and yellow. She was gorgeous. When you sat in the seat and leaned out over the door, the front wings seemed to sweep up and on into infinity almost, they were so long. So too was the bonnet. All the wheels were wire-spoke, with one big, winged retaining nut, and the headlamps sat up on the wings like young searchlights, being at least twelve inches in diameter. I would have loved to have taken her out on the road proper – maybe with soft helmet, scarf and goggles! But at sixteen I wasn't yet old enough.

I was lucky at Grey's really. The lay-out of the service area was in the shape of a letter P. You entered at the base of the upright, then at the top you curved to your right for the workshop, then continued bearing right, through the parking area, rejoining the upright halfway along. Then you could either turn left and make your exit, or right – and do a second lap through the workshop. And a third. And a fourth – and so on. It was a big garage, although the actual workforce numbered no more than about six, excluding office staff and petrol-pump attendants.

Very few houses were built with garages then, the automobile being comparatively new to the scene at the time they were built, so covered parking space was at a premium. The average rent charged then was half-a-crown per week, and one garage where I worked at a later date could accommodate over two hundred cars under its roof at one time. So you can imagine, I had plenty of room to practice my driving at Grey's – during the daytime when most of them were out – without even going on to the road!

On the very day that I was seventeen, Mr Grey presented me with a provisional driving licence and took me out on the road. Officially. He wanted me to obtain my full licence as soon as possible, thereby increasing my usefulness to the firm. I say *officially* because once previously, I had done a 'naughty'.

We had to tow a big Armstrong Siddeley right across London, from our garage which was north-west to somewhere in the south-east. The Armstrong was hooked up behind our breakdown truck using what we called the 'Ambulance'. This was a solid bar as opposed to a rope or chain, and was much safer. I climbed into the Armstrong, which of course had a pre-selector gearbox, and was told I had to do nowt but steer it, following the breakdown truck. No pedal work to bother with at all – just steer.

About thirty feet out from our garage we had to stop at the traffic lights. And... CRUNCH! The bar had swung sideways, and the Armstrong went into the back of the breakdown truck. No real damage was done but the implications were clearly there. Mr Grey Senior – for it was he who was driving the breakdown truck – pulled in just beyond the lights and got out to come and survey the situation. After some thoughtful chin-rubbing, he turned to me and asked if I thought I could drive the Armstrong. As it happened, I'd had very little experience of pre-selectors up to then, so I felt it would be wisest to say no. Round the block maybe – but right across London? Phew!!

I should point out that the only reason we were towing her at all was that there wasn't another qualified driver available right at that moment, and the delivery was very urgent.

But I *could* drive the breakdown truck, and offered this as an alternative. Mr Grey looked a little uneasy, for he was indeed a very upright, law-abiding person normally, but under these rather pressing circumstances, he somewhat reluctantly agreed to the idea.

There wasn't much of me at sixteen – I weighed only about eight stone – and you should have seen our truck. She was a Packard Straight Eight – eight cylinders in-line that is – and a bit like a tank! Mind you, that would be a really *beautiful* tank, whose motor purred as sweet as a dream. She had a great long bonnet, naturally, and enormous wheels. Like most American vehicles she had a bench seat, and a huge white steering wheel of about twenty inch diameter.

I climbed in, and he looked at me with a frown. I must have looked rather like a five year-old sitting behind the wheel of his Dad's car. But I could see well enough, *and* reach all the pedals and controls, including the big white knob on the end of the gear lever. And I was quite competent at 'double de-clutching' which we all had to be then, for there wasn't much synchro-mesh around generally.

So off we set, with me quite confident in my driving ability, whilst Mr Grey – I suspect – was having kittens in the Armstrong. But I made sure I kept damned close up behind him all the time – for fear of getting lost! I just wouldn't have known *where* I was. But we completed the journey without further incident, and returned to our garage, whereupon I proudly related the event to my fellow workers – and felt quite chuffed with myself.

Not many young people had the opportunity to learn to drive then, not many folk could *afford* a car. It was really only those whose job required them to drive that got the chance. So by the time I was called up for National Service at eighteen, I was one of a very small minority already qualified to drive. Yet I was thirty-three years old before ever I owned a car. And *that* was secondhand.

That garage was a cold place in winter, very cold indeed. It was wide open most of the time, and we had just two coke-burning stoves to heat the whole place. These were great, when you were fairly close up to them, but when you weren't – well, you just wouldn't have known they were there at all. So when tea-break came you can imagine where we were to be found.

Some time earlier we would stoke those stoves up, so that by break-time their walls were red hot – *literally*! So whatever food you'd taken with you was speared with a home-made toasting fork, and held to this heat. It curled up into some odd shapes, but by jingo – that sure warmed you up. And by the time tea-break was over, we all walked away steaming like mad, where the fierce heat had affected the oil content of our overalls. It felt great though – for a few minutes – then you seemed to get colder than ever.

Life with Aunt Grace and Uncle Charles was pleasant enough, though not particularly eventful. They were good folk as I've said, and we all got on well with Edna and Jack – the couple upstairs. We'd have some great fun playing cards on Saturday evenings. The favourite game at the time was Newmarket, which always created a good deal of excitement. Yet no matter which way your luck was running you'd neither lose nor gain more than about five shillings by bedtime. Now and again we'd break off to watch something on that there new-fangled television thing, returning to the cards when it broke down, as it pretty well always did.

Every Tuesday evening, Cousin Tony and I would walk round to where Chas and Stella lived, in Stella's parents' house, for another card session. Stella's parents were a couple of 'cards' themselves really, especially her mother who had a very rare, *dry* kind of humour. She used to have us absolutely in stitches. So did Betty – Stella's younger sister. Then there was her friend Sylvia, and a neighbour called Colin, and one way or another we numbered about a dozen. We all sat round their large dining table, and that place fairly rocked. There was always a bit of cheating – from certain quarters – and a steady flow of side-splitting but clean jokes. They really were smashing evenings, and no mistake.

I didn't seem to make any other friends during that phase of my life. I don't really know why – except that I didn't get involved in any other social activity, as I had with Ma and Pop. I went to the cinema quite regularly, and that was about it. Some Sundays, in the summer, I'd persuade Cousin Tony – who wasn't at all athletic really, to accompany me on a day's cycling. We'd go to Rickmansworth, hire a rowing boat for a couple of hours on the river – or was it a lake? – eat our sandwiches and drink our pop then cycle all the way back home, arriving in the early evening, tired and hungry, but quite happy.

Life seemed to follow this regular pattern, pleasant but fairly predictable, and I guess I was happy enough. Then – after a couple of years or so – something suddenly came through the letter box and dropped on to the mat. And what a change *that* brought about. It was a long brown envelope, at the top of which were the large, bold letters O.H.M.S. And in it were my call-up papers.

I knew they were due, I'd had my medical nearly five months previous, and my eighteenth birthday was well past. I'd been classified A1 – and I was not a 'Conscientious Objector' or anything, so their arrival was without question. I *could* have applied for deferment on account of my apprenticeship, as most others similarly situated did. But as I've said, life wasn't particularly exciting at the time, and I knew I had to do this thing sooner or later, so best get it over and done with.

GET SOME IN

O n Thursday 13th April 1950, I and my faithful but now *really* battered old suitcase, set off once again. But I must say I was a good deal more apprehensive about what lay at the end of this particular journey, than I had been of any other so far. Maybe it was because I had no choice in the matter – I was obeying a command. But I drew a certain amount of comfort from the thought that thousands of others would be embarking on this same journey, at this same moment. And most of them would have had nice, comfortable home lives hitherto, with perhaps few problems, and even fewer challenges. They were bound to find it much tougher than I would. Or so I tried to convince myself.

On each leg of my journey I was joined by more and more of these case-toting youngsters – although this I'm sure was the day we all felt we'd become men – so that by the time we arrived at Aldershot, our destination, we were a sizeable crowd. A bit like Northampton on the day war broke out. But there the similarity most definitely ended. No magic, or wonderful sense of freedom would be awaiting us at Oudenarde Barracks, our ultimate destination. Oh no! Bless me no!!

Mind you, there'd been lots of speculation all the way to Aldershot, with the usual hard-nuts vowing *they'd* never be made to conform. They'd swaggered about boldly, but underneath they'd have been just as jittery as the rest of us were. And with good reason too, it turned out.

A roll-call was taken outside the station at Aldershot, then we were ushered into a string of Personnel Carriers which conveyed – or was it convoyed? – us to the barracks, our new 'home'. I can't remember all that happened on our arrival, which I believe was mid to late morning, but I do remember it was a very cold day and snowed frequently. We were given another medical examination and vaccinated.

Then began the long, long business of drawing all our kit and clothing. The Quartermaster's Stores seemed not to be in one large central clump, but rather a series of smaller stores, scattered around the camp, which covered a considerable acreage. So we were marched to the first store, brought to a halt outside, then made to form a single file in order of size. Shortest on the left, tallest on the right. Perhaps this was where we were to be blessed? – as in the song '*Bless 'em all, bless 'em all; the long and the short and the tall*'. But no, as we filed in, there was all this clothing and stuff, sized off in similar fashion, so that as you moved along, what you were issued should fit – roughly. *Very* roughly in some cases!

Then we 'fell in' outside again and formed three ranks, before being marched off to the next store. Then the next – and the next – and so on. Collecting kit and clothing in so piecemeal a fashion made it take most of the day, and it was quite late when we drew the final item. Which was the beret.

This caused a bit of a stir, for everyone was eager to try on the beret. Some guys really loved them – setting them on their heads at jaunty angles, fancying themselves as Tank Commanders and the like. But most of us saw how strange our fellows looked, and were quick to whip them off again. In no way did we wish to be seen in *them* before we had to!

And that wasn't long in coming either. For after our evening meal in the cookhouse we were marched off to the place we came to dislike most – the Regimental Barber's. What they did to us in there was almost criminal. Well, we thought so anyway. They shaved us – close-cropped that is – right up, leaving the teeniest amount right on top! We really did look, and feel, bloody awful, and I can tell you that those berets – pocketed earlier with a sneer – were now donned pretty damned quick in an effort to cover our acute embarrassment. *And* to provide a little warmth, as the snow continued to fall.

At last we'd finished kitting up. Perhaps now we could have a rest, or maybe find out what the NAAFI had to offer tired, hungry lads. No such luck. That whole evening was spent first marking up our kit – every single item had to be either stamped with steel number stamps, or stencilled, with our new Army Number. Boots, boot-brushes, blanco-brush, button-stick, trousers, tunics, socks, shirts, underwear, denims, hold-all, mess-tins, water-bottle, housewife, eating-irons, beret, greatcoat, all our webbing – *everything*!

The housewife by the way, was a little white bag containing needles, cotton, darning wool, etc. Items utterly alien to some guys, who viewed them with considerable unease – and suspicion. I was quite familiar with them of course, having had to sew on my own buttons and darn my own socks from the age of about five.

We then had to learn how to make our beds up, and how to make our beds down. How to fold our kit – each item a specific shape and size – socks 4" x 2" for example, and then how to lay it out for inspection, which we would have to do every day from now on. At about 8 p.m. we'd more or less finished, according to our billet corporal, all we had left to do were our boots. We'd already stamped our number on them, so there couldn't be much to worry about there surely.

How wrong can you be! Those boots were some really tough cookies, and didn't give in at all easily to our demands. They were a bit like 'clod-hoppers' really, in fact a lot like clod-hoppers, with a heavy, orange-peel finish all over. Underneath they had U shaped heel irons – like back-to-front horseshoes – steel toe-plates, and thirteen studs in each. But by morning the toe-caps and heel sections had to be as smooth and shiny as glass. What an impossible task. And we each had two pairs! Didn't they realise we'd had a long, trying day and were utterly knackered? Well yes – they did – but we had right up until lights-out, which was 2230 hours! That – we worked out – was 10.30 p.m. in English.

Candles were issued amongst us, and we were shewn how to warm the areas in question over the flame, then with boot polish and a toothbrush handle, plus a fair amount of spit, beat those little bumps into submission. Once the bumps had been smoothed out, which took quite a long time, you applied a little polish to your duster, then rubbed it into those areas using tiny circular movements, adding more spit, more polish, more spit, and so on till the desired finish had been achieved.

Inevitably, some guys hadn't done everything by lights-out – probably 'Mummy's Boys' – and you could hear the odd whimper as you lay there in the dark, reflecting. What a hell of a day *that* was!

Those boots really were the worst though. I'd cleaned eighteen pairs every day as a nipper – in the Children's Home back in the thirties – but that was child's play to this. (Pun not intended). Yet somehow, we all managed to get to sleep eventually on that night of 13th April 1950, but were quite sickened when we were very rudely awakened early next morning – and found that it had *not* all been a particularly nasty dream.

Reveille on our first day in the King's Army – George VI was on the throne at the time – was at 0500 hours (5 a.m. English) and was indeed an awful shock. Few of us had any idea that 5 o'clock occurred *twice* in the same day. We were hustled and shouted at and jostled outside in just P.T. shorts and vests, and made to run. In the snow. Any romantic ideas any of us may have had about being a soldier were absolutely and undeniably dashed right there and then!

We returned from this run and collected our toilet gear from our barrack room, then made our way to the Ablutions Block. We'd be learning some strange new words in this army, and here was one for a start. This facility was about fifty yards away across a grassed area, and was semi-open. And bloody freezing. The wind just whipped right through the place, with little but our partly-clad bodies to stop it. And guess what – the water was in keeping with the rest of it – ice cold! I was surprised there was a roof on the place, but at least that kept most of the snow off us.

This cold water, and the requirement to shave every morning, whether you needed to or not, soon made our faces and necks very sore. And with our close-cropped heads, we looked anything but romantic. Particularly as few of us had clothing that

fitted anything like, or any idea on how to wear our berets. We *were* what we looked
– absolute rookies.

For the next two weeks we were drilled mercilessly on the 'Square', and educated
into the ways of the army. Basic Training they called it, and I must say, by the end of
it the difference was definitely noticeable.

Our 'Best B.D.' (battledress tunic and trousers) had been tailored to fit properly,
and had the shoulder flashes sewn on. Our feet were becoming more compatible with
the boots, and our blisters little more than a memory. We knew who to salute and
who not to, who was a 'Sir' and who wasn't. And believe it or not, the square-
bashing was becoming quite enjoyable! I was in N squad, C Company. Various
squads were being drilled on the square at the same time, and the competition soon
began to creep in. You saw how clumsy and out of step the others were, and strove to
better them.

We learned how to wear our uniforms and gear to better effect, and every single
one of us was made to become more than just familiar with those two words –
Personal Pride. This extended into our immediate surroundings too, there being a
shield or something awarded for the best kept barrack-room each week. Windows
shone – inside and out – and anything that lent itself to being polished positively
gleamed, including the centrally positioned black stove. One kind of central-heating,I
guess. Our beds were all steel, and closed down to half their length each morning
when we made them 'up'. But it didn't go down too well with us when we discovered
that we had to use our own boot polish to 'bull-up' these beds, which were painted
black.

We received either twenty-four or twenty-eight shillings per week – I can't be sure
now which it was – out of which we had to buy everything. Blanco, Brasso, Boot-
polish, Boot-laces, all Toiletries, Writing paper, Envelopes, Stamps, Cigarettes etc.
That didn't leave much as you can imagine. And no matter how well you kept your
barrack room – even if you held the shield – you always found that an amount had
been deducted from your pay each week, under the heading 'Barrack Room Damages'.
No wonder some guys were perpetually broke.

Us growing lads needed all the extra food we could get, especially with all this
drill and exercise we were now getting. But we seldom had enough money over to
pop into the NAAFI, to top up. The variety and quality of the food in there – the
Salvation Army too for that matter – was excellent. And the odd pint helped you to
drown your sorrows now and again – when you could afford it. For although I may
not be giving that impression, life at Oudenarde was extremely gruelling – very, very
tough indeed. In fact some of the guys were really struggling with the harshness and
severity of it all. Thoughts of suicide filled many a mind in those early days I can tell

you. And if you think I am laying it on a bit thick here, believe me – I am not. It was *tough!* To a slightly lesser degree, it would be the making of many of *today's* youngsters, of this I am certain.

But, as I say, at the end of that fortnight we were a much different set of people from those that had been collected from the railway station at Aldershot. Even the hardest of the hard-nuts had been relieved of most – if not all of their arrogance and swagger. Nobody – but nobody – ever got the better of the Army. The majority of us knew there was nothing else for it but to do our best, 'keep our noses clean', and keep our chins up.

But as early as that, we were counting the days to demob. We really envied the Permanent Staff personnel – who had maybe three or six months service in already.

The results of all this brief, but quite intensive training were to come under the scrutiny of a Brigadier – or some such high-ranking officer – and all his entourage of Brass Hats, on our last day at Oudenarde. This was the Passing Out Parade. We'd been constantly primed up to this occasion by our mentors, (more like *tormentors*) and it was certainly very aptly named. The military band took up position on one side of the parade ground, right opposite the platform where our Brigadier chum and all his merry men would take the salute. In between, filling up the parade ground – which must have covered some three to four acres – was us lot. ''Orrible little men' and 'Nig-nogs' all. Squad after squad, each formed into three ranks, right across the square. I ought to point out that the latter of those two expressions did not have the connotations it might possibly have today. For throughout the entire duration of my service, never once did I come into contact with anyone other than Caucasian. Not that it would have mattered if I had, we are all God's people in my book.

We'd been marched in and positioned in plenty of time – as is the Army's wont – and of course, our visitor decided to be late. The weather had improved a little since day one – fortunately – and now we stood in late April sunshine. And we stood, and we stood. The command had been given '*Stand at Ease*', which as any ex-serviceman knows, is still a position of attention in which one moves nothing more than an eyelid. And *that* in as imperceptible a manner as possible!

I'm not at all familiar with today's Army, but then, in that position, you stood with feet fifteen inches apart, right arm stiffly extended forward and gripping your rifle barrel by the end, the butt being on the ground and in line with the seam of your right toe-cap. And the worst thing a soldier could do, so we'd had drummed into us, was to drop his rifle. An unspeakable crime. 'If ever you drop your rifle' – we were advised – 'for God's sake follow it down. Pretend you've fainted!'

We'd also been advised, fortunately, to occasionally lift our heels slightly off the ground – again imperceptibly – should we be required to stand to attention for any lengthy period. This would ease the blood circulation and prevent fainting.

We stood and we stood. Then suddenly, horror of horrors, we heard the unspeakable being committed – a rifle clattered to the ground! Sure enough, its owner followed, as advised. But this was no sham – the guy really had fainted. Then someone else went, then another, and another. They were dropping like flies. 'Lift those bloody 'eel's' screeched our corporal from the corner of his mouth. I was lifting mine like mad – as imperceptibly as I could – for I was feeling mighty peculiar myself. The rows of heads in front of me, and the rooftops beyond, all began to merge into one dark, swaying mass. I could see nothing but blackness. 'This is it,' I thought, 'here I go'. I tightened my grip on my rifle and kept lifting my 'eels.

One's instinct would be to go to the aid of an unconscious comrade in such circumstances. Perish the thought! In no way could you break ranks, and if they still lay there when you marched off, well, you just marched right on over them.

After what seemed an eternity, and just as I thought I'd had it, the band struck up. At last they'd arrived, thank goodness! We were quickly brought to attention, right turned and quick marched, and the parade finally got under way. The sudden movement just saved me, restoring my consciousness and vision sufficiently for me to see the form of the chap in front of me, which although no more than a blur, was enough for me to follow. I just hoped he knew where he was going. My head gradually cleared and, to the strains of our own Regimental March, we responded to the command '*Eyes Right!*'

I looked at 'His Nibs' as I marched past, and wondered if he cared about all the prostrate rookies his tardiness had undoubtedly caused. Still, I suppose they did have the distinction of having passed out twice in one day!

I must say, it was a feeling of achievement, passing out. And no doubt some were feeling like 'old soldiers' already. Especially when we caught sight of the new intake arriving; a right shower they looked – still in their civvies. 'Get some in, you bloody nig-nogs!' we called out. Fairly inaudibly I might add, for fear of being disciplined.

Following the Passing Out Parade we hurried to look at 'Part One Orders' – which it was one's duty to do every day – to see where each of us was going next. We hoped naturally, that we'd be lucky enough to stay with those we'd made good friends of, but had absolutely no choice in the matter of course. By the way, I made mention earlier of the fact that I did meet up with one of my old Yorkshire pals once again, after leaving Leeds. Well, this was when. Coming back from the cookhouse one day, after one of those 'sumptuous' meals – I thought to myself 'I know that face!' And sure enough it was my old school pal Herbert Unwin. He was just four days younger than me so naturally we'd been called up on the same day. But to go to the same camp, when we lived a couple of hundred miles apart! Our reunion was brief though, for we had different postings from Oudenarde and I never ran into him again.

I was down to go to Blandford in Dorset. Several others from N squad were on that posting, and I was glad to see amongst them my two pals, Geoff Martin from Gazeley, near Bury-St-Edmunds, and Don Whitwood from Norwich. This was an eight-week course, concentrating on driving – and guess what – more square bashing etc.

Before I leave Aldershot I must just recall one incident. Each barrack room, which housed probably about forty, had in the middle of it the corporal's bunk. This was more like a chalet really, a room within a room if you like, and quite private and secluded from the rest of us. So our barrack room was – effectively – in two halves, and each of these halves had in its centre a stove. The corporal had his own open fireplace within his bunk.

One evening he emerged from his bunk and ordered us all to form a line outside his door, each with a mess-tin half filled with cold water, and one shirt sleeve rolled right up. Odd, we thought, but nevertheless obeyed. We'd been in the army long enough to know that you obeyed *all* orders – no matter how odd or even stupid they may seem – and queried them afterwards if you felt the need.

He had one of his pals in his bunk with him, and he'd left the door slightly ajar.

So the first few in the line could both see and hear things from within. The corporal withdrew from his fire a poker, which was glowing red hot. He spat on it, then returned it to the fire saying it wasn't yet hot enough. He also mumbled something else, rather incoherently. But one word stood out clearly enough. *Vaccination*! At which those at the front of the line quickly spun on their heels and moved to the back end. As others moved into their hastily vacated places, the performance inside was repeated. After two or three such performances, the entire forty of us were fighting to stay at the back end of the line, all scared out of our wits. Vaccinated with a red-hot poker? Some were close to passing out – we were such greenhorns we were taking it all in.

The relief was truly heartfelt when the pair of them came out laughing their rotten heads off, confessing to their little prank. We supposed they treated themselves to this laugh once a fortnight, with each 'New Intake', and were very wary of all corporals – *and* lance corporals – for quite some time after that!

As far as square-bashing etc. went, Blandford was just an extension of what we'd had at Aldershot really, only a bit more of it and over a longer period. Plus of course the driving – which to some of us – already skilled in the art ,was good fun and a bit of a skive really. To others it was quite different – horrifying even.

The barracks were called Spiders, presumably because from above they would have resembled the shape of those insects. This of course is purely my guess, but they were quite comfortable really, with the ablutions in the centre or 'body' section. A great improvement on Oudenarde, for now we didn't have to go outside for such facilities. And if your timing was good there'd be hot water too. Things were looking up, although in all other areas the harshness and the rigours continued. But we were gradually becoming hardened to it, and were much better able to take it.

Our performance on the drill square improved, and we became quite sharp. And we were very proud of ourselves. Each fortnight one group finished their course and moved on, and a new group moved in to start theirs. As the weeks passed, we compared ourselves to these new intakes – with all of two weeks service behind them – and grinned at each other. When we'd watched those lads arriving at Oudenarde, on completion of our initial two weeks' training, we'd felt *so* superior. Yet we'd been no more advanced than these lads were now.

We learned various skills – Map-reading, Field-craft etc., and received training on a variety of weapons, leading to a day's shooting on the firing range now and again, which I found quite enjoyable. We had to negotiate a pretty tough Assault Course periodically and were exposed – though very briefly – to gas. This of course was without the protection of gas-masks, high-lighting their extreme value! And we received regular physical training, including a few route marches, some of which were pretty lengthy – twelve miles or so. Yep, life was very full!

When we attended P.T. sessions we fell in outside in the appropriate gear – vest, shorts and gym shoes – and were inspected by the P.T.I (instructor), who was always a corporal. We were still in the process of selection here, so were a mixed bunch at this stage. Rough and smooth together.

One day, the PTI found a couple of guys who hadn't washed themselves properly. I'm sure they'd already received a previous warning, so this time they were for it. They were charged, and sentenced to a Regimental Scrub. This sounded rather drastic to us, but they weren't from our squad so we weren't too concerned for them. That evening however, an N.C.O. poked his head into our billet and called for six volunteers. We'd been in long enough to know also, that you never volunteer for anything in the army, so the response was totally negative. At which, he detailed six of our biggest lads, to carry out this unenviable task.

Apparently – or so we were informed by our superiors – a true Regimental scrub took place in the centre of the Parade Ground. This, we assumed, was in days gone by – the 'good old days'! A bath was placed in position and filled with cold water. The whole battalion – everyone in the camp in fact – was assembled round the square to witness the event. The offender was stripped and plunged into the bath, then scrubbed with bass brooms. What a humiliation! Not to mention the pain. I should think old John Wakeman – he of the regular flogging over the side of the bath in the Children's Home – would have felt he'd got off quite lightly, had he been witness to this.

But on this day, they didn't use the Parade Ground. We'd advanced a lot since those times, and were much more civilised now. Instead, it took place in the Ablutions Section of our hut! But everything else was the same. Cold water and bass brooms were still used, and our six colleagues were made to do the job properly. And the pain and humiliation were still there, for on completion of their ordeal the offenders had to run the gauntlet – past us enforced onlookers – back to their own billets. There weren't so many of us as would have lined the square, but I'm sure this was of little consolation to these guys. They ran stark-naked past us all, their bodies bright red from the scrubbing and goose-pimpled from the stone-cold water. They shivered and shuddered, and sobbed openly as they ran past.

A good lesson to all, you'd say. In no way would anybody lay themselves open to such treatment as that. Yet at a later date, those very same guys were charged with the same offence again. They were punished, but I don't remember a repeat of the Regimental Scrub. Can you believe those guys?

Sunday morning could be a bit tricky at the Blandford camp. Unless you were unfortunate enough to be on guard duty it was your day off. So, as is the way with most young fellows of that age – eighteen to twenty – a lie-in was generally the first order of the day. But pity the fool who chanced his arm after our first Sunday.

The door suddenly burst open – some time before 0700 I think it was – and an NCO entered the room, declaring his requirement of three volunteers, for fatigues. The stony silence which followed brought about the press-gang tactics, for which the British Army was renowned. Most other armies too, I suppose. 'I said I wanted three volunteers' he barked, 'so I'll have you, you and you!'. Just my luck – one of those unfortunates was me.

What a day that was! We stood side by side at a large white sink, scraping new potatoes, all day long, with just the one break for our midday meal. The potatoes were mostly the size of marbles, with just the occasional whopper – nearly as big as a golf ball. They were being prepared for the following day, as was the regular custom. The quantity required seemed incredible, till you worked it out – then it figured. We had to fill a large galvanised dustbin!

We got stuck in and were well on the way to filling it when our spirits were truly dashed. The cook sent in a further FOUR of these bins, all of which had to be filled before we'd be released.

Fatigue was certainly the right word. Can you imagine – scraping potatoes that small – and tossing them one after another into a bin that size, till it was full? Five times over! The fronts of our denims (overalls) were caked stiff with dried scrapings when we eventually staggered back to our billet. Stiff too were our poor hands – *and* sore.

The only sure way to avoid being caught for this monstrous chore was to get up early and be well clear of the camp before 0700. On a Sunday morning! You may be lucky if you just hid up for a while, returning to your bed when you considered it safe. But that carried a great risk for they knew all the tricks, and were expert at playing cat-and-mouse.

Fortunately this was late Spring/early Summer and the weather had improved considerably since the snows of mid-April. So we used to make our way to Bournemouth, and while away the day there – out of harm's way. So we thought.

There is much wisdom in the saying 'moderation in all things'. But some of our chaps, alas, paid little or no heed to such sound advice, for when the weather was particularly nice, with very warm, uninterrupted sunshine from dawn till dusk, they'd strip off and lie on the beach – all day long! Inevitably some of them got sunstroke, and on Monday's early morning muster parade, there was more of the old passing out. They were duly charged – the offence being 'self inflicted injury' – and punished accordingly. Probably 7 days C.B. (Confined to Barracks) or more rotten fatigues. Talk about adding insult to injury – you couldn't win.

Another less pleasant aspect of our situation was the necessity for jabs. We were marching back towards our billets one day – day's duties behind us – when we were suddenly brought to a halt, right outside the Medical Block, and ordered to form two ranks. We were then turned to our right, forming two files. We were ordered to roll up the shirt-sleeve of our outer arm and place that hand on our hip. Thus we filed in.

Progress was fairly slow, no more than a shuffle really, whilst the medics did their foul deeds on those up front. There was the usual speculation and leg-pulling, all the time we were *out*side the building, with the clever-dicks trying to scare the pants off the more timid ones. And mostly succeeding.

But an amazing hush descended once we were *in*side – and could see what was coming. I don't know now what we were being injected against, such things as cholera and tetanus I should think, but even more passing out took place. And these were mostly those same clever-dicks, or big, strong looking guys. They collapsed just before it was their turn, the sight of the needle going into those ahead being too much for them. So they received their jabs whilst in a state of oblivion on the floor. Then you got a needle in each wrist as you passed through the doorway on your way out, a grinning medic positioned each side in wait. Sadistic sods!

Outside – once everyone was through – we fell in again and continued the march back to the billets. Those out first, now the deed was behind them, had been play-acting around in front of those still waiting to go in, pretending to be suffering the effects and staggering about. Little did they know!

It was Friday, as we came to learn was always the case when jabs were given. That way you recovered in your own time, over the week-end. And brother – they knew just what they were doing. I clearly remember sitting at the table in the middle of the billet, writing home to my Aunt and Uncle. After a while I realised that I was the only one who wasn't in bed – and it was only mid-evening. Beds were all a-shake as their occupants either shivered violently, or sweltered, as the effects took hold of them. They were moaning and groaning – *what* a to-do. And they weren't pretending now either! I cannot fathom why I wasn't similarly affected – I felt a bit groggy but that was all.

I remember the next day well enough though. Not that I was ill or anything, but was my arm stiff! I was a smoker then, and I was walking away from the camp when I fancied a cigarette. I popped one between my lips, and went for my lighter, which was in my left-hand trouser pocket. The arm I'd been jabbed in! I couldn't move that arm backwards more than about an inch from the normal hanging position, without agonising pain. So I had to wait until I met somebody before I could light up.

The mess-tins I mentioned earlier were not used on a regular basis, only when we were on the firing range for the day, or field exercises and the like. Regular meals were eaten off normal plates, which were cookhouse property. Our 'eating-irons' (knife, fork and spoon) were our own issue though, and we were responsible for these ourselves. Consequently they were clearly stamped with your own number. When not in use they clipped conveniently together.

When you'd finished your meal you picked up your plates, dishes and eating irons, took them out back and washed them, returning plates etc. to the stack nearby, and irons to your pocket. The facility provided for this purpose was two more galvanised dustbins, each filled with hot water. *Very* hot water. You carefully immersed the items into the first bin – which quickly removed all traces of food, then into the second, which stayed very much cleaner and gave a better finish. This was extremely effective and a most commendable idea.

Until that is, some bright spark caught you unawares, and nudged your elbow when you were swishing your irons to and fro in the first bin, causing you to lose your grip on them. As they were your own responsibility you were forced to retrieve them, which was a very messy and uncomfortably hot business, with your sleeve rammed right up into your armpit. Had it been a plate you could have left it there – but there was no fun in knocking *those* from your grasp. This happened dozens of times every day. Ah well – boys will be boys.

As I've said, the driving part of the course I found quite enjoyable. Irrespective of any previous experience we may have had – including even the possession of a licence certifying that you had in fact, already passed the driving test – we all started from the same point. The training was all taken on 3 ton lorries, and was in three stages. First – The Compound, then the Basic Route, and finally out on the public highway.

That Compound was something. At times it could be slightly dangerous I suppose, at others hilarious. It was completely enclosed by a tall wire fence, and covered an area of probably a couple of acres. The surface was really something else. Nothing but pot-holes and small hillocks. This was formed deliberately of course, for the purpose of developing pedal control. The likes of myself had little trouble with it, and graduated almost immediately to the Basic Route. But you can imagine the antics of the raw beginners. Talk about kangaroo juice!

The Basic Route was fairly tame, just the roads within the boundaries of the camp. Similar to the roads outside mostly, with T junctions and crossroads. But no traffic lights, and practically no traffic.

The final stage was, naturally, the most satisfying. Driving through Bournemouth and Winton, and all the surrounding villages and country lanes. We went three to a lorry usually, one driving – with the D.I in attendance of course – the other two riding in the back, awaiting their turn. This part was, actually, nearly as good as the driving, as you could lean over the tail-board and wave to all the pretty girls. We each managed about two hours of actual driving, being out all day long. At midday the chuck-wagon drew up in its predetermined layby, and our mess-tins came into their own once again. Then it was off for the afternoon in the wagons again.

The Examiners roamed the outside routes, and any pupil deemed by his DI to be ready for the test, could pick one up and take his. The test was the same as that taken in Civvy Street, and the Examiners themselves were non-military. You were quizzed on the Highway Code just the same too.

On my first day I covered the Compound, the Basic Route, the Outside Route and took the test. And failed! I'd inadvertently crossed my hands on the steering wheel as I emerged from a side road – and that was it. I knew – the instant I did it – I just hoped *he* hadn't noticed. But how could they fail me, when I'd already passed the test a year previous? Well apparently they could, and they did. I took the test again on the following day though, and was more cautious. This time I passed.

I wondered what I'd be doing for the remainder of the course now, whilst those lucky blighters were out joy-riding all day. I needn't have worried. We were hit by a pretty significant Meat Strike in London just then – May/June 1950 – and the Army was called in to help out. Several of our DI's were sent up there, plus one of two other drivers I think, but I was not amongst them. I was a bit disappointed over this at first, but soon cheered up when I was made a temporary DI, to help out with the training programme. I can't remember how long this situation prevailed, but I know I enjoyed it.

You were allowed 24 hours of actual driving. If you hadn't passed the test in that time you'd had it, never getting another chance. Or so they told us, and I must say, I never had any reason to doubt the truth of this. Your horizons were greatly restricted then, as you couldn't go on to higher things in our mob – the RASC – without first becoming a qualified driver. You could be a desk clerk, or an 'Issuer'. I never did find out the real meaning of that word – well in that context anyway. Something like a general labourer I think, as it was always them who'd be found cleaning latrines and ablutions and things. Or waiting in the Sergeants' Mess maybe. I was only too glad not to be one of *them*.

After we'd all qualified – those that made it – the interest heightened. We all went 'solo' and in convoy. Truck after truck rumbled through those towns and country lanes, with DR's (Despatch Riders) travelling to and fro the length of the convoy, looking for stragglers and directing operations at crossroads and junctions. The Vehicle Mechanic's mobile workshop took up the rear, so as not to miss any breakdowns. We felt great. Eighteen/twenty-year olds doing all this. And a couple of times we went out on night convoys – solo again – and were out most of the night. What a thrill – and we were being paid for it too! Albeit only four shillings a day – or thereabouts. But of course, life wasn't always this good as a National Serviceman in training, so it was a time to be cherished.

We finished the driving part of the course and went on to finish the other side – the regimental stuff. I was really glad that Geoff and Don had passed everything as well, making good our chances of staying together, also several more of our buddies. We'd been together ten weeks now and the bonds were becoming quite strong. Life hadn't seemed so bad at Blandford as I say, mainly due to the driving. I've been driving now for 45 years – as I write – and have developed a take-it-or-leave-it attitude towards the whole thing now. There are so many restrictions these days, and I am very much saddened to see the courtesy that once was shared by all road users falling into such decline as to be almost non-existent. But then, well, it was so exhilarating. I remember yet the thrill of taking an army lorry out on my own for the first time.

A couple of slight misfortunes befell me during my time at Blandford. The first, for which I was awarded seven days CB, involved the loss of my best boots. They always used that term incidentally – '*awarded*' – as if it were some kind of honour!

On leaving the billet each morning, to get about our day's duties, one man was appointed 'Billet Orderly'. His job was to stay behind and watch over the place, where all your kit was laid out and your personal things in your locker under the bed. Your 'Best Boots' stood, gleaming like mirrors, on a box at the foot of your bed. Like the rest of your kit they were all in perfect alignment with everyone else's, right to the 'nth' degree.

On this particular day we returned from the mornings doings, and I was most upset to find a yawning space where *my* boots should have been. I reported their loss, and, to my utter astonishment and dismay, I was put on a fizzer. Which if I haven't mentioned already is the more commonly used alternative for charge. Or 252.

Up before the Old Man next morning – minus cap and belt – I was helpless. The billet orderly had denied responsibility, claiming he'd left his post for no longer than it took to pop to the loo, or acquire some food or something. Perfectly legitimate reasons – and accepted by the O.C. – but somebody had to be held responsible. And they *were* my boots! So in addition to receiving seven days, I had to foot the bill for a new pair of boots! (Oh dear – is that another pun?) But worst of all was all those hours of hard work that had gone into 'bulling' them up. I now had to go all through that again. And how on earth could I have prevented their loss?

The second occasion was something quite different, but just as unfortunate a hole to fall into. We were on the firing range all day and I was down for Main Guard duty that night. I always enjoyed those days on the range, and had become quite a decent shot with the Lee Enfield .303 rifle, which was general issue then, the Sten Gun – which beyond about five feet was a pure lack affair – and the Bren Gun, which I considered a beautiful weapon. If indeed *any* lethal weapon could be so regarded. But we were only shooting at man-made targets anyway.

We returned to camp after a long but enjoyable day, with dirty rifles and webbing. There wasn't that much time left before Guard Mounting Parade in which to get ready. I needed to shower and shave, then there was the boiling and pulling through of my rifle, webbing to be blanco-ed, which comprised belt, gaiters, cross-straps, ammunition pouches, large pack, small pack and bayonet scabbard. And my boots, tunic and trousers, tie, lanyard, cap-badge, brass buttons and buckles – all needed to be immaculate.

I did all the blanco-ing first, as that needed time to dry before I could clean the brasses. Next my rifle, which took a lot of cleaning after the day's activities, and then my boots. A quick dash to the cookhouse for a little food – there wasn't time for a proper meal – then back to the billet to clean brasses, press trousers etc.

There was just time left for a quick shower and shave before getting it all on and falling in on the Guard Mounting Parade. The morning's shave by the way – no matter how close – was never good enough for guard duty on the evening of the same day. At one of the camps where I was stationed, the Regimental Sergeant Major –

when he was inspecting a parade – used to hold a piece of paper edge on to your face and slowly stroke it upwards. Even the merest hint of a whisker would rasp like a piece of coarse sandpaper being applied to a hard surface, and bring forth those dreaded words – '*Charge this man, corporal!*'

The ritual of Guard Mounting followed a regular pattern. You were thoroughly scrutinised – back and front, top to bottom – by the Orderly Officer. Then came the rifle. You received the order – 'For inspection, Port Arms!' – whereupon you brought your rifle up in front of you at an angle of approximately 45 degrees, into a position a little lower than would be adopted to fire off a salvo at a special occasion. You drew back the bolt, then placed your right thumb into the breech so that your thumbnail would reflect the light up the barrel, affording the Orderly Officer a perfect view of it as he peered down.

I was fully confident. I'd worked damned hard on that weapon, as indeed I had on all the rest of my gear. Imagine then my utter disbelief and despair as I heard those dreaded words being directed at me! I couldn't believe it, that barrel was bloody near perfect.

But it wasn't the rifle he was doing me for, nor any other part of the kit upon which I'd worked so hard. That was all fine. So what then? Apparently, when he'd looked down the barrel, he'd caught sight of a scraping of blanco under my thumbnail! In my haste I'd omitted to scrub it out. Would you believe it? I had to report to the Guard Commander as soon as possible – after the Guard had been mounted – to have my scrubbed thumbnail inspected.

And I received once again – on the subsequent OC's Orderly room – another seven days' CB. And to think, I'd missed most of my evening meal that night too. Still, I suppose it could have been worse. But what a life!

The day following a night's guard duty could be quite a struggle, especially if it was spent in the classroom, rather than out on something active. One such day we were receiving instruction on governors – the type that control the speed of an engine that is – not the bossy type. My eyelids became heavier and heavier as the Instructor's voice droned on and on, and I drifted off into another world.

I was brought up suddenly by piece of chalk hitting my chin. As my head cleared and my eyes re-opened, I found the Instructor looking directly at me, and asking if I'd been paying attention. 'Yes Sarge' I replied. 'Right' said he, 'out you come!' I then had to face the class and repeat all that we'd just been told. Could have been quite tricky really, but my years at 'Power Units' and 'Grey's' saved the day. I didn't get it *quite* right, but my effort was accepted – if a mite grudgingly. Good thing it hadn't been on a different subject – I was getting tired of CB.

The course at Blandford duly came to an end, and a look at Part I Orders revealed that my next posting was to Farnborough – back near Aldershot. This was for a sixteen week Vehicle Mechanic's Course, but needless to say, loads more of the old Regimental Stuff would be included. Sure enough, both Geoff and Don were on this posting, so too were a few others from our original 'intake'. But our number was ever diminishing. Still, it was a comfort to have a *few* familiar faces around you when you arrived at a new place. And Geoff, Don and I had become really good pals by now.

We were beginning to get some in now all right – ten whole weeks in fact. Let's see – ten from seventy-eight – only sixty-eight weeks to go! But *were* there? So we felt less like raw recruits when we arrived at Farnborough, than we had at Blandford. But we were – nevertheless – the new intake. Us that is, and several others who'd come from other camps.

It's amazing how camps varied, one from another. At Oudenarde there'd been quite a bit of space, grass too for that matter. And at Blandford there'd been even more. Farnborough on the other hand, seemed to consist of the drill square, with buildings almost completely enclosing it, and little else. But perhaps the distance of time clouds the mind's eye, and there *was* more to it.

Our barrack block filled one side of the square, and was two or three stories high. Our room was about halfway along on the first floor. There were something like fifteen of us sharing this room, whose only outlook was the square.

Most of the facilities you would need were situated around the square, on one side or another. So you were always obliged to either cross or circumnavigate the square itself, wherever you wanted to go. And you never, ever strolled or sauntered across the drill square. *Strictly* taboo! Consequently, we seemed always to be marching everywhere – in a very 'soldierly manner' – even in our leisure time. Though now and again, when we had a little more time, we would take it easy on a longer route.

Every morning the entire company paraded on the square. The newest intake at the back, the oldest at the front. A new intake arrived every other Thursday, displacing the one whose course had just ended. So your squad progressed across the square, in fortnightly hops, till your final fortnight saw you right at the front. Right under the 'eagle eye'.

The V.M.'s course was quite intensive, there was much to cram into the sixteen weeks. And the level of bull was no lower than it had been anywhere else either, so one way and another we were kept pretty busy. We needed to concentrate very hard during the day – in the workshops and in the classrooms – and at night, after all our blanco-ing, boot-cleaning, brass-polishing, ironing, personal hygiene etc. had been attended to, we got down to our précis. All the day's rough notes and sketches had to be transferred into our exercise books, in very neat text and detailed, accurate drawings. As you laboured away at this task you endeavoured to inwardly digest every detail, in readiness for the eventual *Final Trade Test*. All this invariably took us right up to lights out, but we did occasionally manage to squeeze in a visit to the NAAFI.

All the other side of our training continued as ever – assault course, firing ranges, fieldcraft, physical training, map reading exercises, route marches etc. I don't know how we fitted it all in, but we did.

Morning and afternoon sessions were each broken by the tea-break, thank goodness. This was when the Salvation Army chuck wagon came round, and weren't they welcome. They always had the most scrumptious cakes and snacks on board, all at very reasonable prices, and the 'soldiers' serving them were really nice people.

The lessons themselves were both informative and interesting, but lacked the sparkle and pleasure of the driving course at Blandford. There were no picturesque views from these workshops and classrooms, nor were there any pretty girls to wave to. But I guess it gave us a better chance to concentrate.

One evening the call went out for volunteer blood donors. There always has been a need for blood of course, but in those days we weren't made quite so aware of the urgency. So the response was very poor, no more than two or three names being submitted. Coupled to this I should point out, was this natural reluctance to volunteer for anything, no matter how worthy it might sound. We'd all heard about the guys who responded eagerly to a call for people who could ride a bike, and finished up humping furniture about in the Sergeant's Mess!

A day or two later we were marching back from the workshops when we were brought to a halt and right-turned to face the Medical Block again. Oh no – not more jabs! 'Volunteer Blood Donors, one pace forward march!' bawled our NCO. The two or three guys responded – the rest of us stood fast. 'Come on, you bloody nig-nogs' jeered our friend, 'what's the matter with you – all turned yellow have we?' He then proceeded to call out names from a list. The whole damned lot of us were on it!

Somebody had gone round in our absence and taken every man's name and number from his locker – probably *him* I shouldn't wonder – and plonked it on the list. We didn't mind too much really, but weren't too pleased when we were made to 'Slope Arms' immediately we reassembled outside again, and continue the march back to the billet. That hard little pad they put in the crook of your arm afterwards made it very uncomfortable, trying to hold the rifle in that position. We could have been allowed to 'Trail Arms' under the circumstances. There's gratitude for you.

One morning – on the square – they had a purge on berets. The correct position for the beret was with the rim one inch above the eyebrows, running level right round the head, with the badge directly over the left eye, and the slack pulled down over the right ear. You can imagine the variations that were possible here. The punishment for those in breach of this regulation – on this particular day – was to double off the square back to their billet, then double back again after swapping their beret for their steel helmet. They then had to wear that for a whole week.

By the time that parade was over, a good many heads were steel-helmeted! There were a few headaches that week, as they weren't at all comfortable. I can't think how I wasn't amongst them, for anything placed upon my head always slips over to one side. Perhaps I was able – imperceptibly – to straighten mine up before they got to me.

One chap so punished – Patterson by name and an ex Boy-Soldier – chortled that at least he wouldn't have to polish his cap-badge every day. Don't you believe it. Our sergeant overheard his remark and ordered him to report to him every night, with a gleaming cap-badge in his hand. Patterson was a nice guy. A good height and a matching physique, good-looking and always very well turned out. Quietly spoken, unassuming, and a credit to the army. Yet that sergeant had it in for him for some reason.

For some other minor infringement – probably trumped up – he was made to report after the day's duties in FSMO, then run round the perimeter of the square, lap after lap, until it was decided he'd had enough. And that continued every night for one week. FSMO is *Full Service Marching Order*, and is a condition in which you wear or carry every piece of army and personal equipment you possess. All your webbing, back-packs, rifle, steel helmet. And kit-bag stuffed with all the rest across your shoulder.

Poor old Patterson. But he took it well, and was none the worse for it afterwards. Probably stood him in good stead I should think, for I believe he was one of those sent to fight in the very nasty Korean war.

I won't mention where this next incident took place, as this is purely a collection of memoirs and not an indictment, but we once had a change of RSM at one particular training camp. Our first introduction to the new guy was on the drill square, and we weren't too enamoured with him when he straight away referred to us as rabble. ''Orrible little men' – even 'Nig-nogs' – we were used to and could take in our stride. But we were very proud of our performance on the square, with near-perfect timing to the man.

But he was going to straighten us out – make *men* of us! Where've I heard that before? The fact is, he did just the opposite to one poor lad, who'd been called out for talking in the ranks. This fellow was made to run round the perimeter of the square – as Patterson had – but with both arms stretched above his head, supporting his rifle. The Lee-Enfield .303 weighed 7¼ lbs if I remember rightly, and would become unbearably heavy held thus for a prolonged period. The rest of us carried on bashing that square, whilst the unfortunate squaddie completed lap after lap. As he flagged, he was bellowed at by our friend, whereupon he gathered himself and struggled on, till finally he collapsed. Time can cloud the memory I know, but I am almost *certain* that poor lad dropped dead, there and then.

Whilst on the morbid side of things – although there was more humour in the following incident – afterwards – I must mention a guard duty I was once on. And only once thank goodness. I was still on training, and was sent to stand guard over the Detention Ward at a military hospital. There were six of us on this particular guard, working in pairs, and doing the usual two on and four off. In our off period we were swotting like mad in the guardroom, and trying to grab a few winks here and there. But what an experience my second two hours on turned out to be.

The inmates were all afflicted in one way or another, but seemed mostly to be mentally deranged. 'Nutters' we called them, but with the benefit of hindsight, I can see that this wasn't very charitable of us. They weren't allowed belts, braces, boot-laces and ties – or anything else with which they might harm themselves. And for harm read *hang*, for this was the thinking behind the ruling, based on several fatal incidents apparently. I was actually in one camp, as a visitor – having driven our OC there on business – when they cut down one guy who had hanged himself in his cell. They were too late as it happened. And this was some time later, when my training was well behind me.

The door into this detention ward was very, very sturdy – and heavily bolted. On the *out*side. The two chaps on sentry duty positioned themselves, one either side of the door. When I say either side, I mean one inside, the other outside, in the passage. There were tall windows all along one side of the room – heavily barred – and the loos and toilet facilities were at the end furthest from the door.

I was one of the first pair on – from 1800 to 2000 – with a wee Scots laddie called Jock Dippie. We tossed a coin and he won, electing to go *inside*. I threw the bolts on the outside, turned the key in the lock and sat on the chair provided. There was no contact between us other than a bell, and a light which flashed when this bell was rung – from inside. The two hours dragged by, but we were eventually relieved and made our way gratefully back to the guardroom. 'What's it like in there?' I asked Jock, as we walked along together. I can't remember his reply exactly, but I know he succeeded in putting the wind up me, and I wasn't looking forward to midnight, when we two would be on again.

During our four hours off, the guard commander received a call from somewhere requesting that he send two of the biggest chaps he had, to assist in the bringing in of a very desperate character, who'd just attempted suicide. The other guys were all bigger than Jock and me, so off went two of them. Well – the fellow they brought in looked anything but desperate, in the sense we'd been expecting. He was shortish, very slightly built, and quite subdued. I can't imagine he'd put up any resistance. He'd slashed both wrists and – though we couldn't understand why – placed a red-hot iron against his face. Metaphorically speaking that is, for it was a clothes iron, and I can't say I've ever seen one of those actually glowing red. His wounds were quickly attended to, and he was placed in the detention ward.

Just before midnight, Jock and I were roused from our slumber in the guardroom, and taken to relieve the two who were just finishing their stint. It was pitch dark now of course, and the whole place took on a different aspect. Jock stood back whilst I made my way through the doorway, to take up position on the inside. Was it my imagination, or was that a grin on his face as he slammed the door shut behind me? I shuddered as the bolts were rammed home and the key was turned. There was a very low wattage light-bulb above the door, which cast eerie shadows across the room, and which stayed on all night. I sat on the chair, measured my distance to the bell-push, and prayed that I wouldn't have to use it. Or that it would work if I did!

Assorted grunts and groaning noises were coming from the 'patients', and as my eyes became accustomed to the gloom, I counted something like a dozen beds I believe. The majority of these guys were asleep now, but three of them seemed to have no plans in that direction. One – who was nearest the door – was the new arrival with the slashed wrists, now heavily bandaged, and the face, which had been left uncovered. It looked horrible. He spent the whole time groaning, and picking non-stop at the mess the iron had made. Quite sickening really.

Another, with shaven head, got out of bed, slipped on his lace-less boots and clomped his way up to the loo. What a racket – on the bare wooden floor! Back he came – clomp clomp clomp – but instead of getting back into his bed, he took his handkerchief and went clomping across to the windows, where he climbed up onto a sill and started polishing the glass. During the process, he'd lost his grip on his cordless pyjama trousers, and down they fell. He carried on regardless, a pretty odd sight, and rather unnerving. I managed to persuade him to return to his bed, and sat back on the chair.

Number three was a guardsman, and was he big. His bed was furthest from me and in the deepest shadows. He had a cage over his lower half – under the blankets – presumably to keep the clothes off injured legs. He'd been moaning steadily, but now it began to intensify. It reached such a pitch that I went down to try to quieten him, I didn't want him waking any of the others – I'd enough on my hands as it was.

'Giss a fag!' he demanded.

'No' I replied, lying that I didn't smoke. He groaned louder and repeated his demand. Again I refused, but gave in when his behaviour worsened even further. Peace restored, I returned to my chair. I peered at the bell-push and looked forward to 0200 hours.

Suddenly, number two got out of bed again, donned his boots and made for the windows. I quickly headed him off, but he insisted he needed to visit the loo. Clomp, clomp, clomp. Number one continued his groaning and pick pick picking. The window cleaner re-emerged from the loo, and I steered him back and into his bed. Back to my chair. I listened to them all – snoring and groaning – and envied Jock outside. No wonder he'd grinned! Supposing they all rose up at once and came at me? And supposing the bell failed to work! Oh hurry up, 2 o'clock.

'Giss a fag!'

Oh no – not him again. 'Go to sleep, I've none left!' Groan, groan. 'Be quiet!'

'Giss a fag!' he insisted. '*No – go to sleep.*' He began to get out of bed and I could see just how big he was. I quickly took him a cigarette – and checked how many I had left. I prayed there were enough to last him till 2 o'clock. Another guy got up and went to the loo. This triggered off the window cleaner, and so it went on. By the time 2 o'clock came I was in serious danger of qualifying for a bed myself. It was a bit like the attic in The Homes all over again, with danger lurking in every shadow. Phew! – was I glad to get out of *there*. It was me who was cadging a cigarette then, to calm my nerves. We would no doubt have become quite blasé about it all on further tours, but this was our first, and we all felt the same.

Talking of guard duty, it payed you well to achieve a personal turn-out that just had the edge on everybody else. Well – on Main Guard at Farnborough it did anyway, for they had an incentive there that was well worth going for. They always detailed, for that particular guard, one over the requisite number of personnel. On guard-mounting inspection, the man deemed to have the smartest turn-out was awarded the title of '*Stick Man*'. I don't know the origin of this business, but what it amounted to was that the lucky guy was dismissed from duty, but credited with having completed it. In theory, this meant that if you were awarded the title every time, you'd never have to actually do a guard duty. I was lucky once, and never met anyone who'd been luckier. But you had to try.

My luck was most definitely out on another occasion though. But come to think of it – so would everyone else's have been as well, for it was something that affected every single National Serviceman in the British Armed Forces. And by single, I don't mean unmarried.

It was Farnborough again, at just about the time my course was coming to an end. I was on Main Guard, and positioned right outside the guardroom itself. It was late evening and I was checking the movements of personnel in and out of the camp.

'*Halt! – who goes there – friend or foe?*' It was always 'Friend' of course, which was just as well really, for I don't know what we were supposed to do if the reply was 'Foe!' We had jolly nice rifles – but were *completely* devoid of ammunition.

Anyway, it was pretty quiet, and my off-duty mates were lounging inside the guardroom, listening to the radio. I was quite enjoying it myself too, as the strains came through the open window. Then the news came on – and the bottom dropped right out of my world.

I'd been wallowing in the fact that I'd just completed six months – a third of the way through my service – leaving one year to go. *Lovely*. All downhill now. Then came this announcement – which was like a knife through my heart – stating that the duration of National Service was being increased from eighteen months to TWO YEARS. Forthwith! So my six months was completely wiped out at a stroke. I still had eighteen months to do. It was heart-breaking, it really was. The only consolation was that we were all in the same boat.

The completion of our course at Farnborough – in the autumn of 1950 – coincided with an event of much greater significance, to the world at large, and some of our lads in particular. This was the Korean War. We'd had our final 'Trade-Test', and were making our way – with bated breath – to see the results on the notice board. Had we passed? If so, where were we going next? After six months of solid training and studying, with very little time to ourselves, we were looking forward to being posted to a 'working unit' – where the atmosphere would be much less stressful.

As we neared the board, guys were moving away from it, with very mixed expressions. Some looked positively elated, others utterly dejected – almost in tears. Not because they'd failed the test – much worse – they were being posted to Korea! Most of those on that posting were really quite excited at the prospect – what a change from square-bashing and studying it would be! No, these few with the downcast look were those with problems at home. One of them, a chap from our billet, had a seriously ill mother. Another was about to become a father at any moment, and another's wedding was imminent. Korea later maybe – but not right now.

As far as Geoff, Don and I were concerned, we were both pleased and disappointed. Pleased because the three of us had all passed, and all with a high mark. But disappointed – not because we were down for Korea – we weren't being sent there, but neither were we going to a working unit. We, and two others from our squad were being posted to the Isle Of Wight – which might have been fine but for one thing. It was another bloody training course! We couldn't believe our eyes.

There certainly were some mixed emotions that afternoon. Some were delighted with their postings – to various parts of the world, or maybe just within the U.K. –

but wherever it was it would be to a working unit. Others were excited at being sent to fight in the Korean war. Innocent fools. Others on the same draft – like the three I've just mentioned – were in deep despair.

And us three, well five actually, were absolutely devastated with our lot. Another thirteen weeks' training on a Marine Engineering Course, plus more of the inevitable regimental stuff. We'd had more than enough training and studying already, and who wanted to be a blasted Marine Engineer anyway? And to think – those guys we'd been with at Blandford, the ones who'd progressed no further than drivers, would have been enjoying themselves at various working units throughout the world, for over three months now. Yet look at us. What a bloody drag.

We mulled it over awhile, then hit on the idea of volunteering ourselves for Korea, in place of those not wanting to go on compassionate grounds. After all, we were all single and unencumbered, and really eager to get off this I.O.W. thing. The other guys were quick to agree, and we drafted our application:- 'We, the undersigned, hereby submit this . . .' and handed it to the Adjutant. It was turned down flat! *We* were going to the I.O.W., *they* were going to Korea, and that was that. Bloody-minded sods.

In retrospect of course, I thank God I wasn't sent out there. No wars are nice, but that one seemed particularly nasty, and our lads taken prisoner had a very bad time, so we heard. I have met several who were eventually released and returned home, but none that I knew, and those reports were confirmed 100%. Not to mention all those killed. I have wondered since as to how many of our original intake perished in Korea, and how close us five may have come to it.

Our time at Farnborough coincided with another event of great significance too. And great would be the operative word. It was the Brabazon. We were out on a twelve-mile route march one day, and the homeward stretch took us right past the aerodrome at Farnborough. Somebody looked across and saw her, sitting there dwarfing everything else in sight. Somehow, our NCO obtained permission for us to cut across the airfield, and we were able to walk right up and touch her. What a whopper! I don't remember much about that particular aircraft – I don't think she came to anything much – but I do remember her size. *Enormous*. Well it was then. This little diversion certainly took our minds off our blisters for a while.

So, in spite of no less than five repeat applications for service in Korea, the 'Three Musketeers' – as I began to think of Geoff, Don and myself – were to be found, this day in October 1950, setting out to conquer the seven seas on our journey to strange, faraway lands. Well at least, we boarded the ferry at Portsmouth, to cross The Solent to Ryde, I.O.W. That was a *start*. We looked sympathetically at the other passengers. After all, they weren't really used to the ways of the sea, and us – well, we were *sailors* weren't we? Well, we were going to be – jolly soon.

We were picked up at Ryde and taken by Bedford 15cwt truck to Freshwater. Well, just outside Freshwater in fact – to *Golden Hill Fort*. Now there's a name for the imagination to toy with. Shades of Beau Geste (spelling?) and the Foreign Legion and all that stuff. And I must say, I found it very impressive as we marched under the tunnel-shaped arch that led past the Guardroom and into the quadrangle. Our footsteps rang against the stout stone of its construction, reminiscent of medieval times, and every time I marched under that arch, which was several times every day for three months, I felt a strange kind of thrill. Almost as though I'd been there before – in some previous life.

The quadrangle that this arch led on to was in fact the Drill Square, and the buildings bounding it contained everything except accommodation, ablutions, the NAAFI, and the Motor Transport (MT) Sheds. In here were the Cookhouse/Messroom, Admin Block, Quartermaster's Stores, Armoury, Dog-Kennels, Boat-Stores, and various other things. By comparison with the other places I'd been to so far, it seemed quite small, although the facilities outside the fort itself – but still within the boundaries of the camp – were well spaced, with lots of wide, grassed areas between. And I liked it. Yes – I really liked it, and came to grow quite fond of it over the next three months. So too I think, did Geoff and Don.

The billets were quite good here, though the ablutions etc. were once again separate. The level of bull was just as high as everywhere else, needless to say. The maxim was – 'If it moves, salute it, if it doesn't, *paint* it!' We even had to use boot polish on the soles of our Best Boots, finishing off with a rub of Brasso over the thirteen specifically placed studs, and the toe and heel irons.

But by now, we were well used to all the bull and discipline, and took it fairly comfortably in our stride. We knew exactly what was expected of us, so there it was. But as with Farnborough, the biggest rub here was all the précis-bashing every evening. And of course, we still had to do our share of guard duty, both at Golden Hill Fort, and at Fort Victoria, Yarmouth. There's *another* great name. The latter was where our classrooms and workshops were, and there was a lovely 'old' feel to it all. I loved it, and again felt some strong link with bygone times.

The regimental training continued as ever, but the trade training seemed to become even more intensive. There was no more than a handful to a class, which in itself further heightened the concentration. And at the very outset, our instructor – a very competent Marine Engineer (ME) himself – informed us that he'd had no failures yet, and didn't intend having any from our little group either. So the onus was on us to pass at all costs. Unfortunately, the cost was far too high for one of our classmates, whose name I shall not disclose. I shall instead, give him the alias Ken

Brewster. More of him later.

The general atmosphere at Fort Victoria – as far as I was concerned – was marvellous. The salty smell of the air, the sight and sound of the sea, the constant tolling of the bell-buoys just offshore. As much as I love the deep countryside, so do I love the sea, so of course, the best part of the training by far was that spent afloat.

The training vessels were quite a mixture really, but none of them was very large, although they were all sea-going craft. They ranged from thirty-foot Harbour Launches – each powered by a small Kelvin paraffin engine – through General Service Launches and Fast Motor Vessels, to the largest of all, a ninety-foot ex-fishing vessel – which had also been used as a Royal Navy liberty boat – the MFV 1502. The GSLs and FMVs were about fifty feet in length, and the latter of these two classes was capable of speeds somewhere in the region of 24 knots. We had some quite exhilarating times with these at a later date, up in the Menai Straits. More of this later too.

When first I'd been called up, I was asked if I had a preference for any particular branch of the Services. Every inner instinct pulled strongly towards the Royal Navy – with my great love of the sea – but I made my heart give way to my head, and went into that particular corps of the Army that would enable me to continue in my civilian occupation. So you can imagine my delight now, as I got to grips with things at Fort Vic. I was getting the best of both worlds, always allowing for the great pressure in the classroom.

The three of us settled well to life at Freshwater. I think all the other guys, Shipwrights, Navigators and Ordinary Seamen, felt the same, unexpected thrill attached to the place as well. After all, we'd all joined the Army – yet here we were!

The first thing we had to master was sculling. Some of us had rowed before, in fact I myself was quite competent at that; but none of us had ever sculled. And this was something quite different. You should have seen the antics! The locals and the holidaymakers must have had some really good laughs at us as we flailed around in Ryde Harbour. *'Figure of Eight – Figure of Eight!'* stressed our instructor, but whatever number we tried to etch into the water with our scull, we made little or no headway. And frequently lost the scull. But it was great fun, and as with most things, practice makes perfect – and most of us mastered it – eventually. Memories of Toad, from 'Wind in the Willows'.

Marine engines of today are no doubt quite different, but then, they were as exciting as a beautifully maintained Traction Engine would be today, up against a modern motor vehicle. Although when you were down below, in a rough-ish sea, with the strong smell of diesel oil all around, things could get a mite unpleasant.

My biggest thrill came from the FMVs. They were twin-screw vessels, which means of course that they had two engines, and therefore two propellers. They had Ailsa Craig engines, whose horsepower I don't remember right now, and they were mounted right in the stern. They were, naturally, side by side, each a beautiful match to the other, and each with its own set of controls. The telegraphs were mounted on the bulkhead forward of the engines, and the best instruction from the Skipper up in the wheelhouse would be '*Full Ahead – Both Engines!*' You'd reply on the telegraph, then ease both throttle control levers forward – in unison – then feel and hear the powerful response of the engines. You'd probably get a wet backside then as the bow lifted to the surge, and the stern dipped right down. And you were sitting with your rear end overhanging the transom, so conveniently placed.

We nipped across The Solent occasionally, to Poole or maybe Lymington, where we'd always have a pleasant hour or so ashore. An hour which was spent mostly drinking coffee and playing the Juke Boxes in the Milk Bars, as they were called. And also of course – the *main* thing – chatting up the girls. Now that we were in the Water Transport section of the RASC – now the Royal Corps of Transport I believe – we sported an extra 'flash' on the sleeves of our tunics – the Blue Ensign. A really smart addition, and certain we thought, to capture the attention and interest of the girls.

Of course, they'd seen plenty of Blue Ensigns before, on the sleeves of all those countless trainee Marine Engineers etc. that had gone before us. But those lasses were always nice and friendly, as indeed were most people towards us National Servicemen, or Conscripts, to give us our other name. After all, we had no choice in the matter, and anyway, they all had brothers, sons, boyfriends, who'd been dragged off to do their bit, just as we had.

I did click with one nice lass in Poole, named Rae. But our visits were always short and not that frequent, so nothing came of that, other than a couple of letters. I certainly couldn't afford the ferry across.

Those trips were usually in the Harbour Launches, GSLs or FMVs. One day our destination was a little further out, and our vessel – the *MFV 1502*. By comparison with those fast little launches, the 1502 was a rather lumbering old tub, and was said to roll quite a lot. We nevertheless clambered aboard excitedly, delighted to be going to the Channel Islands, where few if any of us had ever set foot before. There'd be the usual brief trip ashore, where we could each purchase a limited quantity of cigarettes and spirits, which would be exempt from duty on our return.

The weather wasn't too good when we boarded, and as we got under way it began to deteriorate. But up to this point it was no worse than to add a little zest to the trip, and really give us our sea-legs. Our watches were worked out and we settled to the usual training programme. By the time my two-hour watch came around it was getting quite serious, but I think the Skipper had decided it was a better bet to go on rather than turn back.

I descended the ladder to the Engine Room, and set about my business. I can't be certain now what the engine was, but I have a very strong suspicion it was a Widdop. She was a good old job, and quite old I think. She sounded good – if a mite loud, but she created quite a lot of heat and smelt pretty strong. Of diesel fuel that is. She kept you busy, checking all her vital points and oiling bearings and things regularly, which was all good fun under normal conditions. But not so funny on *this* day. We were heaving badly now and her reputation for rolling was well deserved. And with the strong smell of diesel oil I began to feel quite queasy. Which was very unusual for me, for unlike most of my fellow trainees, I hadn't been bothered by sea-sickness so far on the course.

Regular entries had to be made in the Engine Room Log, regarding wind-speed and direction, visibility, sea condition etc. Against the latter I was just entering '*Heavy Swell*', which I felt was a howling understatement at the time, when I had to make a dive for the bucket, just to the right of where I stood. This wasn't in fact a bucket at all, but an empty five gallon diesel-oil drum whose top had been cut out to serve the purpose, and to this day, I still feel it was almost the death of me. As I leaned over it, an even stronger smell of diesel hit me full on, causing me to retch quite violently. I heaved and I heaved, then suddenly, my stomach seemed to seize up solid with cramp, and I could neither breathe – in nor out – nor straighten myself up. For what seemed ages but was probably a few seconds, I stood doubled up thus, feeling absolutely certain my end had come. And barely nineteen years old!

I must have been blue in the face by the time the cramp eased off enough for me to straighten up and move away from that bucket, to where the air was slightly less obnoxious. After a few greedy gulps, I fairly quickly returned to normal. Well, as normal as was possible under the circumstances.

I continued entering understatements in the Log, and looking after the engine – though a little less whole-heartedly than when I'd started out – until my watch was finished. I made my way to my bunk, but found little respite there from the really wild movements of the ship. But at least the air was better than where I'd just come from! I was offered food – albeit Emergency Rations – which I promptly rejected. After the two hours I'd just experienced, tinned bacon and spaghetti did little to stimulate my appetite.

I somehow coped with the remaining rigours of this so-called day return trip, and after something approaching a twenty-four hour battering, relief finally came as we entered St Peter Port, Guernsey. Considering her age the ship had taken it quite well really, and had obviously fared better than we had. But then, she would no doubt have been through this kind of thing many times over, she certainly wasn't as green as us lot. But anything that hadn't been lashed down securely was likely to have been lost.

It was on this particular training trip that we almost lost our class-mate, Ken Brewster, mentioned earlier. I'd come up on deck after another two-hour stint in the engine room. Bracing myself against the howling wind and lashing rain, I struggled my way to the head of the companion-ladder that led down to the crew's quarters. It was pitch dark – I can't remember what time it was – and we were pitching and rolling quite violently.

As I was about to make my descent, my eye caught something glinting in the light that was shed from the wheelhouse. I was desperate to get below and rest up awhile, but something compelled my eye to dwell on this glinting. Slowly, in the gloom, a strange shape began to emerge, not moving at all – other than with the ship – and I was quite shocked to recognise this shape as Ken. What the heck was *he* doing up on deck in this weather? I stood and watched quietly as I tried to fathom the situation.

He was clad in black oilskins and sou'wester, which was of course the cause of the glinting, and stood high on some coiled rope or something, up close to the siderail. He had one hand-hold on part of the structure but his position was extremely perilous, and I soon realised his intention. A sudden movement on my part – or a shout – and he would have been overboard. The rest of us all knew that things were getting on top of him, particularly the intensity of the course. He was a bag of nerves every time we approached a test – he had so little confidence in himself.

Hanging on for dear life, I crossed the deck – as imperceptibly as possible – and laid a gentle but firm hand upon his shoulder, at the time asking him what he was doing. I strengthened my grip as he flinched and made to pull away from me, then, as he slowly released his grip on the rigging or whatever, turned him and moved away from the side, and eventually to the comparative safety of the crew's quarters. He hadn't resisted at all after my initial touch – which was just as well really or we might *both* have gone over the side – lost forever.

He quietly admitted to me, soon after this incident, that I had guessed correctly at his intentions, and had undoubtedly saved his life, although he hadn't been at all grateful for this at the time. He'd definitely intended jumping overboard, and was just trying to summon the courage at the moment of my intervention.

Poor Ken. He was such a quiet, inoffensive chap, and the army was really no place for him. But then, neither would it have been for a good many others, that's for sure. It wasn't through any of our doing that we were here, but here we were, and most of us tried to make the best of it. I think it was mainly just the training period that got most guys down, and in our case this was *particularly* protracted, with one darned course leading straight on to another! And every evening taken up with doing all our bull – *and* keeping up with our précis. Usually right up until lights-out.

Ken nevertheless completed the course, and absolutely astounded himself – and us – by passing. So, as with Geoff, Don and myself, he became a Marine Engineer, Class 3. I just cannot describe the wonderful feeling of relief we all felt. Nine solid months! To be sure, there was no studying *that* night, instead a trip to the pub in Freshwater – I can't remember the name just now – and a darned good celebration.

Anyway – back to Guernsey. I forget what time of day it was when we tied up at the quay, but it was daylight. How subdued we all were now, quite the reverse of the jaunty, excited bunch that had only yesterday boarded the MFV 1502 at Yarmouth. And that included the regular crew-members too! We'd planned to leap ashore the moment we arrived, so that we might take in the town and as much of the island as time would allow. But – once we'd made fast – a strange stillness and quiet came over the ship as we all collapsed gratefully onto our bunks!

But we were all young so of course recovery came quite soon, and ashore we went. We thoroughly enjoyed our visit, which in the event was greatly enhanced by the fact that the storm conditions at sea persisted, and we became weatherbound. For three whole days! It was well that everything was so much cheaper there, otherwise our four or five shillings a day pay would have left us doing little more than window-shopping. As it was, we each had a haircut, bought a few nick-nacks, and as much whisky and cigarettes as we'd be permitted to take ashore on our return. I didn't drink whisky myself, but there were plenty who'd be glad to buy it from me at that price. And of course, several of those back at Freshwater had given us money to buy drink and cigarettes on their behalf.

After three days, we were all fully recovered from the trip out, so the calm, uneventful return journey was quite an anti-climax. After all, we all had our sea-legs now – well and truly – so this was a bit of a waste!

Our skipper had passed back word of our plight from Guernsey, but by the time the news reached the ears of our shorebound contemporaries, it had been stretched a bit – one way and another – so on landing back at Fort Victoria, their goggle-eyes saw us as *Jason's Argonauts* or something, and we were regarded with considerable envy. We wallowed in this hero-worship for a while, then settled down to finishing the course, which as I've said, we all passed. And for the first time throughout our service so far, we felt the sheer delight of seeing our names down for postings to working units – rather than more training courses.

We had so little time to ourselves on the Isle of Wight during our initial stay, that I can find little to say about our off-duty activities. There was just the occasional visit to the NAAFI for a pie and a pint, and the rare trip into Freshwater or Yarmouth for a game of darts with the locals. But perhaps we managed these visits slightly more often than I now remember – 40 odd years is quite a time. I do know however, that there wasn't time to develop any kind of relationship with the opposite sex – even short-term. Other than in my case, the very fleeting romance with Rae, in Poole.

I've had one or two mental blanks during the course of these jottings. I now have another. For the life of me I cannot remember whether Don stayed with us when we went from Freshwater, I.O.W. to Menai Bridge in North Wales, or was posted elsewhere. I feel pretty sure that our original group was now down to three as we boarded the train. Just Geoff, Ken and myself. This feeling is supported by the definite knowledge that Don wasn't with us when finally we were demobbed. We did meet up again later though, when we were on the Emergency Reserve, and had to go back to Freshwater for two weeks each year for the 3½ year duration of that reserve.

MENAI BRIDGE

It was with a good deal less apprehension then that the three of us – Geoff, Ken and myself – settled down to the journey to North Wales. After the previous nine months we couldn't imagine what life in a non-training establishment would be like, but it had to be a lot less fraught – surely to goodness.

After a non-eventful journey, we arrived at Bangor railway station in the early evening. It was now mid-January 1951, and quite dark as we left the train. And raining steadily. The first thing we noticed was that all the locals there seemed to have something on their chests – or in their throats or something – for all the time they were talking together they were constantly trying to clear it. We kept a wary eye on them all for a while, for as Geoff said – ' You feel they're going to *spit* at you any minute!' But we soon found that this sound was made when pronouncing a word that began with two Ls – as in Llandudno for instance – and our wariness soon eased away.

In fact, I for one, found the Welsh people to be extremely nice, and quite sympathetic towards us National Servicemen, *wherever* we hailed from.

There wasn't a great deal to Menai Bridge then – maybe it's changed a bit now – and our camp was small. And I must say, I felt really at home there and fitted in well with the locals. Even learned quite a bit of the Welsh language – eventually. And had a few girlfriends, all of whom were very attractive. Really lovely girls they were.

We were directed to Menai Bridge from Bangor station – by bus – and put off at the far end of the village. The camp, as I say was small, and on a tiny island called Ynys Gant. Or it might have been Gaint – I should know really – for I wrote home pretty regularly in the fifteen months that I was there. But it isn't listed in my large-scale A.A. road atlas either, so there we are. There was nothing else on this island, just the Army. And we soon learned that the English translation of this name was 'Island of Goats' – which was a mite disconcerting to us – and possibly explained the absence of anyone else! Access to the island was by a little elevated road, single width and about 70 or 80 yards long, with a low rail along each side. A bit like a causeway.

All the usual facilities were there, but on a very much smaller scale than those to which we'd become accustomed so far. There were just the two billets, each with about ten or twelve beds. The Sergeants and Warrant Officers had their own mess of course, in a small building which incorporated their sleeping quarters as well. And there were just two Officers – the O.C. – who held the rank of Captain, and the Adjutant, who I think was a Second Lieutenant. They each had private accommodation in the village.

What a difference! I think we totalled no more than thirty – and that included two civilian clerical staff. Plus a handful of us who crewed our little fleet of about three or four craft – moored in the Menai Straits – and who slept aboard. So as you'd imagine, it was quite friendly and fairly easy-going, although proper respect was accorded the Officers at all times – NCO's too where called for. Discipline was also properly maintained, but not in so over-the-top a manner as we'd had in all the big training camps. Yes – this was much more to our liking, and we looked forward to the remainder of our service being spent here.

On our first morning we were interviewed by the O.C. – during which I was asked if I was happy being a Marine Engineer. I made some reply to the effect that I would rather have stayed as a VM in Motor Transport, than gone into the Water Transport branch. He pondered this for a moment then said – 'We're only allotted one VM on our small strength – which we have already. But leave it with me and I'll see what turns up'.

Meanwhile, we were assigned to our places within the unit, and I was quite delighted to find that I was down as Engineer on one of the unit's two FMVs. And would you believe it – Geoff took the same position on the other! I don't recall what happened to Ken just at that time, but I'm pretty sure he wasn't placed on a vessel.

As I said earlier, those FMV's were some really trim little craft, about fifty feet in length and quite fast. The crew was minimal, comprising the Skipper – who was a fully qualified navigator – the Engineer, and usually just the one Seaman. Sometimes your number may be increased for a while – if they had a surplus of personnel on their hands, but this would be only temporary crew – not permanent as we were. These craft – I can't recall what the other one or two were – were all ex-Air/Sea Rescue vessels, used in the war. And they were great.

Being peacetime – and on our own shores – there wasn't any specific role for us to play that I can remember – other than target towing for the RAF down off the west coast. – Aberdovey I think it was. I can't recall anything else, we just took off for a run now and then, and kept everything in tip-top condition. This was where the fun came in that I mentioned earlier.

We tended our engines, and all the other gear that came within our sphere, steering, winch, generator, decking etc. There was little on the vessel that *wasn't* the Engineer's responsibility in fact. But it kept us occupied. Once a month each vessel was subjected to a 407, which was in fact a thorough inspection – the equivalent of the 406 in the MT. So you had to keep them immaculate.

Whereby of course, a great deal of pride came into it as you constantly compared yours with the others, and these runs could get quite competitive. We each felt ours was best – and fastest – although there was no way you could tamper with them at all – like mechanical steroids of some sort – or your own concoction of 'Whizz Juice'. So quite often, had anyone been at a suitable vantage point, they'd have witnessed some pretty exciting 'burn-ups' through the Menai Straits. All unbeknown to the powers-that-be, needless to say. Until the day when somebody cut a little too close to the shore, and ran aground on a sandbank! I can't remember the outcome of that little indiscretion, for it was some time after I'd been re-assigned – to a shore job.

The OC had called me in to discuss further the question of my preference for MT over WT. Quite frankly, I'd almost forgotten about that now – I was enjoying life afloat so much. But I listened to what he had to say.

Our little unit had places on its strength for only the one VM, and one driver. These two places were still occupied – but he was having trouble with drivers at the moment. The one that was there when I came – a big, surly Scot – had been involved in a number of prangs, and as he was close to demob, had been put on something else to finish out. The OC had requested a replacement driver, and was sent a very lively cockney lad named Pete. He was a very likeable guy, but it wasn't long before he too fell from favour – for one misdemeanour or another – and was relegated to general duties, pending transfer.

'So I wondered if you'd like to take over the post of Company Driver for the moment', said the OC, 'and we'll see what develops?'.

Well; what could have been better? I'm not usually that lucky, and I could see straight away that although I'd be giving up my very enjoyable life afloat, it would be for something I'd enjoy just as much – if not more. So I didn't hesitate with my answer, and spent the rest of my Army service in that capacity. Nothing further ever did develop on the VM front, but I never regretted that for one moment. Particularly as a Marine Engineer's pay was considerably higher than that of a Driver – and I was never down-graded!

The unit had two vehicles, an Austin 10 'Private Utility' – PU for short – and a three ton Bedford wagon. The latter was changed just after I took over – following Jock's series of mishaps – for a brand new Fordson. She was a fair wagon, and may have been some improvement on the Bedford – although I did have something of a soft-spot for Bedfords – especially the little 15cwt. But this was well over forty years ago now, and lorries weren't anything like as comfortable and luxurious as they are today – or as well equipped.

There was no heating or ventilation in the cab for a start, although you could swing your windscreen forward, like the peak of a cap. But you then ran the risk of getting your eyes bunged up with insects of course, although the cooling effect was nice. Neither was there power-steering, air-brakes, synchro-mesh, radio, seat-adjustment – other than fore and aft – or anything like that. They were purely functional really, and gear changing was much like square-bashing in a way – all a question of timing – for it was 'double-de-clutching' all the way. And whatever the weather, you had to open the window right the way down and stick your arm out to signal.

Yet given the choice between driving one of those vehicles, in road and traffic conditions as they were then – and driving one of today's luxury jobs in current conditions – I know which I'd go for. But then, that view applies to pretty well everything as far as I'm concerned, for the world is rapidly deteriorating from where I stand. But here I go again.

I switched from one vehicle to the other, according to my workload. The first job each day was to take the MT corporal to the village in the PU, to collect the mail from the Post Office. He'd also post letters for anyone who asked him, mail being very important to us 'fed up and far from home' National Servicemen. I noticed he always wrote something on the back of these envelopes before handing them in, and on asking why was quite amused when he showed me. On those that didn't bear the usual SWALK, BOLTOP, BURMA, NORWICH, etc. he'd write 'Yours till cockerels use lipstick' or 'Yours till herrings wash their feet'. Another was 'Yours till glow-worms use batteries'. There were others which escape me just now, and I don't know what their recipients must have thought! Archie, the MT corporal, must have had his routine changed after a while for I started doing this little job on my own. But he insisted I keep up the messages on the back.

The PU also served as Staff Car, although it was really a small truck with a canvas tilt over the back part. I'd run the OC to wherever he had to go, and collect the occasional newcomer from Bangor station as they were posted in. Once in a while I'd have to go to Shrewsbury – or was it Hereford? – it's so long ago now, I cannot remember.

Anyway, this trip was to attend a Court Martial – when one of our chaps had committed a crime of rather more serious proportions. An example of this was one regular soldier in our unit – a scouse as it happens – who's name I've forgotten now. He'd go off on leave and not come back. Do a bunk as they say. Inevitably he'd be picked up by the 'Redcaps' (Military Police) and returned to our camp. Then would come this trip to Shrewsbury or wherever. The OC would ride up front with me, whilst the prisoner and escort sat in the back. It wasn't a bad little trip out, but it was overshadowed by the sorrow I always felt for the guy, who I believe was having trouble with his marriage.

Following the case he'd be sent to a Detention Centre somewhere to serve out his punishment, then be returned to us to resume his normal service. At the very first opportunity he'd put in a request for leave, and when granted, do the whole thing again. He was quite a nice guy really, a bit like Alan Ladd to look at, but apparently so desperate to get out of the Army and sort his problems out that he was doing this in the hope of getting out on a DD (Dishonourable Discharge). I can't remember the final outcome of this little saga, but I'm sure the Army would have won.

The Fordson – or 'Big-'un' as Archie called it – was used more extensively than the PU, although only a very small proportion of its carrying capacity was generally used.

There was a Royal Artillery camp, about twenty miles from Ynys Gant if I remember rightly, where I used to go regularly to collect supplies, mainly for the cookhouse and NAAFI. I say NAAFI with a smile really, for it was so wee it was more like a little 'snug' in a local pub. And it was run entirely by one of our lads, Don Booth by name. Mind you, no cooked food or the like was obtainable there, just snacks, drinks, cigarettes, writing pads etc. And bottles of ink of course, for if the ball-pen was on the scene then, it certainly wasn't a common sight. I know for a fact that all my writing – throughout my National Service and for several years afterwards – was done with a fountain pen. The sort with a rubber tube inside which you depressed by lifting a little lever on the side, then slowly released, drawing up the ink. We also availed ourselves of the Unit T Tailor at the Artillery Camp – with me doing all the fetching and carrying – and I collected small quantities of coal occasionally, probably when we were awaiting a delivery.

When first I commenced my driving duties, the laundry we used was in Bangor, just a couple of miles away, over the Menai Suspension Bridge, but we soon switched – why, I don't know – to Portmadog, which was more like thirty to thirty-five miles. I did this trip twice a week, taking the dirty laundry in on Monday and collecting it – all nice and clean – on Friday. That journey would take barely half an hour on the roads of today, and in one of today's Heavy Goods Vehicles. But our lorries were governed down to a maximum of 30 mph! Or it might have been 40 – but certainly no more! So of course, it was a whole morning's trip each time, which I thoroughly enjoyed, for it was through magnificent scenery.

You could have put all the little bundles I carried on this trip in a child's pram, and still had room left, so you can imagine how they looked on the back of a great lorry! But there we were, anything other than local routine trips had to be done in the Big-un, so that should the OC need to go somewhere urgently – in my absence – the

PU was at his disposal. I certainly didn't mind, for you got an even better view of everything from this much higher driving position. It was great.

I used to stop somewhere along the way at a nice little café, which was set in a particularly pretty spot. Just tea and toast at first, then one day I had a few extra coppers in my pocket, so had a full breakfast – eggs, bacon, sausage, tomatoes, fried bread, bread and butter etc. It was so delicious I tried to go for it every time after that, but of course, I had to drop back to toast now and then, when funds wouldn't stretch.

Then one day I was extra hard up, and ordered just a cup of tea. The good lady who owned the café questioned this, and when I replied that I just wasn't hungry that day, she gave me an old-fashioned look and retired to the kitchen. She was fairly soon back again, and in her hand was a plateful of heaven – my usual breakfast! She brushed aside my protest as she set it down before me, saying, in her lilting, motherly voice – 'Now you get that down you, you're a growing lad, and I shouldn't think that Army food fills you up properly isn't it!' What was I to do? Mind you, as far as the 'growing lad' bit went, there was little chance of me extending any further upwards. And all that physical stuff I'd been subjected to during my first nine months, had in fact increased my weight by well over two stones. And that wasn't fat!

The next time I stopped there I had enough cash and ordered the breakfast. Up it came – beautiful as ever – but my money was refused! Again I protested, and again I was overruled. 'You lads don't get that much pay, *I* know,' said this lovely lady, 'so you have this on me'. She saw my embarrassment and added quickly, 'And I don't want you going somewhere else in future either, just because you feel awkward about it. It's my pleasure!' There were absolutely no strings attached, just a genuine act of kindness and generosity. Could be she had a son of her own who was away doing his bit for 'King and Country' somewhere, I don't know, but I did meet many other equally kind, warm-hearted folk up there.

I continued calling there – twice a week – for over a year. My embarrassment gradually eased, and there wasn't another café on that little journey anyway. I'm sure I *did* spend some money in there, on cigarettes, chocolate, and so on. I don't suppose that little place exists today, with the way things change. But it most certainly does in *my* memory – and in my heart.

As nice as she was, that dear lady was a bit out with her assumptions on army food I have to say. Well at Menai Bridge anyway. Normal meals were quite substantial enough really, *and* in pretty good variety. Mitchell the Cook, was one of us – a conscript – called up as it happened on the same day as Geoff and myself. He did a good job, and being so small and friendly a unit, was a bit more forthcoming than we'd experienced elsewhere, and you could most times get second helpings. He did all the cooking – and we did all the cleaning – on a rota system.

This was a normal duty, all this cleaning by rota, and was part of what passed as our Guard Duty! Only we didn't have proper Guard Duties at Menai Bridge, instead we had '*Telephone Picket*'. This was worked out in the same way as were Guards, with each of us taking our turn, as designated on the Part I Orders notice board. A Picket comprised three men, and as I say, there were several cleaning duties to be performed each evening.

The Telephone Room would have measured something like fifteen by ten feet, and adjoined the Quartermaster's Stores, which was the first building you encountered on entering the camp. In one corner was a small desk, chair and telephone, the rest of the room was empty except for three iron bedsteads, folded back to half length. It wasn't used all day, whilst the office was manned, but after office hours the Telephone Picket took it over until normal duties were resumed.

I was quite amazed when my first Picket duty came up. The first thing the three of us did was pop next door to the QM Stores and draw a mattress and bedding each! The next step, naturally, was to make the beds down – or was it up – I seem to have lost it after all these years. No, I'm sure it was down. We were each allotted our chores then, by the Duty NCO, which included cleaning the offices, that is, sweeping out and dusting all round, polishing the floors, clearing out the stoves and laying them up for re-lighting next morning, emptying waste-paper bins etc., etc.

Then there was the cookhouse and messroom to do, and everything had to be done thoroughly. Lots of big old pots and pans to scour in the cookhouse, and fire to be kept in all night ready for cooking next morning's breakfast. But there were no spuds to be peeled or scraped – thank goodness – they were all done in a machine. This was a rotating drum, and looked a bit ancient, but who cared – you just tipped the spuds in through the open top, turned the water on I think, then started her up. The spuds all rumbled about with the movement, rubbing the skins off each other as they went, and it was as simple as that. Primitive looking but quite effective. Why couldn't they have had something like that at *Blandford*? But the cook himself did all the spuds here anyway.

Once all the cleaning and fire-laying chores were completed you could relax in the Telephone Room, just answering the phone when it rang. At lights out we used to undress and climb into our beds for the night, just like everyone else – having first rung the Exchange to place an early call for the morning. And that was it, other than just going round putting a match to the fires first thing. And making sure the cookhouse fire was still in of course, ready for Mitch to cook breakfast.

Easy as this sounds, the Telephone Picket *was* the first line of defence in an emergency, and we ought really to have slept with one eye open I suppose. But all incoming calls were usually routine, and nothing ever happened anyway. Until one night.

The '*Cold War*' between East and West seemed to be ever deepening at the time, and we were all a bit anxious as to what the Communists might get up to. Even to mounting an invasion of our sacred shores! We'd just sorted the Jerries and Japs out after nearly six years of struggle and strife, and we certainly weren't about to give in to anyone else now.

So emergency measures were taken at Ynys Gant, and presumably at every other service unit throughout the land too. All *we* knew was that Russian Paratroopers could drop in on us at any time! Our plans were laid – by the OC – and the whole manoeuvre was given the codename '*KNOCKOUT*'. At the OC's utterance of this word it was to be passed swiftly but silently round, so that everybody could immediately take up their predetermined defensive positions around the island, having first drawn ammo and stuff from the Armoury. I must say, it all sounds a bit 'Dad's Army'-ish now, but it was deadly serious then.

Fire power had already been determined for each of these positions – 3 Rifles here – a Bren Gun there – 5 Rifles here – and so on. Simultaneous with the command 'KNOCKOUT', all lights had to be extinguished and radios silenced etc., giving the impression that the island was deserted. And we were to communicate with each other only by signs and whispers.

At 0200hrs the phone rang. My bed was nearest, so after a few grumbles and groans – from all three of us – I stretched out an arm and lifted the receiver. 'Buckingham Palace – George speaking' said I. 'KNOCKOUT!' came the reply. I blinked and said something like 'Do what?'.

'*KNOCKOUT!*' – a bit louder this time. I was only half awake, but wary enough to know that at this time of night such a disturbance was usually caused by one of the lads from an outside phone somewhere. He was probably on his way back to camp – tipsy – and wanting a bit of a laugh. 'Sod off!' I growled and slammed down the receiver. We all snuggled down again, only to be awakened with a start minutes later when the OC burst angrily in on us.

As you can imagine, this was the real thing! Well, not the *real* real thing – with 'Ruskies' dropping in and everything – but real as far as he was concerned. He'd obviously been in a state of readiness himself – when he'd phoned in from his billet in the village – and at my rather frivolous response to his command had whizzed up to the camp post haste.

It was accepted that the Picket slept through the night as a regular practice, and fortunately for me the OC acknowledged this fact and made allowances for my immediate response. But from the moment of his arrival it was *Action Stations*. We tried to rouse the guys in the billets quickly, by shaking them violently and whispering

'KNOCKOUT' right into their ears. Some leapt instantly out of bed, but others responded exactly as I had to the OC. But my '*sod off*' had been mild by comparison. The OC himself was right alongside me trying to shake them out, and was receiving quite an earful! But according to Army law, for one minute following arousal from sleep, a man was deemed to be not fully in charge of his senses, and could say what he liked without being punished. So he was obliged to stand and take it. But after that minute . . .

Well, pandemonium ruled for a while, in the pitch dark. After all – we'd not had to do this before, and it *was* the middle of the night! Nevertheless, after the one minute's grace several guys were charged with insubordination or something, and amongst them was Mitchell, who was a heavy sleeper. Eventually everybody got the message and made for their positions – via the Armoury. It was quite hilarious at times – being pitch dark – and even the OC was accidentally knocked off the elevated footpath that led up from the billets. There was little he could do about that, although we were all quite sure it had been done deliberately. Probably by one of those he'd put on a fizzer!

And there were a couple of other facts that I haven't mentioned, but which were quite significant at the time. The first – it rained the whole night long, and the second, which wasn't so hilarious for me – I had the blasted flu.

At the end of it all we were assembled in the messroom – at about 0400hrs I guess – to hear the OC's verdict on the whole thing. And as you'd imagine, we none of us came off too well. Me worse than most I reckon, for in the course of clambering over a rocky outcrop on the way to my position, my boot slipped on the wet surface and the hand that clutched my rifle came down hard, smashing my finger-tips. One finger had swollen to twice its normal size and was really hurting. Some months later the whole nail came off, and although I've lost several finger nails over the years, the events leading up to the loss of that particular one stand out most vividly. And what with suffering from the flu through all this, I wasn't at all sorry to hit the sack the following night. The guys charged all got jankers (CB).

Going back to the Telephone Picket, this was a very enjoyable part of camp routine on a Sunday morning – as long as you weren't on it, that is. For this was when you had breakfast in bed – with one or two other little luxuries laid on as well – compliments of the Picket. The night before, they would take your order for breakfast and morning newspapers. Then in the morning, between them, they'd cook all the eggs, bacon and sausages, make the tea, go down to the village and collect the papers, then fetch it all down to us in the billets at about 0900.

For convenience your breakfast was all in sandwich form, and the tea was in a two-gallon bucket. And my goodness, did that go down well! As soon as they'd dished everything out they'd switch on the wireless – and in the Winter light the stove – then leave us to it, returning a little later with another bucket of tea for top-ups. And we could all thoroughly enjoy this luxury – unashamedly – for we all had to do a week-end Picket in turn.

And the regular orders for a Sunday morning – amongst ourselves that is – were 'In bed or out of barracks!' What a difference from the training camps. But I must point out here that in spite of all these little easy-going facets of the place, our personal turnout and that of the camp itself were always well up to scratch.

For our leisure moments at Menai Bridge, we had a pretty good outdoor tennis court and a Recreation Room for indoor pursuits. In the latter was a piano – in good tune, a dartboard, and table-tennis equipment. The floor was kept well polished, by the Picket of course, and there were tables and chairs dotted around with our little NAAFI bar in the corner. And didn't we have some great times in there!

On a Sunday in Wales – at that time – nothing opened at all. No shops – other than the newsagent's I guess – no cinemas, dance-halls, cafes, pubs too I think – it was absolutely dead. There were just two exceptions to this condition, one was Church of course, (or Chapel) the other our camp. Every Sunday evening we held a Social in the Recreation Room, to which we invited friends from outside. Needless to say, those invited were all girls, and lovely they all were too. I cannot recall seeing an unattractive lass on Anglesey – Mainland North Wales either come to that – and at these events they outnumbered us by about two or three to one, coming from miles around.

Yup – they sure were some great evenings. We had a record player and loads of records to which we danced – all 78 rpm of course. And with the cookhouse right next door, with the fire always in, you could slip in and make yourself the odd sandwich when the fancy took you – quite unofficially of course. And it goes without saying, there was always plenty to drink, yours truly having fetched same back from the Royal Artillery Camp aforementioned!

We held another social every Wednesday evening which, whilst fairly well attended, never quite matched the Sunday one when there was nowt else to do. And being the Company Driver I always finished up running several of the girls home in the PU – again quite unofficially. So of course, I was well placed to get on pretty good terms with most of them. This sure made up for the first nine months of my National Service!

Pastimes outside the camp were much as they were anywhere else. In Menai itself there was a cinema – was it *The Star*? – I can't remember. There was also '*The Liverpool Arms*' pub, and a nice little fish and chip shop – with a smart restaurant at the back. That was about it really – if there were any other pubs I don't recall them.

We went to Bangor quite often – where there was the added attraction of the dance hall, though I mainly only remember going to the 'Tanner Hop'. This was the name given to local little dance halls at that time. It was a tanner (2½p) to go in, but where the hop bit came into it I'm not sure. But they were damned good places and we always enjoyed ourselves.

Some of the guys would go exploring the surrounding countryside at week-ends, to take in the scenery. I didn't need to – being always out and about. Somehow my journeys seemed to take in the very best parts anyway. I regularly drove through Snowdonia, and all along the Llandudno/Colwyn Bay/Rhyl coastline. Other notable places on my regular routes were Betws-y-coed, Swallow Falls, Conway Castle, Harlech Castle, Llanberis Pass, Chester, various places along the west coast, in fact there was very little of Wales that I *didn't* cover – from Anglesey in the north, to Barry Island in the south, and from the west coast to the bordering counties of Cheshire, Shropshire, Herefordshire, Worcestershire, and Gloucestershire.

The roads were generally very good and well sign-posted, and the traffic mostly light. And as I've said, the scenery was quite magnificent – breathtaking at times – as so many people will have discovered now, with travel being so much within the reach of a good many of us these days. But then, it was for the few, and in my case the added beauty of it all was that it cost me absolutely nothing. In fact I was being paid to do it! Oh yes, I really did enjoy my fifteen months in Wales, and never *ever* lost sight of all its beauty.

On one occasion one of our boats needed a replacement engine. We had our own workshop on the quayside at Menai Bridge, manned mostly by local civilians of the 'W.D.Fleet'. At least I presume they were civilians, for although they wore navy blue trousers and jerseys bearing shoulder flashes, they all lived at home and only worked normal hours. But why that engine couldn't have come from there I can only put down to its size. It didn't look that big in situ, but it certainly left little room in the back of my wagon. So I was given an order to collect it from the depot on Barry Island. Right from one end of Wales to the other!

I was to drive through the night, sleep at Barry the following day whilst the engine was loaded on to my wagon, then return through the next night.

I set off on the outward journey in a pretty powerful thunderstorm, and as I drove through the Llanberis Pass it really was something. Just me, my wagon, and the sheer drama of the elements. I cannot ever remember so stirring a journey in all my years of driving. It was at once both thrilling and frightening – with all the non-stop thunder, and lightning flashing from peak to peak. A truly magnificent and spectacular experience.

The storm had well passed by the time I began my return journey, and although it was still a very beautiful drive – in bright moonlight – I missed the drama of the previous night.

So, that was the pattern of life for me at Menai Bridge, and work-time or leisure-time, I thoroughly enjoyed every minute of it. And to think – I'd made no less than *five* requests to be sent to Korea! Was I glad now that they were refused. I had a number of girlfriends up there, but was serious with only one, whom I may mention later.

This very pleasant lifestyle was quite rudely upset for a while though, at one point. Once again we had a change of Sergeant Major, though I can't remember whether he was RSM or CSM, we certainly wouldn't have had both in so small a unit. I rather fancy he was the latter – Company Sergeant Major. Either way, he felt his number one task in our happy little set-up was to instil a bit more discipline, straighten us all up! Familiar words. Chaps were having to get haircuts right left and centre, and I had to buy a new cap as well. Jankers was dished out for the most trivial offence, and so on.

As I've said, we were on a tiny island, so were of course surrounded by water. The incoming tide would deposit on our little beach odd bits of jetsam, driftwood, and various oddments of general debris. Nobody used that bit of beach anyway, and it was mostly screened by trees, so it didn't bother us at all. But our new friend had different ideas.

He summoned us all together in the early evening – in our own time that is – then had us gather up and load this stuff into a dinghy, then scull out to the middle of the Menai Straits and dump it overboard. When the beach was completely clear we were released and allowed to get about our own business. The following evening we were fallen in again and the whole business was repeated, for subsequent tidal movements had of course brought it all back in again. We kept this up for several evenings, till finally he saw the futility of it all and gave in.

He'd come to us from a big MT unit, and was absolutely *bristling* with bull on arrival. But it wasn't too long fortunately, before he toned down to our more agreeable ways. A little ripple in an otherwise calm sea.

Nothing further stands out in my memory of those times – nothing of any great significance that is. But perhaps I will mention just the one small incident, which I found quite amusing at the time.

I was on Telephone Picket and had drawn the cookhouse-cleaning straw, whilst the other two shared the manning of the telephone and cleaning of the offices. I'd seen to the fire and cleaned up the big old cooking range, and was busy scouring pots and pans when suddenly I was overtaken by the desire to 'spend a penny'. The toilets and ablutions were not that handy to the cookhouse, so I opted for somewhere a bit closer.

Out back was a concreted area, which was the regular parking place for our two vehicles. At the edge of the concrete the ground fell sheer away, to a grassy area about six feet below. I nipped through the back door and made for the edge, and was just beginning to sigh with relief when, from immediately beneath me came a very loud 'Oi!' A bit of scuffling followed this shout – down there in the dark – then all was quiet again. I completed my mission, then returned to my scouring.

I learned later that the 'Oi' had come from one of our sergeants, who happened to be having something of a close encounter with his girlfriend just at that moment – and in just that spot. He couldn't very well make any more of it of course – after his initial shout – without revealing his identity. So although he couldn't quell my mirth, I may well have cooled his ardour!

And so the days passed, quickly but unnoticeably turning into weeks, the weeks into months. Then quite suddenly it seemed, that which we'd longed for so much in our early days was upon us. *Demob*! Only now, I wasn't viewing it with the eager anticipation I'd imagined I would. No sir – not at all. I was happy with this life – and all my friends – both inside and outside the camp. I liked my job, and of course I loved Wales and all its beauty. And as I mentioned earlier, I was fairly well into a serious courtship with one of the local lasses – a particularly lovely girl she was too. And I got along fine with her family.

So I considered the prospect of 'signing on' – for a three year spell as a regular. Purely in the hope that life would continue unchanged, with the possible exception of my marital status. Or there was the alternative of taking digs up there after my demob, and making North Wales my permanent home. The latter of the two held by far the most appeal, but on the advice of several friends I decided to return south – back to my Aunt and Uncle's place, and try to gain a more objective view of the situation from there.

Demob day has always stood out quite clearly in my memory, although there was nothing of any great magnitude attached to it. In spite of the great sorrow I was feeling, there was still a fair amount of excitement afoot. Three of us were going on that day – my long-standing pal Geoff, and Mitchell the cook being the other two. *They* were each like a dog with two tails of course, probably because they had a much more settled home life to go to than I did. And my life at Menai Bridge had been much more of a doddle than had theirs.

We had to go to Crowborough in Sussex to be demobbed. There was a great feeling of relief on that journey, after all, we were practically civilians already. Free men! Just a few formalities. Mind you – these would be conducted in somewhat different a manner then had those as we were leaving the camp at Ynys Gant. We thought that was a bit of a laugh, but our Sergeant Major – whom I shall call McAndrew, as that doesn't sound too dissimilar to his real name – was a good deal less than amused.

The three of us had been told what time to report to him in his office, for final documentation. It was some time late morning, and as our mood was quite carefree – theirs rather than mine of course – we decided to nip down to the village and while away the time in the Liverpool Arms. We were on very friendly terms with the Landlord and his good lady, also the regulars, whose company we'd enjoyed so much over the past fifteen months. The pub was right close to the jetty, and one or two of our W.D.Fleet friends managed to pop in as well I think. We laughed and we drank, and we drank and we laughed – then suddenly the phone rang behind the bar.

'It's your Sergeant Major' said the landlady, 'and he doesn't half sound cross! You're to get straight up to the camp – at the double!' We finished our drinks, in quite leisurely fashion, after all – what did it matter now – and ambled back to camp.

She was right – only he was a bit more than cross – he was hopping mad. Well, we couldn't be serious with him – the mood we were in – in fact we just grinned at him and made a few wisecracks. We were never likely to see him again anyway. But our behaviour, though only mildly mocking, was *most* irregular for the British Army and would normally have landed us in pretty dire straits.

So we left Menai Bridge behind us and went to Crowborough, and from Crowborough, we each went our separate ways – after saying our farewells. I sure was going to miss Geoff, we'd been close pals for the entire two years, and had gone through quite a lot together – especially during those first nine months. But there we are, life goes on and we go where destiny wills.

So it was back to Aunt Grace and Uncle Charles for me, but now I had every bit of my Army kit with me, for I now had to serve 3½ years on the Army Emergency Reserve – as previously mentioned. I'd made the journey all the way from Menai Bridge – via Crowborough – in FSMO! All bar the rifle that is. I don't know what the neighbours must have thought as I yomped up the road. It was good to be back – particularly to feel free – but I longed to be back in Menai as well. But I *must* be objective about it all, I kept telling myself.

I took a job straight away, although it wasn't the one I'd left when I was called up. Mr Grey – from the garage – had stressed how much he wanted me back on completion of my National Service, both when I'd left and each time I'd visited when on leave. But being out and about all the time as I had been for the past fifteen months had left me feeling very unsettled, and I just could not envisage my days being bounded by four walls all the time. So the position I'd taken now was really no more than a stop-gap (although I stayed there for two years) – but turned out to be the first of some two dozen or so jobs I was to take, from then up till the time of writing.

I quickly readjusted to civilian life again, and quite enjoyed the job, which entailed quite a bit of driving every day – albeit only within the local area – and meeting lots of people. I wrote to my love back in Menai, and she replied. But as the weeks went by our letters became less frequent, until sadly they ceased altogether. But then, we were still quite young, she in her late teens and me not long out of mine. We'd maintained our line of correspondence long enough however, for me to learn that within four months of my departure the camp on Ynys Gant was disbanded and the guys were all split up.

So I did right to decide against signing on. Who knows *where* I might have ended up? One thing's for sure – I would never have had as enjoyable a time as I'd had at Menai. But I've often wondered what the outcome would have been had I opted to settle there immediately after demob. But then – we can ask such questions of ourselves all through life!

JUST THE JOB

About a year after my demob I met Mary, who lived quite close to my place of work, which was an Off-Licence in North-West London. I used to see her quite often as I came and went the shop, and eventually we got talking. We soon began dating and after another year or so, marriage started to feature in our conversation.

My job was easy, and as I've said, quite enjoyable, although handling crates and casks all day was heavy enough. But I was young, and very fit, and I've always enjoyed a job that requires a bit of physical effort. Forty odd years on my feelings haven't changed, but the heart is a bit more willing than the flesh now! However, nice though the job was – and good the long-term prospects – the pay right then wasn't that good, certainly not conducive to setting up home. This was the early fifties, and things were still done properly then – thank goodness!

So, after two happy years at the Off Licence as Driver/Salesman, we decided I should seek a job whose income would give us a better start. But before I get on to that, I must just mention one incident that occurred in that first job. Well, first since returning to Civvy Street that is.

About two or three times a month we'd have a party to cater for. This would be either a wedding or an engagement, or maybe a 21st birthday. And quite a number of people would have a party to celebrate their demob too. Usually a local hall would have been hired, but sometimes it would be held at a private house.

On this particular morning I was delivering the stuff to a private house, for a wedding reception. The front door of the house was quite close to the pavement, and my rat-a-tat on the knocker soon attracted the attention of a bunch of youngsters who were playing close by. 'Wotcha doin' Mister?' they inquired, as they watched me open the back doors of the van. The lady of the house – the bride's mother – had shown me exactly where and how she wanted everything laid out in the hall.

It was a fair-sized hall, and lent itself nicely to being used as a bar. And it had all been very tastefully prepared for the occasion with good quality wallpaper and smart paintwork, above a beautiful Axminster which continued right on up the stairs. I stacked all the bottles as instructed – beers, wines, spirits etc., and set all the fancy glasses out on the tables provided.

The kids – now on the doorstep – watched in wonderment as I kept coming and going with crates and boxes, and I fancied I sensed a touch of hero-worship creeping into their gaze. Remember, I was only just into my twenties, and I *did* go the cinema quite a lot!

Now for the climax......The Barrel. I'd played up to my audience and deliberately left this till last; my '*pièce-de-résistance*' if you like. Well of course, it wasn't a real barrel, not in the true sense of the word. I'd never have managed that! It was in fact a firkin, which at nine gallons is a quarter-barrel, and heavy enough. They were all made of oak then, not aluminium as I believe today's are. But the kids didn't know what size it was – to them it was a big barrel, so they were no less impressed.

'Wow!' they chorused, as I heaved it easily up and on to my shoulder and carried it in. They watched agog as I positioned it on its stillion by the foot of the stairs. I went back out to the van to fetch the tap, and the tools I'd need for its insertion. '*Wossat*?' they gasped – eyeing the mallet. 'You just watch' I answered smugly.

Before driving in the wooden tap – with two or three swift movements of the mallet – you had to loosely insert the 'spile'. This was a small tapered wooden plug used for venting. A softwood core was provided for this purpose – appropriately positioned on the barrel's side – which was knocked through with a blunt screwdriver or suchlike, prior to the spile's insertion. It was all a very simple job, and with practice you could carry out the whole operation in a few seconds, and not spill a drop. And I'd had plenty of practice by then – was something of an expert in fact. The kids looked on excitedly as I raised the mallet.

Well, I don't know what was wrong with the contents of that cask, but directly my screwdriver pierced the core there was an almighty WHOOSH! And I was instantly blinded. Not only that, my hearing went too! For a few moments I was totally flabbergasted – and as you can imagine, worried sick about losing my sight.... Then, as I rubbed at my eyes, they began to clear, and needless to say I was extremely relieved. But this feeling of relief alas, was immediately replaced with one of utter horror – as I took in the scene about me.

The entire area of the hall and stairway was splattered – absolutely running in fact – with a foul, sludge-like substance. All over the ceiling it had gone – as that firkin did a first-class impression of Vesuvius – all up the walls and over the carpet, the fancy glasses – everywhere! Nothing had escaped, including me. It was this sludge of course that had filled my eyes, and as I wriggled my ears clear with my fingers I could hear my little friends on the doorstep. Absolutely splitting their sides.

Some hero! I must have looked a right stooge – for that horrible sludge was all in my hair as well. And didn't it pong! I don't know how those poor people got over that disaster, but I'm happy to say it was a one-off for me. Occasionally a bottle would explode on the shelves back at the shop, which made a proper mess of course, but was infinitely less embarrassing.

I buckled to, and took the rogue cask back to base, returning soon afterwards with a replacement. The kids were back in an instant at the re-appearance of my van, and hopped about excitedly as I approached the moment of truth. But to my great relief – *and* that of the bride's mother – they were to be disappointed, as this cask responded normally to my tapping. And honour – I felt – had been restored, not only in my eyes but theirs too, if a mite grudgingly. I never did discover why the other one had gone off, but I'll not forget that incident as long as I live. I laughed as much as those kids had afterwards, but was fair 'frit to death' at the time, and no mistake.

Something else worthy of note during my time on that job was *The Great London Smog*. This was dreadful, and despite most of us wearing 'Smog Masks', a good many fell victim to it. These masks cost about one shilling each, but could be prescribed by doctors where considered necessary. And you could get refills for them too, which was just as well, for they clogged up pretty quickly in that foul stuff. It was that thick – a good pea-soup would have paled in its shadow. I oughtn't to make so light of it really, for it really was serious.

Heating and power were still largely provided by coal and the like – both in industry and in the home – where we all huddled round the open fireplace. So the air, in winter, was quite heavily laden with pollution, and when a particularly dense fog descended, you can imagine the result.

The year in question would have been either 1953 or 54, and this smog caused a great deal of chaos, as we all tried to get about our business – as well as acute discomfort and, I'm sure, premature demise, of a number of old folk. Visibility was right down to little more than a couple of feet a lot of the time, and that is no exaggeration believe me!

Our routine varied little in the shop first thing each day. We started work at 0930 – better than office hours – and whilst Jim, the Assistant Manager and I humped crates and cases up from the cellar to re-stock the shelves, and put up the orders for that day's deliveries, Mr Footer, the Manager, prepared the previous day's takings for banking. He had the wireless on in his little office behind the shop, and it was always particularly nice at that time of day, with Housewives' Choice on the Light Programme.

At about 10 o'clock I'd pop next door to the baker's shop and bring back some scrumptious cakes and rolls, and then we'd brew up and have our 'elevenses'. Or should it have been tensies? Whichever, it was always a nice, leisurely business – after all, the shop didn't open until 11 a.m. I think it was, being subject to the Licencing Hours, and went on until quite late evening, with a two or three-hour break in the afternoon. I don't recall the exact hours of opening just now, other than the cosy 0930 start.

When we and the shelves were quite replete, Jim and I set off in the van to the bank. It was only a couple of miles away, and we were usually back within the half-hour. But not during that smog era we weren't. Dear me no!

The first really bad morning we both climbed into the van, then Jim climbed straight back out again. She was an old Standard Twelve, with a fairly long bonnet of about 3'6" I'd guess, and strain as we might, neither of us could see beyond it. We considered the wisdom of undertaking the journey at all, but concluded that if these conditions were to prevail for any length of time, all that money should be safely tucked up in the bank.

So off we set, with Jim walking in front of the van, and me straining my eyeballs out to keep sight of his hand, which rested on the front end of the bonnet. Even so, I occasionally lost sight of it and ended up laying myself across the passenger seat, with that door held open a little by my left hand, whilst I tried to get a fix on the kerb. And thus we crawled, with my gaze switching from Jim's hand to the kerb and back every couple of seconds. Talk about kerb-crawling. We never even considered the danger of my driving in so awkward a position, with Jim immediately in front of the van as he was.

It seemed more like a thousand miles than just the two, and took hours, for each time we came to a junction we lost sight of everything and floundered helplessly. But everyone else was in the same boat of course, so apart from the tremendous strain on our eyes – our whole bodies in fact – there were plenty of laughs to be had. *Afterwards.* We sure were glad when conditions eventually improved. But the mirth was tinged with sadness for as I say, I'm sure a good many would have perished before their time.

I left that job – somewhat reluctantly – after a couple of years, and took up my new position as Accounts Clerk in a Tottenham Court Road accounts office. This was with a very busy Radio/Electrical Wholesaler, and suitability for the job was determined by the result of an aptitude test which all applicants were given on their interview. This test was mostly mental arithmetic, with questions coming in pretty rapid succession. It's a good job maths was one of my favourite subjects at school, for as I say, I got the job.

But before I leave the Off-Licence entirely, I must just mention the first of my annual Army Emergency Reserve (AER) summer training camp escapades.

As I've said previously, the duration of the AER – on completion of our National Service – was three and a half years. After that you were relieved of all your army gear, and re-classified as an 'N' Reservist. Later still, as you became older and others came up behind you, you were moved back further still, becoming finally a 'Z' Reservist. I don't know what happened after that – nothing was ever said about it to my knowledge – and for all I know I may still be a 'Z' man. I hope this is not the case however, for I am well out of practice with the bow, and it's even longer since I slung a good shot! Not to mention my shield – which I think has rusted away in the garden somewhere. But I jest of course. My shield's up in the loft with my quiver.

My first camp as an AER man came whilst I was working at the Off-Licence, and I was summoned back to Freshwater I.O.W. I didn't reckon much of this as a way of spending my summer holiday – back in the classroom and bashing that old drill-square again! But at least I'd meet up with some old pals again so there should be a few laughs.

We were picked up as we left the ferry at Yarmouth, and transported to Golden Hill Fort, and sure enough – there they all were. Geoff, Don, Jake, Dippie, Yorky, Spud – and some that I hadn't seen for a good deal longer. The normal accommodation was all fully occupied by full timers of course, for National Service was still in full swing, and would be for several years yet. So home to us for the next two weeks would be under canvas atop a grassy slope. They were bell-tents, with about six of us to each if my memory serves me right, and a hurricane-lamp hooked to the centre-pole. And by the time we'd grouped up with our buddies and settled in.....well.....it wasn't going to be *too* bad was it? After all, what's a bit of square-bashing and all that when you're amongst friends? And as Jake said – 'A little bit of pain never hurt anybody did it?' (I'm still trying to work that one out!)

This was Saturday, and by early evening most of us were ready to go off somewhere to celebrate our reunion, after all, there was all tomorrow untouched yet for things like 'bulling up' our kit and writing home etc. So off to Freshwater we did go, and into the pub whose name I still can't remember.

And didn't we enjoy it! What with the drink, and the company of old friends – not to mention the Juke-Box in the corner, from which came all the good old songs and singers of the day. Names like Frankie Laine, Anne Shelton, Doris Day, Guy Mitchell, Patti Page, Eddie Fisher, Lita Roza, Johnny Ray, Jo Stafford, Tony Bennett. It was great.

Eventually we made our way back to camp, on foot and in the dark. And all of us *quite* tiddly. A short distance from the camp entrance the footpath began to rise, leaving the road ever lower as it did, I can't remember why. Suddenly somebody loomed up in front of us, coming from the opposite direction, and as I did my Sir Galahad bit (or was it Sir Lancelot?) and stepped aside, there in the dark, I stepped clean off the path altogether and dropped to the road below. I landed on my feet as it happened, though with quite a jar, but all seemed to be well. Well enough at any rate for me to keep pace with a cyclist who happened along at that moment and was heading in the same direction as us. I don't know why I ran with him as I did – just for the fun of it I suppose, as you do at that age – but it caused me to reach camp a bit ahead of the others.

They duly caught up with me, then we all booked in at the Guardroom and made our way the half-mile or so to our tents, up on the hill. My left ankle tingled and throbbed a bit, but I made it, and we all settled into our beds – the base of which was a palliasse. Which for the uninitiated is simply a straw-filled bag, which in our case was laid directly onto the ground. With our groundsheets beneath of course as a barrier against the damp. A bit hard maybe, and home also to a few creepy crawlies, but we were quite oblivious to all this as we were more than ready for sleep anyway.

Which was hard luck really, for a group coming in later than us – and probably even more tiddly – decided to release a few guy ropes in passing, and you can imagine the pandemonium *that* caused as we all fought to extricate ourselves. And re-erecting a collapsed bell-tent – or any other type of tent for that matter – when you're in such state as we were – *and* in the pitch dark! Well....think about it.

But we did it – after a fashion as they say – and just about managed to grab a few zeds (zzzzzzz) before the night was over, which was just as well for me, for it was just my luck to be on Guard Duty the next day (Sunday). And this was a training camp remember, so guard duty wasn't the cushy old thing we'd had up in Menai Bridge. I can't remember now what time Guard Mounting Parade was – probably about nine-ish I should think, under the circumstances – but I do know that it was held in the MT sheds near the camp entrance, about half a mile distant.

I stirred stiffly on my palliasse, and noticed that it was daylight outside. I checked my watch – 0700. Almost instantly I realised I must have quite a bit of trouble with that ankle, for it was now hurting quite a lot. And I was on *Guard*! I thought I'd best check it out as soon as possible – early though it was for a nine o'clock mounting – and brother, what a sight. It had swollen to almost twice its normal size, and was turning all colours. And I'm one who doesn't bruise easily! Some people can spot a bruise on themselves and have no idea where it came from. Not me.... I reckon if you hit me with a fourteen pound sledgehammer you'd not see where! Other than an almighty lump I shouldn't wonder.

Despite the hour I could see I was going to have trouble making it by nine, so I decided I'd best get up and at it right away. And what a performance it was trying to gain the upright from that palliasse – right there on the ground. With a normal bed I could have swung my legs sideways and let my feet dangle, before slowly bringing my weight to bear on the dicky ankle. 'Put a sock in it!' groaned one of the others as I stumbled and 'ouched' – 'some of us are trying to sleep!' 'Lucky you' I thought.

I weighed up the situation. The ablutions were down the hill a way – the cookhouse about half a mile in one direction – the MT sheds half a mile in the other. It'd want some doing – I could see that!

I grabbed my toilet gear and towel and struggled outside. *Crikey* that hurt! And I can see me now – creeping almost backwards down that slope to the 'wash-house'. It was an hour before I returned, and I was in quite some pain now. And I had news for Jake – him and his 'little bit of pain never hurt anybody'! Geoff stirred as I groped my way back inside the tent, and when he saw my ankle he couldn't believe it. 'Bloody hell' he gasped – 'you can't go on guard duty like *that*!' – no doubt forgetting so soon after waking that this was the army, where you 'do' first and complain afterwards.

There was no way I was going to make the cookhouse for breakfast – and I'd not stand a celluloid cat in hell's chance of making the MT sheds in time if I *tried*. It would take me all my time as it was – even if I pulled out *all* the stops! Somehow I managed to dress and get all the gear on, but that boot was sheer agony. I nevertheless broached the journey to the MT sheds – holding little hope for my chances as I hobbled painfully on, and suddenly the answer to last night's little conundrum came to me. It was *Sir Limpalot*! Well, if it wasn't then – it damned well was now.

The Guard Commander was just about to give the command 'Fall-out' as I rounded the doorpost and hobbled into view – the Guard Mounting Ceremony (minus one) completed. The Orderly Officer glared at me and demanded an explanation – which was fair enough. But before I could utter more than half a dozen words in reply he drowned me out with those dreaded words – 'Charge this man corporal!' – and strutted off. 'Bloody hell' I thought – after all the effort I'd put in, *and* all the pain. And no damned breakfast either!

I was detailed off for duty at Fort Victoria, Yarmouth, which was a slight comfort for I would at least be away from the main guardroom at Golden Hill Fort. We clambered aboard the 15cwt that was to take us – although clambered was hardly the word in my case – and off we set.

Patrols were worked out by the Guard Commander on arrival at Fort Vic and we more or less settled down to it, though again – I'm stuck for adjectives! By the time the Orderly Officer did his rounds, some time late evening, I'd just come in from my second two-hour patrol, and had eased my boot off. The ankle both looked and felt terrible – and my foot had now twisted outward about sixty degrees off the norm. And it was quite clear that it wouldn't be coming back for some time. He checked with the Guard Commander, then turned to me and my off-watch companion. 'Any problems?' he asked – in the usual cursory manner, never really expecting other than a 'No thank you, sir' in reply.

'I'm afraid so, sir' I answered, lifting my ankle up on to the bunk. One glance was enough from his nibs. 'My God man' he came back – 'you must report sick with that as soon as possible – however did you do it?' I took my second shot at an explanation, and of course this time he did me the courtesy of listening. He repeated his instruction that I report sick. 'There lies the problem, sir' I replied – 'Sick Parade is at 0830hrs and I'm afraid I shall be unavailable'. 'Unavailable? How come?' he queried. 'Well, if you remember, sir' I began, with a certain amount of satisfaction, 'you put me on a fizzer this morning for being late on parade. And O.C's Orderly Room is at 0900!'

And if you – the reader – are wondering whether it mightn't have been just possible to squeeze the one in before the other, let me tell you, we had no medical facilities at Golden Hill Fort......our M.O. was based at Ventnor, about twenty miles and two bus trips away! So what with the consultation itself, and all the travelling, it was at least a morning's outing. Which, if you weren't hurting too much could be quite a pleasant interlude, particularly in summer!

'Oh good heavens' replied the Orderly Officer – sounding more human by the minute – 'you can forget the charge – you must go sick with that ankle!' I was tempted to point out that I'd have a job to go sick *without* my ankle – but thought better of it. I was excused my last patrol of the night – four hours hence at 0200 – which was just as well for there was no way in which I was going to get that boot on now! She was *well* up.

The charge was officially dropped, and somehow I saw the rest of the night out. Back to Golden Hill next morning, on sick parade – then off to Ventnor. I can't remember quite what the MO did with it, but I finished up with it quite tightly bandaged, and was handed a chit on which he'd scrawled the words '*Sedentary Duties*'. I made my way back to camp – wondering what sedentary meant – and reported to the CSM. He looked at my chit, frowned, then turned to one of the clerks. 'This man will be 'Company Runner' for the rest of the day' he advised him – 'see that he's kept busy!' Clearly I wasn't the only one unfamiliar with the meaning of that word. Either that or he was mad.

What an afternoon – I couldn't believe it! And neither could the MO next morning when I reported sick again and popped along to Ventnor. For 'Company Runner' is the perfect description of that job, whereby you dash from one part of the camp to another with messages. Why they couldn't use the damned *phone* I don't know!

But the CSM had in fact done me a favour – in a roundabout way – for this time the MO scrawled three much nicer words on the chit – words that I understood perfectly, and which read – '*Excused all Duties*'! So the rest of the fortnight was entirely mine – the only disadvantage being that I wasn't allowed out of camp. But we had a good NAAFI there, so I didn't do so badly in the evenings.

And in the daytime, the weather being glorious the whole fortnight through, I was able to lollop around on the grass outside the tent all day – in just my swim trunks – where I acquired a really great tan all over – much to the chagrin of the CSM when he came round on 'billet' inspection each morning. But there was nowt he could do about it! And when I say all over, I mean of course with the exception of a couple of areas. And from where I lay I could just hear the sounds of my pals as they sweated and bashed that old drill square about in the distance.

So I enjoyed my holiday after all, and somewhat more than my pals I'll wager as they struggled with their swotting up in the classrooms. But my ankle was an age returning to normal, and not at all easy to work with on the Off-Licence – what with humping crates up from the cellar – and the driving and all. But I managed, and the ankle was fully restored in time for the next year's camp, and those that followed.

But I still have the odd twinge there – forty-odd years later – especially when I've been pushing myself too hard. My 'Achille's Heel,' no doubt.

So, back to Tottenham Court Road...

I enjoyed the work well enough, which was calculating percentages and discounts all day long. And all in the head of course – there were no calculators about then! But I wasn't too keen on having to wear a suit and tie all the time. And I disliked intensely being shut in an office till 5 p.m.

The office wasn't that big, but was very busy, and housed nine of us – including the boss. In the summer it could get quite stuffy, for as well as not having calculators, there was no air-conditioning either. Nope – there were few creature comforts about then, compared with present times, but we beavered away with little complaint. Well we did in that office anyway, with the boss in constant attendance.

At the desk immediately in front of mine sat a young Polish woman, mid- to late twenties I'd guess. She had a nicely rounded figure, slightly on the full side – exactly to my liking as it happens – and a full head of jet-black hair. A handsome face, with a certain nobility about it, and a very attractive accent completed the picture. She was indeed a most comely young woman. But what a tartar she could be if anyone upset her. As often they did, although usually quite unintentionally.

This would mostly be when the weather was blistering hot and the office more like a greenhouse. We were in the front of the building – first or second floor up, and immediately above the road, which was always choc-a-bloc with traffic. Somebody would open a window – and that would do it. Either the papers were being blown off her desk, or she was being choked by the fumes, or deafened by the noise! Quite justifiable complaints really, but arguably preferable to the heat and stuffiness. The times she stomped across that floor and slammed either the door or the window shut. And nobody argued with her, not even the boss.

It was most unconventional at the time for male members of the office staff not to remain properly dressed all day, but it became too much for me I'm afraid, and off came the jacket and up went the shirtsleeves – chance the outcome! Strewth – even in the *Army* we adjusted to 'Shirtsleeve Order' throughout the summer. I needn't have worried, for my pal Don quickly followed my lead, and in no time at all it was shirtsleeve order all round the office – boss and all. The women of course could always dress comfortably, adjusting as the weather changed, but ever remaining smart. A very different world from today's! Well, in a good many cases anyway, particularly amongst the younger ones. But why our female counterparts had this privilege I've no idea, unless it was simply to brighten up the day of the average warm-blooded male. Yes – that would have been it.

Backing on to Don's desk was the one occupied by Mrs Box. She was a sweet little lady, small and round, with silver-grey hair but a young face, with rosy cheeks. She wore spectacles, but these couldn't conceal the ever-present twinkle in her bright blue eyes.

There was a 'No Smoking' rule in the office, which must have been great for the non-smokers – few though they were – but not for Mrs Box, who certainly didn't figure amongst that category. As in fact, was the case with Don and myself. But us two, being young and nimble, could nip downstairs now and then for a quick drag by the back door. This little life-saver was a bit too much for dear Mrs Box though, so when midday came she was through that door on the dot – then lost in a pale-blue fog for almost the entire dinner-hour.

We dined each day – Mrs Box, Don and myself – in a busy but nice restaurant just across the Tottenham Court Road, about a hundred yards up from the office. Even before we reached it she'd polished off her first cigarette, and was busy lighting up the next. I can't remember now whether or not she smoked between mouthfuls – as indeed some of the other diners did – or just between courses, but she certainly made up for her hours of abstinence. What a dear little soul she was.

Nowadays I'd find it all totally abhorrent, being a 'born again' non-smoker for so many years now, but then, it passed unnoticed – so was accepted.

That office wasn't really as Dickensian as I might have made it sound, but the atmosphere *was* always quite sober and business-like when the boss was in – which was most of the time. It relaxed a little on his occasional absences – and this was when Don and I used to team up as a whistling duo. Mostly we'd treat everybody to *Rachmaninoff's Rhapsody on a Theme of Paganini*, working away as we whistled needless to say, until the glare of Mrs Whatsit-offski became so penetrating as to dry our lips up. And her a Polish woman too! Although hang on – Rachmaninoff was Russian wasn't he? But I must say, in all honesty, she wasn't a bad person to work with really, and I got on okay with her. As I say, the size of that office was no bigger than the average sitting room, so we were pretty crammed.

Which brings me to the travelling. I was living in North West London, although I'd moved out from my Aunt and Uncle's place, and was in digs a few miles away. The daily journey to and from the office was quite something. I began by using the good old London buses, which wasn't too bad going in to work, but a real swine going home. I don't mean the actual journey home, that was okay – quite relaxing in fact – I mean the business of actually *catching* one of the darned things. Standing in the bus queue there in Regent Street – having walked down from Tottenham Court Road – there'd be a total absence of No 6s for ages, then a whole convoy of them would turn up, pretty near all full. We all went mad, and after a few weeks I'd had enough of it, and opted for the Tube.

And what a hair-raising experience that could be! As I made my way down into the bowels of the earth, on that first day, I got as far as the stairway leading down to my platform – and no further. The mass of bodies ahead of me had filled the platform completely, then backed up the stairs to where I stood. Trains came and went quite frequently, so we soon began moving – but slowly. It was no more than a shuffle at first, becoming rather more urgent as we neared the edge of the platform and people tried to position themselves where they figured a door would be when the train stopped.

Pressed shoulder to shoulder as we were on that platform, there'd be no chance of boarding a train unless a door *did* stop right in front of your face. Well, not at the height of the rush-hour there wouldn't, and it was then that I had the misfortune to be caught up in it. As you neared the white-painted line marking the very edge of the platform, with the crowd behind you still pressing urgently forward, it was difficult to see why people weren't frequently jostled over and on to the lines. It certainly was a bit more than frightening at times, as you stood there with daylight beneath the very toes of your shoes and a surging mass behind you. But I never witnessed any such accident during the time I used that service, nor did I ever hear of any. Which I find truly amazing.

As I reflect, I see humour in certain instances of those times. But at the time they were anything but funny. Such as the time a train drew in and stopped – with a doorway smack in front of me. Having been far less fortunate the past few evenings I could have jumped for joy – that is – had my fellow sardines been able to permit such movement!

My joy was short-lived however, for immediately the doors slid open, those within – trying to get out – and those behind me, fighting to get in, came slap bang up against each other. It was like a tug o'war in reverse, and I was right there in between. Of course, those outside should have waited for those inside to get off, but so desperate were they not to miss their opportunity! A kind of whirlpool developed -with me at its centre – and as we rotated and surged to and fro, I at last found myself on the inside. Whew! What a relief. But hang about – as we continued to whirl and swirl I found myself heading back towards the platform again. Back and forth we went, and round and round – like a bloomin' rugby scrum – with nobody wanting to give way. Eventually the doors struggled their way across to the closed position, the train pulled out, and there was I – right back on the bloody platform! I could have howled.

For several weeks I subjected myself to this daily nightmare – if you know what I mean – then, as with the buses, I decided enough was enough. I bought myself a bicycle. Few of us could afford the luxury of a motor car in those days, and those that could seldom ran to more than an old banger to start with. Most of us wouldn't have given the idea a thought even, till we were well on the way to thirty – if then!

This was some bike that I'd bought – so it seemed – though to me it was purely for the purpose of getting to and from work. It was a Claude Butler, and light as a feather, with a chequered strip on the frame – such as the police have on their caps – and very narrow rims. I bought it second-hand and didn't pay a great deal for it, so was surprised to learn of its value. Not that it made any difference to me, I just used it for the purpose intended. This too was a bit hair-raising at first, riding amongst the busy London traffic, but I soon settled to it and became quite an expert. Apart from the fumes it was a much better journey, and far more predictable as regards timing.

About a year after I started that job, and with the wedding date fixed, Mary and I began flat-hunting. As with cars, you couldn't afford to get into house-*buying* – as they seem able to do these days almost as soon as they leave school! – so you had to look for rented accommodation. Which wasn't always easy to find, just where you wanted it *and* at an affordable rent.

We hunted awhile, then with time closing in on us and no success, I spotted an advert for a job – with accommodation – back in North West London. It was a clerical job again, but much more varied than the one I was doing. But one of the qualifications required was the ability to type. I'd never typed in my life, but we needed that flat so I fibbed and said I could. After all, I could coax a tune or two out of the old ivories, and it couldn't be that much different? I attended an interview and was offered the job, and after seeing the flat, which was unfurnished and just around the corner, I accepted. The salary too was more attractive, which helped even further.

So I left Don to whistle on alone, dear Mrs Box, Mrs Beard, Mrs Whatsitoffski,

Jim behind me and the others, and took up my new position – shortly before the wedding date. We bought some good quality furniture and carpets, which we installed as soon as I'd decorated the flat right through, and moved in just as soon as we returned from our honeymoon in Cornwall.

I settled into my new job which was, as I say, much more varied and very interesting, and was quite happy with life in general. The only other people in the office were the boss – who with his brother owned the business – and his son Roy. Roy, who would have been early middle-age, was a brilliant shorthand typist, amongst his many other business attributes, and had finished his time at Pitman's College as 'Star Pupil'. Featured on the front page of the local paper and everything he had. And he and I were to share all the typing duties! My God – what had I done? I was sure to be found out – up against him!

The bulk of the typing came at the start of each month. We were a garage by the way, and in addition to the customers who came to us for repairs – and to purchase new cars – were those who used our rather large covered parking area. A small rent was charged for this privilege, and the bills were sent out monthly along with those for repair work etc. Which meant a total of something like 250 – 300 bills having to be typed out every month, as we could accommodate well over 200 cars! Not to mention all the envelopes.

Luckily for me, I started there just after the month's bills had all gone out, so I had a bit of breathing space. I was also fortunate inasmuch as the pair of them went home to lunch every day, so I had a full hour in which to master the art of typing. Well – not exactly *master* it of course – but maybe become proficient enough to gain a certain amount of credibility at the start of the following month.

'I'm a bit rusty' I fibbed, as we duly came to this mammoth task. 'I haven't typed for ages!' 'Okay' replied Roy, 'you do the calling out, and I'll do all the typing this time, then we'll switch round next month'. Terrific! I'd gained another whole month's practice, and by the time the month had elapsed my efforts were reasonably acceptable. But not a patch on Roy's of course, but then, he wouldn't have expected me to have been in *his* class would he! However, the boss declared my typing to be a whole lot better than his own, so that was good enough for me.

Roy and his father dabbled very much on the Stock Market, and sat studying the *Financial Times* for ages each morning before getting on to their broker. Luckily they always left this paper behind at dinner time, and that's what I used for my typing lessons. I memorised all the positions on the keyboard of that heavy old Imperial, and buried myself in the rather heavy-going text of that paper as I punched away, albeit one-fingered at first. Come to think of it, little's changed in that department, but I get by. Anyway, as I say, all the time I was there nobody was any the wiser. I probably just made Roy look even more brilliant. But there we are, a bit of bluff pays off occasionally, especially if it's sprinkled with a fair coating of luck as well, for I don't know what I'd have done had I been required to do some typing straight away!

Life became fairly routine once I'd learned all the different aspects of the job, but as I've said, I was happy enough and got along fine with everyone who worked there.

The workshop staff comprised three, the foreman and two younger fellows. In their quieter moments these two would indulge in the inevitable horse-play, throwing odd bits at each other and things like that. One day they became a little too enthusiastic and started throwing pieces of rag that had been dipped in waste-oil, all black and sludgy. Back to that in a minute.

The office, stores and workshop were in a block – positioned in that order – going from front to back of the premises, with the parking area all around. Rather like an island. The office looked out over the forecourt, with showrooms flanking the Pump Attendant's little kiosk, then the road beyond. Entry to the office was up some steps and through a door in the front. The workshop had a roller-shutter on each side.

On this day, one of the lads was stalking the other down the side of the block, his hand clutching this filthy, smelly, oil-soaked rag. As he neared the corner at the office end he heard a movement, whereupon he lunged forward and hurled this disgusting object at his pal.

Trouble was, it wasn't his pal – it was the boss, who'd just emerged from the office and was descending the steps. And sadly for our friend, he scored a direct hit! You should have seen the boss' suit. All of which led to a hastily inserted advertisement for a couple of new mechanics. As I say, boys will be boys. Pillocks!

We had a second branch about a mile or so away, though this was just a filling station, but with quite a bit of covered parking area again, and I started relieving on the pumps for a couple of hours each evening after leaving the office at five. Both branches were open for petrol twenty-four hours a day, seven days a week. The extra money was handy, and there was no self-service in those days, so there were quite a few 'tips' to be made on top.

It was at about this time that Charles, my father-in-law, began talking about his approaching retirement from the Metropolitan Police Force, in which he held the rank of Inspector. And when suddenly he took a spare time job in a pub as barman, we realised that his thoughts on retiring to a little pub in the country were more than just a dream.

He had a good friend who ran a big pub in the Edgware Road, though this wasn't the one in which he himself was working, and it wasn't long before I swapped petrol pumps before tea, for beer pumps after tea. The whole idea being that when Charles and Stella, my mother-in-law, realised their dream, it would include us. As it happened, Mary had already done a stint of evening work behind the bar some time previous, and was quite adept at it. So there we were – all getting 'boned up'.

About 70% of the customers in my pub were Irish, the rest a mixture of English and Welsh, and I must say, it was a very nerve-racking experience at first. Not that nationality had anything to do with it mind. But it wasn't anything like as easy a business as the T.V. soaps would lead us to believe, where raw beginners look fully competent and at ease straight away, and know the price of everything without ever having to look it up or ask! Then there's the question of knowing which glass to use for which drink – wine, spirit, liqueur – when to use the 'six-out' measure as opposed to the 'three-out' and so on. Yes – pushing a spirit glass up under an 'optic' is *one* thing!

Anyway, they could see that I was dead green at the job, and took full advantage of this fact, just for fun. Theirs rather than mine need I say. As I've said, it was a big and very busy pub – there were seven of us behind the bar – and that was only on weekdays. This number was swelled some at weekends, when they got really busy, but didn't include me.

It was as bad as, if not worse than being on the stage, although I've never actually been on stage to make a true comparison. In a shop, such as the off-licence, people entered, made their purchases, then left. Here they stayed, and seemed to spend the whole evening watching us behind the bar. I don't suppose they were actually *watching* us, just looking our way without seeing. Except of course, when they could cause you to make a right goof of yourself!

I was shown the rudiments of the job on my first evening, and told to shout if I had any problems. But you learn the ropes much quicker if you just lunge right in and get on with it, putting up with the odd blunder or two. So off I went.

And blunder number one soon came, when I was asked for a pint of Porter. This was a nice dark brown draught beer, still very popular then in those parts. But with the soft Irish brogue of this particular customer, the last syllable wasn't really audible at all and I thought he was saying 'A point o' port'. So I hunted through the bank of bottles on the shelf beneath the optics, and found a bottle of Port. I started to pour it into a pint beer-glass, with him looking on the whole time, and when I'd filled it to the very brim he said – in a somewhat louder voice, '*And what the divil d'ye t'ink that is?*' I looked at it. 'A pint of Port' I replied confidently.

'Port-*er*' he said, rather more distinctly this time, and loud enough to attract a fair bit of attention. 'PORT-ER!' Of course, they all fell about over that didn't they. So too would he have done I guess – had he actually drunk it!

Number two was to a much lesser degree, but no less embarrassing. 'A point o' Macks' said Paddy. I thought for a few seconds. 'Ah, I know what he wants – he wants a pint of Mackeson.' I poured it and slid it across the bar.

'*Begorra Bejasus*' he boomed, '*what in Hivvens name d'ye call that?*' With the attention of practically the whole pub focussed upon me once more, I learned that he'd actually been saying 'A point o' maxed', which further translated became 'A pint of mixed'. And that, in those parts was the normal terminology for a pint of mild and bitter! Later on, in West Kent, the same drink became 'A pint of two's', and I've no doubt there are as many variations on the name of this particular drink as there are counties in this 'Merrie England' of ours.

Although now, some four decades later as I write, fings aint wot they used ter be in pubs – more's the pity. Those, that is, that haven't been turned completely into eating places. What a sad loss – the good old traditional English pub – with its skittles, darts, shove-ha'penny, dominoes, cribbage etc. And occasionally, at weekends mostly, the good old sing-song when someone was coaxed on to the old joanna. Ah me!

I'll never forget 'The Spotted Dog' at Neasden though. That was a really swish place in the early fifties. I don't know what it's like now, or if it still exists even, for I've not been up that way since. They had a smart, beautifully tuned piano there, that on reflection might well have been a Baby-Grand I should think. It was certainly a long way from the more usual honky-tonk upright that's for sure. It was in the Saloon Bar, which was a large, richly-carpeted bar with lovely dark, polished tables and comfortable seating. Flowers and a few other niceties added to the style, comfort and sophistication of the place. They had a resident pianist named Ted, who played lovely, easy background music all the time, but would break off to play 'special requests' – popular or light classical. And the popular music of those times was to me, really great. They were indeed most pleasant evenings. But I digress.......

Back to my inauguration in Edgware Road, at 'The Rifle Volunteer', I think it was called. The one counter commanded all the bars – the very large Saloon Bar, the slightly smaller Public Bar, the little Private Bar – or Snug as it was more commonly called – and the Off-Sales, round the corner at the end. The seven of us whizzed around as we attended everyone's needs, although initially I served all but the Saloon Bar.

At one end of the counter that looked into the Snug, we kept a fair number of spirit glasses – all polished and upturned on to a nice clean white glass-cloth. Why they were stacked there like that I can't really remember now, but they did look nice. They were in regular use, probably kept there just as a matter of convenience. I was busy serving somebody when Mick entered the Snug and came to the counter. He was a big chap with dark wavy hair, wearing a black overcoat. Well, it was *he* that wore the coat, not his hair. (Just felt I should clarify.)

Disregarding the fact that we were all busy he called out 'Gimme a point o' maxed!' 'Be with you in a few seconds Mick' I answered as I whizzed by. At which he took one of these little spirit glasses and dashed it to the floor. 'A point o' maxed!' he repeated. 'Yes yes' I replied, 'in half a tick when I've finished here!' Smash! – another glass. 'A point o' maxed!' Smash! And so it went on until one of us could quickly nip over and serve him. Our nice little stack of spirit glasses suffered quite a reduction in those few seconds. Yet Mick wasn't an aggressive man, in fact I can't recall any of them being so, in spite of their number. That's just the way he was I guess, for by and large they were a pretty decent crowd and gave little real trouble.

Midway through your session Alf, the landlord – an extremely nice gentleman – sent you off with a pack of fresh-cut sandwiches, and a drink of your own choosing, for your break. This was well-earned and taken in the Billiards Room, (a good place for a break) which led off from the Saloon Bar. What a difference. In here were two full-size tables, soft lighting – other than directly over the tables of course – and a whole heap of peace and quiet. All you'd hear was the gentle chinking together of the balls. This certainly was a welcome interlude, especially on those first two or three nights. But I quickly got the hang of it all and soon came to really enjoy it.

Especially at such times as when a particularly gorgeous lady came into the Off-Sales one evening just before Christmas. It fell to me to serve her, and she asked if we could oblige her with a few stamps for her Christmas Cards. I was glad we could, for this apparition turned out to be none other than the stand-in for Sabrina, the beautiful, well-known star of those times. At least, that's what I was told, and I must say, she certainly was most adequately equipped for the part. And how!

I carried on quite contentedly with this life, the office during the day, and the pub in the evenings. We'd settled into the flat, and Mary was quite happy with her job as Cashier in a biggish furniture store. Then all of a sudden, Charles' retirement was upon us. And so, after two happy years at the garage I once again bade farewell to my workfellows, as we weighed anchor and set course for West Kent, and the pub where Charles and Stella were to be the new 'Mine Hosts'.

On the morning of Thursday, 7th February 1957, two large furniture removal wagons drew up outside '*The Prince Albert*' in Tonbridge, following our arrival with Charles, who had just been and acquired his Licence. It was quite a cold day, but we were all oblivious to anything so prosaic as weather – it was all so exciting. A totally new venture. But with the excitement came a certain amount of apprehension. Our whole future lay behind those doors, and we'd not had as much as a peep yet. At least, Mary and I hadn't. But in we went, and what a hubbub it all was on that first day.

The pub was already open for business on our arrival; I think someone from the brewery was standing in. Just as well, for we had to go headlong into everything. The complete inventory had to be taken, customers had to be served, prices learned, cellar-work attended to, fires tended – all at once. We didn't know where anything was, and of course, none of us would have had much sleep the previous night.

As is – or at least was – customary on such occasions, as many regulars as could make it turned up, a) to give the new landlord and his family a good coat of looking at and b) – to receive a free drink. Mind you, *we* wouldn't have known who were regulars and who weren't at that stage, we just gave them all a free drink and hoped they were all being honest with us. But human nature being what it is... And on top of everything there was the installation of two separate lots of furniture to supervise. Whew! Yet Stella somehow managed to rustle up a meal for us all at the end of the morning session, for which we were more than ready. How we got through it all I shall never fathom. Not referring to the meal of course.

'A pint of two's' said somebody. 'A pint of what?' 'A pint of TWO's – MILD AND BITTER!' I grabbed a glass and made for the pumps. 'Not that glass! I've got my own – it's up there with those.' He nodded towards a shelf upon which stood several glasses, each bearing a colourful transfer. 'Mine's got a sailing ship on it.' As I sorted through a miniature armada of sailing ships he suddenly cried 'That's it – the one facing west!' We'd eliminated Percy's, which had slightly different sails – Ernie's, which was on an easterly heading – and Charlie's, which had a tiny chip on the rim, and so on.

'Should be fun' I thought, as I filled and handed him his glass. He took it, then swung round to face the window, lifted it up to the light, and peered suspiciously through it. 'Anything wrong?' I inquired, half expecting to see newts or tiddlers darting about in it. 'I'm just checking' he grumped. 'Strewth' I thought, 'if they're all going to be like this!'

'Bloody cold in 'ere' piped someone in the Public bar. Which wasn't at all surprising really, for the fire in the open grate was all but out. Charles tracked down the coal-bunker out back and lifted the lid. Empty! Bar a bit of dust on the floor. He brought some of that in, then set about finding the nearest coal merchant.

'Haven't you got anything to eat – a ham roll or something?' came another. No we hadn't – just crisps and nuts and things, and some cheese biscuits. 'Hmph!' – he moaned – 's'pose that'll have to do then!' Maybe they thought we'd brought coal and bar-snacks and things with us on the removal wagons!

Charles was upstairs sorting out the removal men when the bitter went off. By which I mean of course, the barrel had run dry and needed changing. We called up to him and he went down to see to it. 'Bloody Hell!' he yelped as soon as he reached the bottom of the cellar steps – 'look at this!' The cellar floor was under several inches of water, presumably storm-water which had seeped through the drayman's flap in the pavement above. It wasn't harming the beer in any way, but none of us was equipped with wellies or waders. We managed to find something to use as duckboards, and temporarily got over that one, but began to wonder 'what next?'

We finally sat down to the meal that Stella had prepared for us, having locked all the doors at the end of our first session – and reviewed the situation. We sure had come in at the deep end and no mistake – particularly down in the cellar. I began to think my fears about newts and tiddlers may quite possibly have been well-grounded after all! But we had a good many laughs as we swapped experiences, and were – if truth be known – quite looking forward to the evening session. By which time we had the fires sorted out, the cellar a bit more under control, had memorised some of the glass armada out in the bar, and made our beds! We felt sure we'd all be more than ready for these at the end of *this* day.

We gradually got to know all the regulars – *and* their little idiosyncrasies – and settled down to this very different, but no less pleasant way of life. But it was of course – by its very nature – a business that wasn't without incident.

The 'Angel Hotel', which was a hundred or so yards away on the corner of the High Street, was a typical country town hotel of the day. Travellers and Reps used the overnight facilities quite regularly, and I think there were a few longer-term residents. The bars were open to non-residents as well, and it was a pleasant enough place in which to while away some leisure time.

They sold one particular line there that had its own small, but very dedicated following. And it was something that we weren't selling at the P.A. This was 'Scrumpy'. But I think it must have been a bit more than most other scrumpies, for those who drank it did so to the exclusion of any other drink, and regulated their intake most rigorously. And there was no way in which they could conceal their particular drinking habit either – had they have wanted to – for their complexion took on a colour all its own, in various shades of purple.

We learned of this situation some time after we'd settled in, but thought little of it at the time. Then, for reasons best known to themselves, the proprietors of The Angel decided to discontinue this line, and directly we heard of it we located the supplier and got some in. We needed to boost our sales anyway, which had dropped with the departure of the previous landlord, which was quite normal.

Sure enough – over they all came, quickly adopting our pub as their new local. They were a decent little bunch really, and each of them knew his limit and stuck rigidly to it. Some could take only a pint and a half, others two pints, but I can't recall anybody going beyond two and a half. I must say, it was very pleasant stuff, so smooth and easy to drink. It would be very easy to overshoot – which did happen occasionally – but not within this little group. Mind you, they'd take a very long time getting through their quota, so sales weren't improved a great deal. I guess The Angel knew what they were at.

At about noon one day, Charles and Stella were having their meal and I was looking after things out front. It wasn't too busy just then – about an hour before the lunch-hour influx. The Public Bar door opened and in came this character – and I *mean* character. He was quite tall, quite elderly, and quite scruffy. He had several days growth of white whiskers on his very weathered – or very dirty face, and this was long before the days when lazy people could hide behind the 'designer stubble' tag. He wore a long black tatty overcoat, scarf, flat cap, and very well-travelled boots. Wispy white hair hung beneath the cap, and he carried a bundle of some sort. He could have walked straight off the set of 'Wurzle Gummidge'.

He approached the bar, and asked me if we had any decent cider. 'Draught' he added quickly. 'I don't want any of that bottled muck!' His quite polite voice and general manner were much more pleasant than his appearance, so I suggested this 'Rubberlegs' – as the regulars called it. He called for a pint, paid for it, and sat down at a table. I warned him of its potency, which he shrugged off with a sneer.

'I've just walked all the way from Folkestone' he proclaimed, 'and I'm ready for this.' At which he up-ended his glass in about one tenth of the time the others normally did, and returned to the bar for a refill. He again shrugged off my warning and went off to set about this second pint, with obvious enjoyment. I slipped through to the back to put Charles into the picture, and he duly intervened when our friend came over for a third pint.

After a bit of argy-bargy he settled for half a pint this time, and when he came back for more we said a firm, but good-natured no. We pointed him at the door, and off he tottered – reluctantly – leaving us to grapple with the remainder of the day.

He reappeared the following morning, looking rather more subdued now. 'I'll have just *half* a pint of that stuff' he said, nodding ruefully at the cask on the counter, 'then I'll be off. You were dead right about how strong it is' he added, then went on to tell us how he'd got only as far as Boots the Chemist – just up in the High Street and opposite its present site – when his legs folded beneath him. He collapsed happily in their doorway and promptly nodded off. This would have been about one to one-thirty and there were a good many people about. The police were called, and they duly ran him in to the local cop-shop where he was clapped into a cell for the remainder of the day, and all night, then released next morning on payment of a five bob fine. Which was quite a sum then – at least the equivalent of four or five pints of cider I should think! Where he made for after that I've no idea, for we never saw him again.

But we did see the odd 'Diddicoy' or two. I should think that's a most outrageous misspelling of the word, but I don't think I've ever actually seen it written. And it doesn't appear in my dictionary either. But local Kentish folk will know what I mean.

They're no different from anyone else really, when you get down to it, we're all trying to earn a living in one way or another. Their way may be a little unorthodox by general standards I suppose, and many folk are a bit wary of them. But I've always got on all right with them. Well – perhaps there was the odd exception or two.

Like when Charles and Stella had gone out for the evening. It was their night off, and Mary and I were looking after things – with me actually in charge. We were aided by a new barmaid on this occasion, a Scottish lass, well-built, and I should think about mid-thirtyish. We ourselves had all had the benefit of previous experience when first we'd faced these particular customers, but this wasn't the case with her. She'd had not a whit; a very raw beginner.

It turned out to be a busy evening. I think actually it was also '*Thrift Club*' night, when certain locals came in to pay their dues into some or other savings fund – probably a Christmas Club I guess. It was nowt to do with us actually, I think all we did was provide the facility for the club's treasurer or whatever to do the collecting. Most members stopped for a drink whilst they were there, though this was mostly just a 'quick half'. Just a little act of courtesy I think, in recognition of our hospitality. Of course, we usually did a bit better out of it when pay-out time came!

There were a good many regulars in as I say, and I was a little uneasy to see amongst them someone I shall call Fred Taylor, which of course wasn't his real name, but one I choose as substitute – you never know – he may still be around! He was a well-known local character, bit of a dealer I think, with a reputation second to anybody's. It was said that he entered the 'Gents' at The Angel one evening, and came up unexpectedly behind an old enemy of his. This chap was just standing there, doing what he had to do, when Taylor plunged a knife into his back. How serious this was – or indeed how true – we weren't too sure, but we didn't really relish having him in our pub. And this view was shared by all four of us.

He'd brought several pals with him – of similar ilk but unknown to us – and so far they weren't stepping out of line in any way. Taylor approached the bar for another round of drinks when both Mary and I were serving, so it fell to our new lass to deal with him. She was, naturally, quite nervous, being right there in the limelight, and her hand shook as she held a glass to the cider barrel on the counter. She nonetheless completed the order and took his money.

A few moments later his voice boomed out – drowning out the rest of the customers and drawing everybody's attention. 'Oh yeah!' he began, 'and what's *your* little game then? – this ain't bloody Guiness!' I moved over quickly. 'What's wrong Fred?' I asked, trying to quieten him down a bit, but he was having none of it. He was centre-stage and meant to make the most of it. 'This ain't bloody Guiness' he repeated, turning back to his buddies for support, and they were more than ready to egg him on. 'I asked for Guiness' he shouted, 'and she's given me an ordinary stout!' 'Yeah, yeah' they all chorused. 'But she's *charged* me for a Guiness!' he went on.

I pointed out to him that our new barmaid was not too experienced as yet, and had made a genuine mistake. I offered to rectify the error, but he wasn't letting go that quickly. 'Bloody twisters!' he bawled, 'charging for Guiness and giving you ordinary stout. No wonder you publicans can drive about in fancy bloody cars!' The bar was dead silent now, even the Thrift Club had frozen in mid-stream. I tried to reason with him, but on and on he went.

'Right' – I said after a while – 'I'd like you, and your friends, to finish your drinks and get off these premises as quickly as possible. And don't come back!' I added. 'Oh yeah!' he responded, 'and just who d'you think *you* are? Where's the landlord?' 'You're looking at him' I replied, 'it's Charles' night off and I'm in charge at the moment. And I'm telling you to clear off. You're barred – and that's official!'

It went to and fro a while – with the regulars resembling a crowd of tennis spectators – and when finally I picked up the telephone receiver, threatening to call the police, they grudgingly left. But not before he'd told me – for all to hear – what he planned to do to me if ever he came across me outside the pub. 'I'll knife you, you bastard!' he promised, then slammed the door.

A babble of voices instantly followed their departure, and a bit of a cheer went up. Clearly we weren't the only ones glad to see the back of Fred Taylor. 'You wouldn't have had to worry, had he turned nasty' said one, 'we'd have been right there behind you.' Which was a comfort – all the time I was on the premises!

I did in fact run into Fred Taylor again on a later occasion, and in a different environment, but I'll not go into that yet. And returning from their evening out, Charles and Stella were both delighted that he'd been barred, and gave their full support.

Seven months after our arrival at the Prince Albert we had a night of fairly strong winds. Nothing like the hurricane of thirty years later in 1987 – but strong enough to register. It hadn't bothered us very much during the night, in fact I personally knew nothing of it until I responded to an urgent banging on our door next morning. It was well short of opening time, but I thought I'd best see what it was all about.

'Have you seen your T.V. aerial?' – asked a little lady in an anxious voice. I followed her gaze, and was most perturbed to see the thing hanging precariously over the edge of the roof – immediately above my head. And I was standing on the threshold of the Public Bar doorway, which – we hoped – would soon be subjected to the stampeding feet of incoming customers! Furthermore, this doorway led immediately on to the pavement, which was pretty well used by the general public. Television was all black and white then of course, and the aerials were much larger and bulkier than the neat little things of today. The cable was dead taut across the roof, and it was only that which kept the aerial from crashing down on to some unsuspecting passer-by. Or worse still – a customer as he approached the door – brandishing a nice fat wallet!

I thanked the lady for letting us know, and as it was the aerial to the set rented by Mary and myself – rather than Charles and Stella's – I got straight on to the hire company. They agreed to send somebody out right away. It had been raining steadily all this time, and unfortunately showed no sign of letting up.

I surveyed the area all around us to see how many more aerials had been dislodged, and was quite amazed to see them all intact. Which led me to the conclusion that the initial installation of ours must have been a bit of a slap-dash affair, after all, these others had been in place a good many years in most cases. Still, we were insured.

By the time the Service Van arrived we were open, and had several customers in, though we hadn't exactly seen anything of a stampede. And you can guess what the main topic of conversation was. 'Have you seen your aerial?' they asked, one after another. The two chaps from the hire company came into the bar – having quickly weighed up the situation – and I gave them each a drink, hoping the rain might stop whilst they sipped. But it didn't, so on went their oilskins and sou'westers and up they went. 'Sooner them than me!' said somebody, as it bounced knee-high off the pavement. The rest were quick to agree.

They were back in just over the hour, having completed their mission, and I gave them each another pint, and expressed my thanks. 'Bit dodgy up there, wasn't it?' I asked rather unnecessarily. 'Not half!' replied the one in charge, as he scribbled something on a form and slid it across to me. 'Ah, you want my signature I guess,' said I, picking up the pen. 'That's right' he replied, 'and there's fifty bob to pay.'

I thought I was hearing things, so asked him to repeat it. Which he did. 'Fifty bob' he said! I pointed out that we were insured through the company. 'It don't cover that' he came back, 'that was blown down and that's classed as an "Act of God"!' This annoyed me, as I mentally pictured all those still-upstanding T.V. aerials surrounding us – to which I drew his attention. 'Nothing to do with us' he countered – 'fifty bob!'

I stood firm, and an argument ensued. The customers had been observing all this of course, and it now went dead quiet as they all sat back in anticipation. 'Oh well, I'll have to go and ring my firm' he declared finally, and off he went. He returned after a while. 'What's the verdict?' I asked, somewhat apprehensively, and was stunned when he replied – 'If you don't pay we've got to take it down again. Like I said – that comes under "Act of God"!' 'Act of God my foot' said I, 'more like an act of bad workmanship in the first place – all these others around us have been up for years – not seven months like this one!'

Well, it turned out that these were the very two that had actually erected it, though I didn't recognise them now. But then, we'd been so snowed under during those first few days. The rain continued – in fact it was fairly tipping it down now – and we argued on. They weren't at all keen at my slur on their workmanship, and were not backward in letting me know it. The audience twitched as our voices rose. 'Are you going to pay, or are we going to take it down again?' they demanded. All eyes looked directly at me. 'Do what you will' I answered, 'but I refuse to pay for shoddy workmanship!' At which they spun on their heels and stomped out. I watched them through the window. On went the oilskins and sou'westers again – by jingo, they needed them now for it was raining stair-rods – and up they went.

Conversation resumed in the bar the minute they'd gone, and the chuckles indicated that the customers had all thoroughly enjoyed this little diversion. Furthermore, they all seemed to agree with my views on the situation as well, which was quite reassuring.

Shortly before closing time, which I think was two-thirty, we saw their van pull away and I went out to take a look. Sure enough, there was my aerial, hanging perilously over the edge of the roof again, immediately above the door to the Public Bar. Rather like the sword of Damocles! We duly closed, and as we sat eating our lunch and mulling things over, the rain suddenly stopped and the sun shone through.

After lunch I went to the builder's yard just a hundred yards down the road from us, and borrowed a couple of ladders. Much as I hate being up on rooftops, I nevertheless climbed up, and with heart a-pounding, managed to fix it. It's the one and only time I've ever done such a job, but some years later, long after I'd gone from the pub, I noticed my aerial standing as firm and proud as any of those around.

As a boy, I'd always envied those from normal homes who had piano lessons. I'd have loved the opportunity myself, yet ironically, the majority of those lucky devils would have given it up at the drop of a hat. They hated their daily practice hour at home, regarding it as nothing less than hard labour, as, I suspect, did most of those who were obliged to suffer it with them!

Little wonder then, that during my time at the P.A., after – as it happened – the sad break-up of my marriage, I decided to make up for lost time and enrol for piano lessons. This I did with a very nice lady teacher named Mrs Doone, who taught at her home in Pembury Road. At the end of my first visit I was given a book, and told to practice the first piece – in between finger exercises of course – upon which I would be tested next time, a week later.

There was a four-hour period between the morning and evening sessions in the pub when we were closed, and this gave me an excellent opportunity to get down to my practice. And didn't I enjoy it. So much so that I soon developed a routine whereby I'd have all the cleaning up and shelf re-stocking under my belt by just after closing time, giving me almost the entire four hours to myself. And my childhood yen was certainly well-founded – for I did indeed spend all that time practising each day. I was in heaven.

I'd buttoned up the first week's lesson on that first day, and by the end of the week was half-way through the book. As a consequence, I felt rather restrained after two or three weeks, for I hadn't disclosed any of this to Mrs Doone. Which was a pity really, looking back, for she may well have set me to something a little more advanced. Instead, I just added to my legitimate practising by playing popular music of the day – in my own amateurish way – which would doubtless have horrified that good lady. But events were soon to overtake this most enjoyable pastime anyway, forcing me to give it up. But oh! Did I enjoy it while it lasted.

Our piano was just the usual upright, as would have been found in most pubs, but it was kept fairly well tuned. It stood at first in the Saloon Bar, where it was seldom used. Then somebody suggested we try it in the Public Bar one Saturday night, so Charles and I, being ever-willing to oblige, manhandled it out of the one bar, along the pavement in front of the building, and in through the doorway of the other. Phew!

As the evening session got under way, a woman sat on the piano stool and began to tinkle. She was a quite ordinary looking person – could have worked on a farm – or possibly in a local factory. Clearly, she was no pianist, but her output was none the less recognisable, and people began to sing. I can't be certain but I believe this was pre-arranged with Charles. In any event, he paid her for her efforts at the end of the evening – that I do know. We behind the bar slogged though the usual busy Saturday night session, and the customers all went home quite happy. Well, for the most part I should say. You can't please all the people all the time, as my old Grand-pappy used to say. Well, that's not strictly true of course, for I never knew either of mine. But I'm sure one of them would have said it – if I had!

The pianist, whose name was Lil, came to collect her reward, and as I looked at her she smiled – revealing just one solitary front tooth! She was instantly christened 'Pickle-chaser Lil', and this name stuck to her, but was never uttered within earshot of her. Weren't we awful!

Sunday morning saw Charles and yours truly humping the piano back along the pavement to the Saloon Bar, where it reposed gracefully till we came for it the following Saturday. This involved quite a bit of effort as you can imagine, but it seemed to be paying off. Pickle-chaser Lil arrived and duly took up her position on the stool, sipping a pint as she considered her repertoire. Eventually she set to, then, about halfway through 'Nellie Dean' the Jenner Boys turned up. They came from the nearby village of Tudeley, and there were several of them. And with their wives and a few other relatives they made a sizeable crowd.

With them they'd brought a set of drums, which one of them -was it Pete? – played in accompaniment to P'C' Lil. The whole effect appeared to be most acceptable to the majority of our customers, who, not having heard the likes before on these premises, seemed to regard the whole thing as something akin to 'Saturday Night at the London Paladium'! And our till kept ringing away, so everyone was happy. Well again – for the most part – for there are always one or two aren't there!

These 'musical' evenings were quite successful, enough at least for Charles to decide after a few weeks to leave the piano in the Public Bar for the time being, which saw the last of the twice-weekly hump, thank goodness.

One Saturday I'd just opened the doors for the morning session, and was quietly counting the till float or something. Ann, our cleaner, had just left and the place looked all smart and sparkling as usual, the Saloon Bar with its dark, solid oak tables and rich red-patterned carpet looking particularly swish. Stella had popped out to buy the material for bar-snacks – bread rolls, ham and so on, and Charles was upstairs shaving, having just finished setting everything up down in the cellar. I don't think Mary was there at the time.

The Saloon Bar door opened and a peak-capped head peered in. 'You open yet?' it inquired, looking round the empty bar. 'We certainly are' I replied, whereupon it swung back the other way and called out '*It's okay – they're open!*'

My goodness – what an avalanche that brought upon me, for unbeknown to me, this head belonged to one of the drivers of two coaches that had just pulled on to our little car park. I don't know how far they'd come, but the passengers came surging in and made straight for the toilets! Queues formed right across the floors of both Saloon and Public Bars, whilst others stood two or three deep at the counter hurling their orders at me. I tucked into it, and as soon as I could get near the communicating door to the private quarters I hollered out a pretty forceful 'HELP!'

Charles came quickly down, so quickly in fact that half his face still sported shaving soap. He grabbed a cloth and quickly wiped it off, displaying half a beard instead, and buckled to the task. Shortly afterwards Stella returned from the shops and joined us. The place calmed a little as their various needs were satisfied, but for a while there it was utter pandemonium. After what seemed an age, but was probably no more than about 45 minutes, they upped their glasses and made their departure.

Peace returned, and the three of us looked first at the bars, then at each other. What an almighty mess! If Ann had returned just at that moment she would have resigned on the spot I'm certain. The tables, bar-tops and floors were absolutely littered, and I should think almost as much liquor had been spilt as had been consumed, in the mêlée. That lovely Saloon Bar floor was now a bunch of puddles, interspersed with crisp packets, chocolate wrappers, cigarette packets and dog-ends – some still smouldering.

We quickly set to and spruced it all up again, but I for one wondered if the now bulging till was really worth it. The thing was, coaches were normally accepted 'by appointment only', and these two had come on spec – catching me unawares. But Charles made sure they knew the score as they left! I shall certainly never forget *that* little incident, it was like being in two different worlds for a while, or watching a whirlwind pass slowly through. Still, it provided us with a talking point for a time.

Shortly after we'd taken over, probably a few months – when everything was up and running smoothly – I went in search of a day job. This had been previously agreed amongst us, as we didn't envisage the pub takings being sufficient to support us all.

So I became Secretary to a well-known farmer at Tudeley. A good many men were employed there, for as well as tending our own farm we contracted out men and machinery to other farmers, who I suppose didn't have all the equipment they needed to do it themselves. And the farmer himself had various other interests within the local community, so one way and another I was kept quite busy. I enjoyed this job immensely, for it was very varied and interesting, and for the most part I was on my own all day. And the hours were quite cushy – so I was well able to take my place behind the bar in the evenings. Another case of two different worlds.

The absolute peace and serenity of the day was broken only by the occasional bleat, snort or grunt, although sometimes the animals joined in too! I jest of course. Then at times I'd hear the anxious lowing of our prize Aberdeen Angus bull, as he was coaxed into the 'crush' to receive one sort of attention or another.

It was exactly my scene and I loved it. My little office was in the oasthouse overlooking the farmyard, of which I had a good view as I sat at the desk under the window. I could see old 'Equilad of Tebworth' (the prize bull) in his stall, or in the crush as the case may be, and John the stockman as he tended him and all the other animals when they were in off the fields.

What a contrast the evening was, with all the jolly banter and general hurley-burley in the pub. But these two occupations went well together in my case, affording some sort of balance between the various facets of my make-up. And I thoroughly enjoyed both.

But all good things – so the saying goes – come to an end, and this proved true a few months later when my marriage suddenly and totally unexpectedly broke up. No details here, but suffice it to say I was absolutely shattered as the 'bolt from the blue' struck. I carried on working at the farm awhile, but the solitude, hitherto enjoyed, now gave me far too much room to brood, and I became very depressed. So, after having been there only a few months I had to give up this lovely, tranquil part of my life and return full-time to the pub, where the diversions – some of which I've already mentioned – were far too many for me to remain in the dumps too long. Well, all the time we were open that is.

Thinking back to the farm, the complete contrast between it and the pub hit me even before I set foot on the place. I was on my way to the initial interview with the farmer, and left the bus at the top of Bank Lane. I started walking down the lane in search of the farm, and I could have been the last person on this planet at that moment, for there was neither sight nor sound of another living soul, save for the birds. It was indeed *most* peaceful.

I rounded a bend, and suddenly all this changed as I came face to face with an enormous pig! He, or maybe she – I didn't have time to notice – was strolling up the lane as I strolled down. We were on the same side, and the sudden confrontation as we met head on startled us both, stopping us dead in our tracks.

For a few moments the tranquillity of the scene was completely shattered as the air became filled with ear-piercing squeals and 'Bloody-'ell's' – as we reacted to the shock. Then, having given each other a jolly good coat of looking at and satisfied ourselves that there was no further cause for alarm, we each, with a few grunts, oinks and phews, continued on our separate journeys. It was the pig by the way, doing all the grunting and squealing. Yes – I'm sure it was!

Not that I am averse to the close proximity of animals mind you, under normal circumstances. But when you're all keyed up for a job interview – only minutes away – and one lands slap bang in front of you, well – I mean to say!

I thought I'd best advise the farmer of my rather unusual encounter right away, and he lost no time in sending the stockman in hot pursuit of the errant pig – lest it reach the main road. The interview followed and needless to say, I got the job. All was peace and serenity again as I retraced my footsteps to the bus stop at the top of the lane – the stockman having successfully recaptured his quarry and returned it to the farm. But I approached each bend mighty warily, none the more for that!

I took that job at probably the best time of year I guess, for there were little lambs everywhere, and bluebells and daffodils in such abundance that I was able to keep all the vases in the Saloon Bar filled, and those upstairs in our living quarters too. I took the bus to work for a short while, then out came the Claude Butler that I'd ridden across London each day from Kensal Rise to the Accounts Office in Tottenham Court Road. But what a different journey this was.

The first part of it – the Tonbridge end – is quite different now what with new roads, bypasses, industrial estates, roundabouts and various other modifications. *Then* – in 1957 – I used to cycle down Vale Road, with the high wall screening the railway on my right, and cottages right the way down on the left. I'd meet little traffic, mostly cyclists and pedestrians really, for the road didn't go anywhere much beyond the Sewage Farm, in fact I think it petered out altogether just past there. It served Strawberry Vale and Lodge Oak Lane, and little else if I remember correctly.

There were no commercial or industrial premises at all until you reached the Ba Ba works, which I seem to think was something to do with carpets, but I can't really be sure now. Then there was the South Eastern Tar Distillers, (SETAR) both these places being on the right. I can't remember now whether there was anything else on that side. Opposite was The Distillers' Company, where I worked at a later date and which must have covered a few acres of ground, and next to this was The British Flint & Cerium works, which later became Creffields I think, and is now Huntings. There might well have been other name changes in between, in fact, it could quite easily have changed yet again, it's a year or two since I've been close enough to notice.

On my bike I was past these few places in just seconds, then I slipped through an opening which led immediately on to the Sewage Farm. This I crossed, keeping to the narrow, beaten track on the perimeter just inside the hedgerow, across the lane at the far side, over Postern Park (or Farm), then with a few more bits of cross-country work I was nigh on there by the time I hit the road again. A very pleasant ride, and infinitely preferable to the rat-race of London. Even the old bike seemed happier, especially on the homeward run when you couldn't see her saddle-bag or carrier for daffs and bluebells.

I can enlarge little really on anything much about that job, well as far as the other members of staff went anyway, for I saw them only for a few brief moments on those mornings when they'd come in for fresh instructions, having finished the job they'd been on. Some mornings there could be three or four of them – which would bring about a fair bit of chit-chat and good-natured leg pulling – other mornings none. My boss – the farmer – came in for just long enough to run through any extraordinary requirements of the day with me, sign a few cheques maybe, then he too was gone till next morning. This usually took no more than about twenty minutes. Friday afternoons were quite different though, for that's when they all came in to collect their pay packets. That outside wooden stairway which led up to my office took a bit of pounding then – especially as they went back down it – with all the extra weight in their pockets!

So, back to full-time working in The Prince Albert again; with Mary having gone my presence was needed anyway. It was a bit awkward at first, having to parry the inevitable questions that came across the bar, but I took it in my stride. But I was quite melancholy – in between sessions – for quite some time. Then one or two of the lads suggested I get out and about a bit, and invited me to tag along. I was soon one of the crowd again, and really had a ball for a couple of years, at the end of which I was pretty well recovered.

A few months after my return to The Prince Albert – when I'd started getting out and about – I decided I ought to seek employment elsewhere, thus removing the difficulty Mary was finding when she wanted to visit her parents. There was absolutely no pressure upon me from Charles and Stella to do this – quite the contrary in fact – we'd always got along so well. But you have to face up to situations don't you?

One of our occasional Saloon Bar customers was an elderly Scottish gentleman who owned a Newsagent/Tobacconist/Confectionery shop just up the road, on the corner of Avebury Avenue, right opposite The Angel Hotel. He'd pop in for a quick wee dram on his way home some nights. He did wholesale as well as retail, and as we chatted across the bar one evening, he suggested I might like to work for him as his 'Traveller'. This of course was an old name for Representative, but more specifically the sort who would cover considerable distances, spending more nights in hotels than in his own home. I found his offer – which did not, fortunately – come under that category, most appealing. So I accepted.

The so-called travelling was all *very* local, mainly just the town itself and all the surrounding villages, and took only part of each day. So I spent some time in the shop most days, usually first thing when folk were dashing in for newspapers and cigarettes, and possibly a few sweets and things on their way to work. I quite enjoyed this little interlude, and came to make even more acquaintances than I'd already made at the pub.

That first hour was always very busy, and evokes another never-to-be-forgotten smell whenever I think back to it. For although we sold a great many cigarettes and packets of hand-rolling tobacco, we also sold a fair amount of the coarse tobacco known as '*shag*'. This was kept loose in two large clear-glass jars with knobbed lids, one for dark shag, the other for light. You'd remove the lid to weigh some out, and the aroma – trapped until that moment – would waft straight up your nostrils. Most pleasant. Come to think of it they were all pleasant smells in that shop, and reminiscent of the early Woolworths stores referred to previously. Snuff was still fairly popular then too, but came a poor second to shag. Well in that shop it did anyway.

The pleasure of the travelling part of the job was further heightened by the vehicle I used. This was a dark-ish blue and black Austin Eighteen saloon – of about 1937 vintage – so elegant and so reminiscent of my pre-National Service days at Grey's Garage in the late 40's. I spent half the week going round to all my calls, which were about 80% pubs and 20% village shops, just taking their orders, then the other half of the week delivering them! A nice, friendly, cushy little number, and I was sorry when it came to an end a few months later.

The biggest of these orders – which were just cigarettes, tobacco and chocolate – would have fitted comfortably into a regular sized breadbin, and there were practically no parking restrictions whatsoever in those days, so you can see, it was a right doddle of a job as well as being a 'nice little earner'! But alas, the boss made an overnight decision to retire from business, and his successor had no plans to retain the wholesaling side.

One of my calls was 'The Albion' pub in Hadlow – though it goes under a different name now – and I already knew Bill Gough, the landlord, from previous acquaintance. It was just at this time that I had decided to move out of the P.A. altogether and take lodgings elsewhere. But my furniture presented rather a problem, as I didn't want to part with it just then. Thankfully this problem was soon solved, when Bill and his good lady wife offered not only accommodation for me, but storage for all my furniture as well – all under the one roof.

Another of my calls, just up the road from The Albion, was Hadlow Garage, owned and run by Mr Elsey. I can't be certain now of his Christian name, but it was either William or Wilfred – the latter I fancy. Right at that time he was thinking of taking on someone to look after the pumps and forecourt, hitherto tended by himself, so almost overnight I'd left Tonbridge and was now both living and working in Hadlow. And shortly after this my divorce was finalised, so it was changes all round. Back to bachelorhood, back in digs, *and* in a new job. Funny old life – innit?

I don't know why now but it was about this time that I started working evenings back at the P.A. I believe Charles and Stella needed the extra help, and most of my friends were still in that area anyway. Here – hang on a minute – I'd been here before hadn't I? Garage during the day – pub in the evenings. It certainly *is* a funny old life!

A reader of these jottings could well be forgiven for gaining the impression that jobs and I were never more than a short-term affair really. But whilst the truth of this is undeniable, I must say – in my own defence (should I need one) that most often the cause of such situations was beyond my control. What with moving around a fair bit

– south to north, north to south, National Service, London to Kent, domestic
upheavals, and people retiring and swiping the job from under me! Well – stands to
reason dunnit?

Chaps who'd been soldiering on in the one job since school would frown at me.
'You ought to settle down in one job' they'd say, 'and make something of yourself!'
Or – 'You might be sorry one day, when you're coming up to retirement!' Well, this
all sounded rather boring to me – I've heard of forward planning, but at 26 years of
age it also sounded ridiculous. It certainly would today, in the nineties, when nobody
can be sure of their job from one day to the next. And anyway, it's just as well we
don't all think the same, for what suits one.....

'You've had *how* many jobs?' some would ask incredulously, trying to intimidate
from me a confession of shame. But, whilst I am not particularly proud of my record,
I am most certainly not ashamed of it. Overall, I would have to admit to being
thankful for it really – for I have had so many experiences of people and places –
albeit all within the U.K., and have learned so many different things. The maxim 'All
work and no play makes Jack a dull boy' surely cannot apply to that particular Jack –
the 'one of all trades'. For though he may, in some cases, be 'master of none' – he
hasn't let the rest of the world slip by unnoticed. And whilst a little knowledge *may*
be a dangerous thing – surely 'tis better to have loved and lost, than never to have
loved at all? A bit profound maybe, but *I* know what I mean!

And in any case, Hadlow Garage was only my thirteenth job – I was to at least
double that before hanging my boots up. So settle back.

The job at the garage was okay, but not too exciting, although there was the
occasional incident to liven things up a bit. The workshop was run by Mr Elsey's son
Doug, who was ably assisted by a local lad named Dave Burt, who was eighteen. So
we were three in number basically, with Mr Elsey in the office at the far end mainly.
Doug was nine years my senior, and Dave nine years younger than me, though why I
mention this I really don't know. It just seemed significant at the time.

Woodfords, the village baker's shop – which flourishes yet – ran two or three
delivery vans then, just round the local area. One of the drivers was Frank Blake,
who lived opposite The Albion pub and looked as though he was well due for
retirement. Another was Mr Sharpe (I think), who either owned or managed the
shop, I believe, and who was also quite elderly. The third was a chap more our own
age, a lively, chirpy sort named Dennis. Woodfords had a credit account with us, so
we saw them all quite regularly when they came in for a fill up.

I guess it's safe to say now, for he left that job many years ago, that whenever
Dennis came in, either Dave or I would wheedle some cakes from him, and decent
chap that he was he never let us down. And he always gave us two bags, each

containing six delicious cakes – usually doughnuts, vanilla slices, cheesecakes and the like. These the two of us scoffed just before our morning tea-break. We'd eat six apiece straight off – then sit down with our tea and sandwiches! Blooming hogs.

Frank Blake would never give us any – for reasons of his own I guess – and we wouldn't have dreamed of asking Mr Sharpe. Of course, Dennis didn't come in *every* day, and in his absence Dave would pop down to the shop and actually buy some – the two of us having clubbed together and somehow managed to scrape up enough for about a dozen. These would be in greater variety than the freebies were – the fact that we were paying for them allowing us the privilege of choice – but they never really went down any better. My goodness, they really were good. It's amazing how you can tuck it away at that age.

Business was usually quite steady at the garage, both on the forecourt and in the workshop, but now and again there'd be slack moments. Then out would come the broom or the paintbrush, or maybe window cleaning equipment. But Dave didn't think much of these as alternatives, he'd far sooner use the time for fun, and occasionally he'd persuade me to play ball with him, the ball being a rolled up rag tied with string. But *not*, I might add, soaked in waste oil! We'd stand one each side of the fairly empty workshop, just throwing and catching.

On one such occasion, it seemed to be coming at me a trifle hard, and noticing a devilish gleam in Dave's eye, I stepped up the pace at my end too. Harder and harder we went, then suddenly Dave ducked, and the inevitable happened. My delivery whizzed straight through the window, which as luck would have it was closed. It was he who was at fault really for not catching the damned thing, but I had to accept the blame, being the last to handle it!

I summoned the courage and went – cap in hand – to confess to Mr Elsey, who was, fortunately, a very kindly sort. I think he was a little surprised at me, an ex-Representative, indulging in such tom-foolery, but he very graciously accepted my apology. 'I can assure you it will never happen again' I promised, as I made my grateful exit.

I resisted Dave's attempts to draw me in on two or three subsequent occasions, but my resolve was finally broken a few weeks later. This time however, we were kicking a tennis ball against a wall that had no windows in it – other than just the one – very high up and out of the way. In no way did we wish to run the risk again. But, boys will be boys – and though we started off very gently – our confidence grew, as the ball was striking well below the window. And of course – I miskicked the ball and it ricochetted off some solid object, though not the car of a customer I hasten to add, and winged straight up at this window, for all the world as though it had been programmed. *Ker-ash*!

I couldn't believe it. As we both looked up in horror I was wondering how on earth I'd explain *this* to Mr Elsey – so hot on the heels of my most solemn promise. Nobody could be that forgiving. 'Oh well, it's been nice knowing you,' I said to Dave as I braced myself for what I knew could be the only possible outcome. But Mr Elsey remained true to form – bless him – for not only do I live to tell the tale, I carried on in my job too! But nothing on earth would have induced me to break my promise this time. The boss had stood the cost of the first repair, and although I insisted upon bearing it this time, it never came to that, for that little window – which served very small purpose anyway – was simply boarded up.

I was unlocking the petrol pumps one Spring morning, when the corner of my eye detected a small movement. And there, bobbing falteringly around on the forecourt, was this dear little baby House-Martin. He was quite well-feathered, but too young yet to know what his wings were for. He'd obviously fallen from a nearby nest, yet fortunately appeared to be unhurt. But he was now in grave danger of his luck running out, as vehicles began trundling in for petrol. So I quickly found a nice clean carton in which I made a makeshift nest with soft, clean rags, and popped him in. I placed the carton on the counter near the till, where I'd be able to keep an eye on him.

He watched me coming and going, and seemed quite happy, but I figured he must be getting rather peckish by now. So I placed the carton atop the privet hedge – just outside my door and about four feet high – in the hope that his parents might feed him. This was a great success, for it wasn't long before they found him and began topping him up. I brought him back into the office now and again, and we became quite pally – so much so that I could place him upon my shoulder – where he'd sit quite happily whilst I went about my normal business. The customers were most amused.

At five o'clock I finished for the day, and a word with Mr Elsey, who took over from me then for the final three hours of opening time, put my mind at ease. For he had a disused Budgie cage in the house into which he agreed to place our little feathered friend for the night, and pop him indoors – just until he'd learnt to fly and could rejoin his family.

This also worked well, and next morning we placed him on the hedge for his breakfast – back now in his carton. I returned him to my shoulder for a while to give his parents time to tend his brothers and sisters, then back on to the hedge. Sometimes I'd just leave him on the counter for a while, and he seemed happy enough with these arrangements. We repeated the procedure with the cage that night, and followed the same routine the next day. And all the time he was growing bigger and stronger.

When I arrived for work on the third morning, Mr Elsey hadn't yet brought him out from the house. So I went out to unlock the pumps – and I was heartbroken. For there was my poor little friend – as flat as a pancake! Apparently he'd managed to climb out of the carton, then hopped from the counter to the ground. This had happened the previous evening whilst Mr Elsey was busy serving out front. He'd then wandered off outside somewhere, and was nowhere to be seen when Mr Elsey locked up at eight o'clock, so it was presumed he must have discovered what his wings were for and gone to rejoin his family. Mr Elsey called it a day and went indoors for the night. But the poor little chap had obviously found his way – undetected – onto the forecourt, just before the last of the customers had pulled away. Upset me for a few days, that did!

I was out front one day, and looked up to see a small, canvas-topped pick-up truck limping in on three – so to speak. One of its rear tyres was almost as flat as that poor little bird. The truck was loaded to the brim with greengrocery, and was clearly more than slightly overloaded. The driver stopped at the airline, and when he stepped out I recognised him instantly. He was none other than Fred Taylor – he who had threatened to 'knife me on sight' when I'd barred him from the Prince Albert a year or two previously. 'Now for it' I thought, as I made my way across.

He seemed not to recognise me as he asked if I'd re-inflate his flat tyre for him, but he never used our garage anyway, so perhaps that was feasible. 'That'd be a dodgy thing to do' I advised him, 'with all that weight on it could quite easily explode before we got very far!' 'I've only got to get as far as Tonbridge,' he replied – as if I didn't know – 'and *I'm* prepared to risk it if you are!' 'Well – I have warned you,' I said, reaching for the airline, 'I'd stand back a bit if I were you!'

I pressed the trigger, feeling decidedly uneasy as the vehicle began very slowly to rise, creaking ominously as it went. Then, as though I was trying to prove my point – BANG!! Even though I was half expecting it, I near jumped out of my skin when it came. So too did Mr Taylor! 'Well – I did warn you' I pointed out, half expecting him to get all pear-shaped. But he didn't seem too perturbed. 'Would you mind if I leave the truck here whilst I nip into Tonbridge on the bus and pick up another wheel?' he asked. I agreed – as long as he wasn't too long – it being a bit of an inconvenience to other customers wishing to use the airline – and I wondered why on earth he wasn't carrying a spare on the truck. Probably so that he could increase his payload I shouldn't wonder.

I jacked up the truck and removed the wheel, so as to speed things up on his return, which in the event, was about two hours later, ours being an hourly bus service. Then, with replacement wheel on and jack removed, he asked how much he owed us. 'Ah forget it' I replied, 'it's all part of the service', whereupon he slapped a pound note into my left hand and shook me vigorously by the right. 'Good on yer,' he said, 'you're a pal!' He climbed in and started her up. 'All the best mate' he called, as he pulled away, and I've not set eyes on him from that day to this. That was about thirty-five years ago as I write, so a pound was worth something then. And a jolly sight more acceptable than a knife in the back!

Throughout this little drama I noticed with some interest – and a good deal of relief – that he never once displayed the slightest sign of recognition, although my appearance hadn't altered much I'm sure. Although wait – I did sport a full beard in my pub days, and I was now clean shaven – so maybe.... Anyway, I'd certainly recognised him, so perhaps we were *both* being prudent!

Which reminds me of another incident concerning diddicoys. This was also at Hadlow Garage, and took place during 'Hopping', which, for the benefit of those not acquainted with the term – is the Kentish name for the season when hops are picked – late summer/early autumn. This was the late 1950s, and still some time before the colour and spectacle of countless hand-pickers had been replaced by modern machine-picking. As well as local pickers, people came from London by the train-load, making it a working holiday, which at the time was still the only break many of them had from their concrete jungle. And for the most part they loved it – insects and all! And the season generally lasted about six weeks.

A truck pulled on to the pumps for fuel, and I nipped out to serve. It was unmistakably a diddicoy wagon, one look at the driver as he stepped out being enough to confirm this. But as usual, he was polite enough and payed up without any question. He started to climb back into the cab, then backed out again. 'I'd better take a bottle of that oil' he said, nodding toward a stand which held some unmarked bottles.

This oil was 'commercial' engine oil, delivered to us in bulk and normally issued from a hand-operated pump on the forecourt. It was low cost stuff and used mainly in the engines of vans and lorries, as its name would imply. For expediency, we would fill as many of these plain, stoppered or screw-capped bottles as we could find – with a measured amount – and place them on this stand for quick and easy access. Having emptied the contents into the customer's engine, we could then refill them when convenient and return them to the stand. But for reasons I cannot now recall, these bottles were not that easy to come by, and I was under strict instruction not to allow them to be taken off the premises.

He was disappointed when I said that I couldn't let him take the bottle, and that I'd have to pour the contents into his engine there and then. 'No, no – it ain't for this motor' he responded, 'and don't worry about yer bottle, I'll bring it back next time!' Against my better judgement, I took him at his word and allowed him to take it – after he had paid for the oil of course. Back to this in a mo.

There is a small triangular piece of land on the edge of the village, between the river and the 'Prince of Wales' pub. Every Hopping would see several diddicoy families and their vehicles taking up residence on this field – all by previous and proper arrangement of course – and if you hadn't known it was hopping time before, you'd have known then, for that field was normally empty outside of those six weeks – save perhaps for a couple of grazing horses. Our friend with the oil bottle was one of these folk, although whether or not they went and did any actual hop-picking I don't know. Perhaps it was just a guise – somewhere to drop anchor for six weeks?

Anyway, back to the garage. A few days later the same fellow came in – with the same truck – only this time he happened to have a couple of his mates with him. No problems, I put the fuel into his tank as requested, but before paying he again asked for a bottle of oil. 'Where's the bottle you borrowed the other day?' I asked. 'You promised you'd bring it back!' He looked at his mates, then back at me. '*Me?*' he replied – in mock astonishment – 'I never 'ad no bottle off yer, you must be finking of somebody else!' Well, we both knew this to be untrue, and I flatly refused his request. He began to argue, but I stood my ground, so his pals joined in. They could see I wouldn't be budged and started to get nasty. 'All this fuss over a tu'enny 'a'penny bloody bottle,' growled the driver, and in a way I was in complete agreement with him. But rules are rules, and there was a principle involved anyway, not to mention the preservation of my job. So that was that as far as I was concerned.

Eventually, seeing the futility of their efforts they gave up and began to climb back into their truck, glaring and growling at me as they went. But before the driver himself joined them, he came right up close to me and gave me a real good 'eye-balling' – to use a present-day expression. 'You just wait till I catch you off these premises,' he glared, 'Then you're gonna get it. I'll break yer bleedin' jaw for yer!'

Nice, I thought, here we go again. Hopping was all but done with for that year, so I figured my days were numbered, and a pretty low number at that. But you just have to carry on don't you!

I ought to mention here that I'd now left my digs at The Albion, and sold all my furniture – which was good quality stuff – to Mrs Gough herself. I'd been happy enough there, comfortable too, but it was interfering somewhat with my social life, which was still centred mainly on Tonbridge. But I'll not go into that just now.

So I was now cycling to work in Hadlow each day from my new digs in Tonbridge. I slip this little bit of info in just here because it is, in fact, relevant to the half-finished account of the oil bottle. Two months prior to which, incidentally, I had begun courting my wife Margaret – I am happy to say. She drove a scooter at the time, which was then a very popular mode of transport. Unless of course, you were a 'Rocker'. Hers was a very smart blue Vespa, and with her red riding mac and white crash helmet she was not only a very attractive little package, but quite patriotic with it.

We both finished work at five, but as hers was based at Yalding she entered the actual village of Hadlow – on the outskirts of which she lived – shortly after I'd passed through it, whereby we missed each another by just a few minutes. I didn't reckon much of this, so even though I cycled back out from Tonbridge most nights, to get about this courting business, I used to wait for her. I'd set my bike at the kerb, just short of the Prince of Wales and right opposite the Brewery that was there then, and sit and wait for her. We'd chat awhile when she arrived, then each get on our way. Ain't love grand.

As I sat waiting one evening, the diddicoys began pulling out from the small field. Hopping was over and they were moving on. They turned right as they emerged on to the road, causing them to drive right past me. One or two trucks went by, then a black Ford Zephyr pulled up suddenly, right opposite me. Horror of horrors – it was *him* – the one who'd promised me a free face-lift! He looked at me quite decisively as he flipped the door handle, and I noticed that all his seats were occupied. 'Bloody hell,' I thought, as I dismounted and braced myself, 'here it comes!' Suddenly I was wishing I'd let him have the damned bottle and chanced losing my job. It would've saved this!

Looking me straight in the eye he strode purposefully across the road, then, when he was about two paces short of me he raised his right hand.... and offered it to me! I wasn't too sure as to what might follow, but I responded to his gesture and took it – gingerly. 'Well, so-long pal,' he said cheerfully, at the same time shaking my hand most warmly – just as Fred Taylor had. 'It's been nice knowin' yer – see yer next 'oppin'!' And with that he was back in his car and away – he and his pals all waving and smiling at me as they went.

What an anti-climax. But one, I must confess, that I was not at all *un*happy about! For on the day he'd been deadly serious, there was no question about that. There just ain't no accounting for some folk is there.

Looking on the lighter side of those days I am reminded of the Mynah bird that belonged to either Ted or Mabel, who lived in the old detached house next to the garage – on the Maidstone side. This property has long since gone, having given way to the Old People's Bungalows that now occupy the site. On fine days, this Mynah would be put outside in his cage, where he had a commanding view of all around him, including passers-by. He was quite an age I believe, and had been a common sight on such days for years. So his initial attraction had waned quite a lot by the time he and I became daytime neighbours. He was just part of the village.

But what even regular passers-by couldn't fail to notice were the very loud, and very shrill calls he made. He could make you jump pretty wildly if he caught you unawares when you were up close. I got used to this whistling, probably didn't notice most of it, but one call he *could* put me on edge with was his 'wolf' whistle. He seemed quite able to distinguish between the sexes, which I suppose wasn't too difficult then as girls wore skirts or dresses most of the time, and lads had sensible haircuts, though the latter of course, is purely a matter of opinion. Anyway, every female that walked or cycled by got the full benefit of this particular whistle.

Which was fine – all the time they knew from whence it came. But if I happened to be out there at the time, well, I could get some pretty black looks occasionally. I soon learned to laugh it off of course, but one occasion I didn't find too amusing was when a woman I shall call Phoebe,which – for the sake of propriety was obviously not her real name – came along. I'd seen her passing several times, and more than once she'd given me the 'glad eye'. But she certainly wasn't my type and I didn't fancy her at all, so I gave her absolutely no encouragement.

Then our Mynah friend put his oar in. '*Phwe-Phwooo!*' he shrilled as she approached. She looked straight at me, flushed, then with a flutter or two of her eyelashes and a demure kind of smile, carried on by. I glared at our friend in his cage.

This was before I'd moved out of The Albion, and before I'd met Margaret too, so I was in the habit of catching a bus at about seven each evening in Hadlow, as I set off for Tonbridge and the Prince Albert. That evening, as I took my seat on the upper deck – being a regular smoker then – she suddenly appeared and sat in the seat alongside mine. She tried to make conversation, and wasn't at all put off by the one-sidedness of it. 'Oh well,' I thought, 'bear with it – we'll be in Tonbridge in a few minutes'. But bless me if she didn't follow me right to the pub! Fortunately for me I was behind the bar and only had to speak to her now and then.

She kept up the pressure for a while – even pinched my sweater one night from the pub. I couldn't find it when I'd finished work, so thinking somebody had taken it in error – or even stolen it – I gave it up as lost. A day or two passed, then up popped Phoebe at the garage and handed it to me, all neatly folded, having taken it home and washed and ironed it for me! The darned thing was perfectly clean when she'd nicked it. I continued to resist her advances, in as polite a way as possible, and eventually thank goodness, she gave up. Phew – yet again. But I kept a jolly close watch on that caged trouble-maker for some time after that!

Once again I was in a job where I met lots of people, and practically all of them local at that. Which was great really, for I soon got to learn all the local history, geography too for that matter.

Vehicles were ever changing then, and it was at this time that 'Bubble-Cars' appeared on the scene. One of our workshop customers had an Isetta, which was a three-wheeler – two fore and one aft – with entry from the front. The front was all door – half of which of course was screen, complete with wiper – similar to today's hatchbacks but hinged at the side rather than the top. The steering column was attached to this door, so when you opened up to climb in or out the steering all went with it, being either hinged or swivel-pinned lower down the colum, I suppose – I forget now. Neither can I remember the actual carrying capacity – people or luggage – but it was, naturally, quite minimal.But they were well-equipped nonetheless, and I for one thought they were great, and real fun to drive. And of course, it mattered not if you had no garage, you could just as easily shove it in the dog's kennel. Well – very nigh.

Another customer had a Messerschmitt, which again was a Bubble-Car, but different in shape. Whereas the Isetta was quite round – bug-shaped I'd say – the Messerschmitt was long and slim by comparison – more ant-shaped. It had the same wheel configuration I think – two fore and one aft – and entry was from the side. You lifted the entire cockpit cover up – it being hinged on t'other side – then pulled it back over yourself once you were in. Your passenger, if you had one, sat right behind you – they were too narrow to sit line-abreast – and I'm afraid I found them just a little claustrophobic. Even so, they were still quite fun to drive, but for me the Isetta had a comfortable edge. But I never let the chance to drive either of them pass.

T'was the same with two-wheeled motoring. Britain's roads then bore only British motor cycles – well – at least 99% I should say. Glorious names like Norton, Triumph, B.S.A., Matchless, A.J.S. etc. But just about to burst in upon us were these Japanese machines, each of which sounded like a swarm of extremely angry bees. Or perhaps one very large one. Their noisy, high-pitched rasping sound came as a most unpleasant assault upon our ears, after hearing only the beautiful throaty tones of our own bikes. Not that I'm criticising the build or general performance of the Hondas, Kawasakis etc., for they are indeed most sophisticated and efficient pieces of machinery. If only they weren't so darned noisy, especially the smaller ones which seem to race through countless, rasping gear changes to achieve speeds little beyond those attainable on a decent push-bike! Perhaps I exaggerate slightly, but I do find this particular aspect of them most offensive.

But such is life, some thirty-five years later. One dreads to think what it may be like thirty-five years hence. But then – I suspect I shall be in a place where it is unlikely to worry me then. Our once-peaceful countryside, comparatively speaking that is – now seems to buzz with the dreadful noise of countless, demented chainsaws that have escaped their owners and are running amuck.

Just prior to these machines however, we saw the return of the Autocycles of the thirties and forties – only now they were called 'Mopeds' and had gears and things. They weren't particularly fun to drive though, other than to very raw beginners maybe. They were however, quite functional and economical, and a good alternative to going to work by bus. But great fun indeed were the 'Scooters', of which the only names I now remember are Vespa and Lambretta. Margaret and I had two Vespas – one after the other that is – and enjoyed them immensely, either driving *or* riding pillion. As well as being fun they were quite practical too, you could dress up to go out somewhere, and arrive almost as smart and unruffled as you'd left. And crash-helmets didn't become compulsory till a good many years later, although Margaret had very sensibly worn one right from her very first moped – before I met her. The fairing – legshield and screen – protected you very well against the elements, and the only way you were likely to get wet was if you were stationary for any length of time. And only then if it was raining!

The hall next to the garage – on the Tonbridge side – was still the main village hall then and was well used for all the usual functions. Dances, weddings, amateur dramatics, concerts, clinic – to name but a few. And at the time of which I write, Tuesday was a very significant day of the week in the village hall – for young and old alike – though I think mainly the younger element really. For this was the day the 'Mobile Kinema' hit town. I never actually attended a show myself, but I'm sure it was enjoyed far more than the derisory sniggering from some of the village lads would suggest. They were at least quite well in advance of the old Magic Lantern Shows, although I'm certain that even these would have been well received by most folk, in their day. But you know what lads are!

Right opposite the garage was 'Great Elms', which was a poultry farm owned by a gentleman whose surname was Newton-Thomas. At the point where the farm bounded the road stood these very tall trees, and although I never really took stock at the time, I would imagine they might have been – as the name would imply – elms. If not then, then probably at some time previous. How sad *their* passing, with this wretched Dutch elm disease. A great loss to the English countryside. Whatever they were – elm or not – they were very tall, the ideal place in fact for a rookery. Which is just what it was, and oh boy – didn't they give you an earful most of the time. But even then – they never seemed able to drown out my dating agency friend – in his cage at the end of the forecourt!

Once in a while, I believe, a bit of a shoot was mounted on these rooks. Whether or not it was a cull during nesting time, or simply just to put something different on the meal table, I really can't say. But I shouldn't think the poor old rooks thought much of it. Nor indeed would the grey squirrels that quartered up there with them, when it was their turn. As everyone knows, these greys were imported to this country – from America I believe – and are so much hardier than our native red squirrel that he was soon ousted. Whether or not this was total I am not well enough informed to know, but I certainly haven't seen a red in the wild for many years. Anyway, these greys were largely regarded as pests at the time – in our area at least – and a bounty of one shilling per tail was being offered. So now *their* dreys were being peppered from beneath too.

Being one who has a very high regard for all forms of life, I myself never took part in any of these activities; the only 'shooting iron' I've ever handled was my army rifle. Oh, and the Bren and Sten of course. Neither in fact was I ever a witness to them, so I cannot guarantee the authenticity of this particular observation. But it was quite the topic of conversation at the time. That I do know.

But all that is long gone now, having given way to the inevitable housing development. And at roughly the same time as this took place, Hadlow Park – a little further on – also fell to the developers, although these were properties of rather more distinction, larger, rather secluded, and rather expensive. But there we are, change is inevitable I suppose, though in most cases I'd say more's the pity!

And change it was that brought about my leaving of Hadlow Garage after just two years. As with the previous job (the 'travelling'), it was a change of management that did it. Mr Elsey decided it was time he too retired, and as his son Doug had no inclination toward taking the business over, he upped and sold it. It was an Esso station up until then – although Mr Elsey actually owned it – but Esso were not prepared to match the offer he'd received from the Regent Oil Company – so – overnight it changed to Regent. Of course, further changes have taken place since.

So, with the arrival of the new Manager – Mr Wilfred Hawkins – and his family, that is – his good lady wife, their son David, daughter Valerie, and Daughter-in-law Polly, yours truly became surplus to requirements once again. But they were very nice about it – apologetic too – and had advised me some time in advance. So I was able to fix myself up with job number fourteen before I actually left.

I must point out the coincidence here, for although well over thirty years have passed since then, I think they were the only two Wilfreds – Mr Elsey and Mr Hawkins – that I've ever met in all my life. Yet one succeeded the other in a little village garage! The only other Wilfreds I can remember hearing of are Wilfred Pickles – he of 'Have a Go' fame and newsreading on the wireless during the war – and the children's comic character in 'Pip, Squeak and Wilfred!'

Thinking of wartime newsreaders, three others come to mind along with Wilfred Pickles. These are Alvar Liddel, John Snagge, and Bruce Belfridge, though I expect my spelling is incorrect regarding the first two. I can hear them now, especially at the end of the first reading when it was repeated – 'at dictation speed'. No doubt there were other newsreaders, but their names escape me now – fifty-odd years on! But I digress – again.

One of our regular customers at the garage was the locally based 'Landscape and

Turf Company', the proprietor of which was Mr Harold Morris. I'd see him occasionally – at least once a month when he came in to settle his account – but much more often would I see the lads who worked for him, when they came in to fill up the lorries and vans, and take fuel and oil away in cans for the various equipment used in the turf-fields. They were few in number at that time, but they came across as a good bunch, and I got on well with them.

Upon hearing of the impending change at the garage – and how I was to be affected by it – Harold invited me up to his house one evening for a chat, the outcome of which was my acceptance of his offer of the position of Secretary on his company. He had plans for expansion, and was in fact negotiating a change of premises right at that time. These plans were however, slightly futuristic regarding my new position, for the office from which I would operate was still just so many lines on a drawing board, and it would be several months before it actually materialised. And I needed a job now. So we agreed that I should 'fill in' with the lads in the turf field, or on such landscaping operations as were then in progress, until the office was ready. I thought this was a great idea, for not only would my position as secretary draw benefit from this very useful insight into the actual 'wheels within' so to speak, but I would be in the best of all environments as far as I was concerned – the open air. And deep in the beautiful Kentish countryside most of the time to boot! I couldn't wait.

And so, the beginning of March 1960 saw me falling in with the rest of the lads one morning, as I squared up to the brand new challenge of job fourteen. I had scant knowledge of what was to come, yet I couldn't help feeling that I was on the threshold of the most exciting, most enjoyable, and most fulfilling experience yet. And although hazard and hardship lay ahead, this feeling was well founded for those hazards were more than compensated for by the many pleasures drawn from that particular kind of life. Make no mistake – it was hard work – *bloody* hard work at times, but there existed a tremendous camaraderie amongst us as we struggled, shoulder to shoulder with one problem or another, or simply enjoyed a drink together after work. A camaraderie I have never experienced in any other job, and as I've said, number fourteen was barely halfway down the list in the final tally.

I know rose-coloured spectacles can bend the memory a little, but I still say they were great times. To be honest, none of us was actually going to make his fortune at it, but the rewards were fair. Hard-earned mostly – but fair. And there are other things in life equally as important as money – very much more so in fact – but money is, unfortunately, a very necessary evil in our 'civilised' world. But I suspect that so many people miss out on so many of these things in their dedication to its pursuit. There is much wealth in life that is nothing whatever to do with money or material possessions. Well that's my view anyway.

Joining Harold's company in March was just right really, for it was still quite early in the season. Turf cutting and laying is best done in Spring or Autumn, avoiding the very dry conditions of Summer and the frosts of Winter, although we couldn't always adhere to this strategy. Which was where most of the hazard and hardship came in.

I would say Spring must be the favourite season of most people, and it most certainly was in the turf field, although progress could be quite severely hampered early on by ground conditions after a very wet Winter. But we were generally favoured by the strong winds of March, which dried the surface and enabled us to move about on it, but didn't affect the area immediately beneath, where the hitherto dormant roots were now beginning to buckle to the task of supplying the nourishment necessary to bring forth the lush new growth above.

Ours wasn't cultivated turf – as would be grown for special purposes such as bowling greens and the like – it was the turf best suited to the general requirement – lawns, playing fields, verges, etc., and was always sheep-fed. So we constantly had sheep running with us, and in Spring, all those delightful, frolicsome lambs. The sheep were vital to the quality of the turf inasmuch as their relentless gnawing at the top worked wonders on the root and fibrous growth below, which was so prolific that you could lift a turf and shake it like a doormat. Grassland that had not been thus grazed would just crumble when cut, and not handle at all.

And of course, nature saw to it that the sheep added even further to the lushness of the growth by replacing some of the goodness they'd taken out. Which meant of course that you were handling this 'fertiliser' quite a bit as it lay on the top, so you could get quite messy at times. But it was well worth it, as too were the zillions of wriggling worms you handled when you lifted the fresh-cut turves, one at a time.

I daresay we all ate some of these worms now and then, though quite unwittingly mind you. For it could be a very muddy business at times, and our clothes became well caked with it as we loaded the turves on to pallet boards, or waiting lorries. And in this clinging mud would be lots of worms – or rather bits of worm for the most part. So when you sat down for a bit of 'scran' – with your open lunch-box on your knees – bits of dried mud and worm would occasionally drop from your clothing straight into it. And if you weren't watching what you were doing!

I gave up smoking a good many years ago now, but in those days we were still relatively unenlightened as to the real perils of the habit. And didn't we enjoy a cigarette as we took a short break now and then. I used to 'roll my own' – as did most of the lads – so bits of worm would drop into my open tobacco tin as well. There they would dry and shrivel up, and become mostly indistinguishable from the tobacco next time I opened it up. So I expect I smoked as many worms as I ate – probably more in fact – for my tobacco tin was opened rather more often than my lunch-box. Yet whenever I see any of my old pals from those times, we all appear quite normal to each other. Older certainly – but normal. Although come to think of it, I met Bunt the other day, and he did seem to be wriggling about a bit as we stood chatting!

I referred to our lunch as scran, because this is what we called it, amongst other names, such as mungee, elevensies, or even lunch. But in fairness to those who were kind enough to put it up for us – wives, mothers, grannies – I must say this was an ill-chosen word really, for the contents of our lunch-boxes were anything but makeshift – which is the true definition of the word.

We had a new chap start one Monday morning, and at lunchtime he sat along with the rest of us under the hedge, as we set about our lunch-boxes. He opened his and looked at the contents. 'Oh no!' he groaned, in obvious disappointment, and promptly tossed them over the hedge. On the following day at lunchtime he opened his box and took out a sandwich. 'Oh no – not again!' and these followed yesterday's. This went on all week – a quick look, then 'Oh no!' – and over the hedge they went.

Come Saturday, which was a normal working day then, we all sat down for lunch and Harry – our new chum – joined us as usual. We all watched expectantly. But this time he opened his box, and without so much as a glance at the contents, lobbed them straight over the hedgerow again. The birds and other wildlife must have been in clover! The rest of us looked at each other, then Bob piped up. 'What's going on Harry?' he asked with a frown – 'all week long you've looked at your sandwiches, moaned, then chucked them over the hedge. Today you've dumped 'em without even a look – *or* a word!' 'Simple' replied Harry – 'the wife puts 'em up all week, but on Saturday she likes a bit of a lie-in, and I have to put 'em up for myself. So I didn't need to look today – I already knew!'

On my first day I had to take old George to Teston, where we were due to start cutting the following day. The track inside the gate was well rutted from the farmer's own tractors, and needed building up with hardcore – so that it would withstand the continuous pounding we'd be giving it for a while as somewhere between 70 and 100 lorry-loads trundled off the field. George, whose surname was Chapman, was a well known local character who joined us from time to time when we had stonework or paving to do, for this was his forte.

He was in his late fifties, which seemed incredibly old to the rest of us of whom I – in my late twenties – was the eldest. The others, being several years younger than me, noticed this age gap even more than I did, and were rather reluctant to work with him, for he was known to moan a bit occasionally. But I have enjoyed the company of older people all my life – revelling in their yarns and stories of the old days – of how they lived, how they played, how they worked, the methods they used – and the tools. So of course, I didn't mind working with the old chap at all, for he kept me very well-informed as to all this stuff, and some of his sayings were most amusing. Oh dear – I've just realised how I'm referring to him – 'old chap'! It occurs to me that not only have I reached the age George was then – I've notched a few more on top! Shouldn't be allowed!

Having ensured – through the combined efforts of George and myself – that egress from the field would be problem free (famous last words), I teamed up with Harold's son David next day for a stint in the turf field. The turf was first mown – beautiful smell – then cut to its regular size of 3'x1'. Cutting the width was easy enough for this was done by machine. You just needed a reasonable eye to follow the previous cut. But they were cut to length by hand, which was a different kettle of fish altogether, and could be quite painful at times. The tool used for this operation was called a 'Race' – and was home-made. It was simply a length of metal pipe whose end had been formed into a curve, resembling a hockey stick – and split. A knife was inserted through this slit, pointing downwards and angled at about 45 degrees, then secured in this position with clamping screws.

A guide-line was pegged into position, and you inserted the knife into the turf alongside this line. Then with your left hand halfway down the race, applying a firm downward pressure, and your right hand at the top end, holding it tightly into your groin, you moved forward. In optimum conditions a well-sharpened knife would slice through the turf like a hot knife through butter, and you'd race to the end of the line – maybe thirty or forty yards long – in no time at all. Then you'd move the line over three feet and race back, repeating this procedure till you'd finished your cant.

But as everyone knows, conditions are seldom optimum on any project, and in our case the major problem was stones – just below the surface. For when you were thrusting forward behind the race, the top end of it held tight into your groin, and you hit a stone...... 'YEOWW!' And most fields were stony to a fair degree. The height of summer could produce similar problems too, when the soil was bone-dry and rock-hard.

But later on we updated our machine, to one which rendered the race obsolete. For not only did this machine cut the width of the turves, it cut the length too. Furthermore, its output was more than double. Stones and hard ground still gave *some* problems, but what a relief to our groins – knuckles too for that matter!

Once the turf had been cut it was lifted and stacked so that the lorries could drive between the stacks and load up. In very wet conditions it would be stacked on pallet boards, then fork-lifted on to the vehicles by tractor, somewhere on firm ground. So when conditions were reasonable, we'd cut and stack as many as we could, in rows about ten feet apart, ready for the lorries as they came and went throughout the day.

And what a back-breaking task the stacking was! On that first occasion – working with Dave – we took a row each, about ten feet across from each other as I say. Then, with backs bent to the task, we didn't straighten up till we'd stacked a thousand each! Dave was well used to the job, for though only sixteen or seventeen at the time, he'd been working at it some years – outside of school hours of course. 'Phew!' he puffed, as he completed his row, turning to see that I was right up there with him – just stacking the last few.

'Strewth!' he exclaimed, 'you've done well – people aren't usually that quick first time off'. But what he didn't know was that my back was absolutely screaming out for mercy, and was the devil's own job to straighten, once I'd stopped. But I'm one who's always risen to the challenge – although in this case perhaps I should say stooped – not wishing to be regarded as a passenger, and I'd used him – fit and well used to it – as a pacemaker.

After a short rest and a smoke it was heads down and away again, and my back felt as though it had just lost an argument with a steam-hammer! We broke off now and again to mow and cut some more – a most welcome relief – then down we went again. I don't know how many we cut and stacked that day, probably no more than a good day's workload, but it seemed like several million to me, and I don't know how I ever got through it. I went home to my digs in Tonbridge positively knackered, and all I could do was clean myself up – with much difficulty due to the stiffness – have my evening meal, and crash right into bed. And this was the regular pattern for my first week or so, after which my muscles and sinews and things began to get accustomed to it and I came through the pain barrier – thank goodness. Now I was well able to steam along, and started to really enjoy it. It was still hard work mind, and I was seldom completely free of aches and pains, but my goodness, that first week really was something else.

My first painful experience I suppose was to do with fingers. When the ground was quite wet – as it mostly was early in Spring – our finger-nails would become packed with mud as we slid them beneath the turves to lift them. This was no great problem for a while, but as we went on – especially when we were very busy and didn't have time to clear it – it packed ever tighter as we dug relentlessly into it, and began to lift the nails from the nail-beds. We could do nowt but continue on, and working in gloves was quite hopeless, so by the end of the day our nails would be standing quite high, and you can imagine how painful this was. Pain which continued when you tried to dig or scrub it out when you got home.

Most other pain was connected with the extreme cold of Winter. But overall I wouldn't say it was a particularly painful job, once you'd got used to it, there were more aches than pains, but as I've said, it was such a great life that we paid little heed to that side of it, regarding it as payment for the privilege I suppose.

I think I was only three to four weeks into the job when Harold moved to his new premises, about a mile and a half outside the village. This was a nice little bungalow set in about seven and a half acres of apple orchard. The bungalow itself needed a certain amount of restoration and improvement I seem to remember, and we had to clear an area which we would need for our yard. There was an old black sorry looking shed on this spot which we pulled down so that we could make a start on our own building programme – which would include my office! The apple trees – of which there were some four hundred and fifty I believe – would eventually be cleared to make way for the market-garden development which was to follow.

By the way, that bit about the sandwiches going over the hedge each day – well – you can believe it if you like. Actually I just threw it in to liven things up a bit. But everything else that I've written is true, to the best of my knowledge and belief that is.

Following my inauguration into the turf field, I eased into the landscaping side of the business in a fairly natural way, though this again was very hard work at times. But it was constructive, and at times artistic, and I found it quite fulfilling – although I can't say the same for my back, which has never been the same since! Being an experienced lorry driver I went out delivering sometimes, which was particularly enjoyable, for not only was I getting the best of the south of England scenery, my back was resting in the driving seat at the same time, although the old Leyland 'Comet' that we had then was light-years away from the comfort and sophistication of today's wagons.

So, this was how it went then, in that Spring and Summer of 1960. In the turf field, out on landscaping projects, delivering turf – throughout London and the Home Counties – grubbing out fruit trees, digging out for the footings of our new buildings. And always in good company, for they were as I say, a really great bunch of lads. Lads, by the way, covers the age range from sixteen to sixty five! And as my office began to take shape, I found myself viewing it with mixed feelings, for whilst I was still looking forward to getting my teeth into the job I'd originally undertaken to do, I knew I was going to miss all this.

Well, it so happens that I have a natural 'eye' for level, or at least I did have before I was forced to succumb to wearing spectacles, and this was an invaluable asset on the landscaping side of the business. Harold was quick to notice this, and it set him thinking. So, after about six months, with the office well into construction, he approached me one day in the turf field. 'I've been doing some thinking' he began, 'and I've decided that with your mechanical skills, and your natural eye and everything, I'd like you to stay where you are – but in the capacity of foreman.

There'll be a pay increase of course' he added quickly, 'so what do you think?' I must say, this came as a total surprise to me, and knocked me sideways somewhat. 'What about my original appointment as secretary?' I asked in reply. 'Oh, I've decided to engage a woman for that job' he countered, 'you're too useful where you are!'

Well, I don't know whether I should have been glad or sad at this revelation, but I stepped a little out of character, and responded to my first impulse, which was to hand in my notice – right there and then. I can't say exactly what it was that triggered this impulse, but Harold wasn't too pleased. We had a bit of a 'discussion' on the subject, but were unable to reach agreement, and in due course I left. just like that! And I'd been *so* happy.

Looking back, I suppose it was all down to principles – which can sometimes be a mixed blessing – but you can't help the way you were raised I guess. But though I left with a heavy heart I nevertheless prepared myself for the next challenge – which in retrospect, was an experience worth having – though not *too* long-term, for it required a good deal of energy most of the time, which isn't quite so plentiful when you get older. I'm all for keeping fit and active, but this taxed even the youngest of us.

So in the autumn of that year – 1960 – I became a 'Process Worker' at 'The Distillers Company' in Tonbridge. This was all research and development work in the field of chemical engineering, where, amongst other things, we tried to harness the waste products from other industries, and turn them into something useful. There were two or three stills in operation whilst I was there, and the one to which I was assigned leapt up through six floors. Each floor would have been something like about forty to fifty feet square, and was made of steel mesh – so you could in fact stand on the ground floor and practically see the roof. Each floor was built around the still as it soared up through, and supported all kinds of associated equipment – pots, tanks, pumps, control gear etc. A rather large and very complex monster. Well, that's how I first viewed it anyway.

Initially, I was put on day-work for a short period, assisting the plant fitters who were constantly modifying everything throughout the plants, as one experiment followed another, and this was interesting enough. But having to wear more clothing than I'd been used to wasn't at all enjoyable, especially when it included a steel helmet, which was compulsory on the plant because of the open flooring, and rubber gloves. No more would I feel those gentle breezes on my bare skin, or wallow in the smell of fresh-mown grass.

But the company paid considerably higher than most others in the area, and Margaret and I were saving hard for our marriage the following summer. So I determined to give it a jolly good try.

The stills ran non-stop – day and night – right through until the run was finished, unless of course we had a breakdown. As a consequence it was necessary for the operatives to work on a three-shift basis, which was totally foreign to me, especially when I had to try to sleep in the daytime. We worked seven days, then had between two and three days off before commencing the next shift. There were no tea-breaks at all, and only twenty minutes for our lunch break. And in that twenty minutes we had to remove our protective clothing, wash our hands, dash across to the messroom, have our food and drink, and our cigarette, replace barrier cream and protective clothing, and be back at our posts on the plant – sharp! And didn't we have to steam along either side of that break!

There were two sides to this job. One was when the still was running and needed constant attention, the other was when it was shut down on completion of a run, and needed stripping down, cleaning, and generally preparing for the next. A shift – or crew as we were called – comprised about seven or eight, of which four were process workers. These were numbered one to four – number one being the most senior. So on each crew you had your opposite number, and on changeover you simply picked up where he'd left off. There were four crews, giving full cover at all times.

The most hectic time was when the still was running. There were check-points everywhere, throughout the six floors – temperature gauges, pressure gauges, flow-rate recorders, liquid levels, rotating pen-charts etc. At regular intervals – say half-hourly on average – we had to visit all these points and enter readings on a log sheet. Samples also had to be taken from various other points on the still at the same time. When you'd completed your log sheet, you took these samples to the laboratory – about a hundred yards up the road – for analysis. They'd give you the results of the samples you'd given them half an hour earlier, which you took back to your plant for comparison. You may then need to make a few adjustments here and there, to maintain a steady course.

So what with taking forty to fifty readings over the six floors, two or three samples and dashing up to the lab with them, then making the odd adjustment on your return – every half hour – it was rather like the painting of the Forth Bridge really. No sooner had you completed one set – it was time to start the next. Up and down, up and down – my goodness, we must've been fit. Actually, we did have a medical check once a month, which included blood-pressure, weight check, blood and urine sample analysis etc. We sure did have to whiz around on that job and no mistake. But as I say, the pay was good and once you began to understand the workings of it all, it was very interesting.

The other side of the job came sometimes as a drag, sometimes a relief, for you weren't tearing around like a greyhound all the time. The worst of it would be like on the Sunday afternoon, for example, which was the first day of the late shift, when I reported for work having just eaten a substantial Sunday dinner. I met my oppo on the ground floor of the plant. 'Still's shut down' he said, 'and I was just about to climb into the big glass-lined pot on the third floor, to start cleaning it out!'

'Oh no!' I thought, for it was a nice day out and the temperature inside the building must have been well in excess of ninety degrees. And inside the pot it would be even higher – on top of which I'd have to wear full protective clothing, rubber gloves, and clumsy breathing apparatus, whose stout convoluted hose had to come up out of the pot, right across the floor, and out through a window to the outside air. We worked in pairs on this part of the job for safety, your partner standing over the open man-hole into the pot, watching you closely and holding your life-line. This was a stout rope, the other end of which was attached to a broad leather belt around your waist. The idea being that should you be overcome by fumes or heat, or whatever, he could haul you up and out. You changed places about every twenty or thirty minutes so that you had a rest, and a chance to cool down a bit, whilst you watched over him. What a job for a hot Sunday afternoon, replete with roast beef and Yorkshire pud! Still – rough with the smooth – it could be something much more comfortable the next day. You could but hope.

Tonbridge was quite badly hit by flooding that year, soon after I'd started this job in fact. My first real taste of it was when I reported for duty on the night shift, and found my crew-mates gathered on the road outside. The floods had hit our firm and we couldn't get in. Fortunately the stills were shut down at the time, although there was still very important work to be done everywhere. Flooding was no stranger to Tonbridge in those days of course, in fact, it was a fairly regular visitor. So our longer-term personnel knew just what to do in such circumstances – contingency measures having been firmly established – and quite soon a high-slung, narrow-tracked vehicle, such as might be used on a farm, came to our aid, ferrying us across the short causeway which led on to our site. 'Damn and blast!' groaned Jim – 'I was hoping they'd send us home!' Joking of course. I think.

Suitably clad for the occasion, we spent most of the night on the ground floor, raising things up above water level – which was none too easy a task in places – and at times you could imagine you were way out at sea on a large, storm-stricken vessel as you waded thigh-deep in water. But here of course, the water wasn't rising. Or was it?

On our plant – which was numbered P3 – we had a good many pumps, some pressure, some vacuum, mounted on low concrete plinths on the ground floor. These were now submerged, and we had to first locate – then partly dismantle them so that we could bring them up on to dry land. Locating them wasn't too bad, you simply traced the pipework back. But trying to release the fixings and power connexions without your head going under – well, that could be tricky.

At about 0200 I watched Jim Tidy – our number three – swim past, and thought of all those lucky 'normal people', warm, dry, and fast asleep in their beds. But there we are, it made a break from routine – and like everything else on these pages – gave me something to write about.

On another occasion – night shift again – we had some modifications or maintenance work to do on the ground floor of P3, which involved some quite prolonged use of a pneumatic drill, of the kind used by road-workers. The noise was absolutely indescribable! Just imagine it – *in*side the building – which was, by virtue of the open flooring, hollow right up to the roof – about sixty feet up – with nothing whatsoever to absorb or deaden any of it, everything being either steel, stone or glass. We took it in turn to operate the drill, but it mattered not whether you were on it or off it – the whole plant was dominated by this abominable racket! What a night that was – it must have been days before our heads cleared and we stopped shaking. But again, it was something different. Whenever I see people wincing as they pass road workers using these drills – outdoors – I think to myself 'my goodness – you should have been *there* – you'd have done more than wince!'

When we were on night shift – late shift too for that matter – we still had just the one twenty-minute break throughout the shift. But now there was nobody on duty in the canteen to cater for us. So we each had to take it in turn to be 'Cook' for the day – or night – being released from the plant about sixty minutes before breaktime to prepare all the food. Had the meal been the same for everybody, it would have been relatively simple – once you'd found your way around the kitchen – but this was never so. Some would order a good old fry-up – like a breakfast – others would want something with chips, like pie and beans or maybe sausage and eggs. Then there'd be beans on toast, soft roes on toast, bacon sandwiches, or eggs boiled to just the right degree. Some might just want soup. And you always had to make both coffee and tea.

As you can see, there was never anything complicated, even to a raw novice like me, but timing was absolutely crucial – there being so little time in which to tuck it away. Everybody expected their meal to be ready for them the instant they appeared, also that it be at its best, which wanted some doing with everyone coming at the same time – and all wanting something different. And remember, by the time you'd reached the table nearly half your breaktime was gone! And most of us smoked.

But there we are, we all had to do it, and by the time you'd washed up afterwards and left it all ship-shape and Bristol fashion, you'd had at least a two-and-a-half hour break off the plant, which helped to shorten the night.

I had a rather unsettling experience on that job one day. I'd come to the end of my night-shift – everything seemed to happen on that shift – and as things were ticking over quite nicely on the plant, I decided to walk across to the workshop where I knew my oppo would be getting ready to come and relieve me. In this instance it was Ernie Chivers, who was one of a large, well-known Tonbridge family. His brother Bob worked there also, on one of the other crews.

We stood talking a while as I advised him as to the situation on the plant, and as we chatted he took out his 'baccy' tin and began to roll a cigarette. Then quite suddenly, when he was in mid-sentence, open tobacco tin still perched on his raised knee, he just slid sideways and fell to the ground. I thought he'd passed out and quickly raised the alarm. Each crew had in it a qualified first-aider, as well as a qualified fire-fighter and another qualified in matters of civil-defence, and our 'medic' was in the locker room right next door. He heard my shout and was there in an instant, but alas – it was too late. Poor old Ernie had popped his clogs right there as he spoke with me, and was actually dead before he hit the ground. Artificial respiration was tried and resuscitation equipment rushed to the spot, but all attempts to revive him failed.

Poor Ernie – he was so pleased with the bungalow he'd just built, or *had* built, in readiness for his retirement a few years hence. But then, I suppose it was a nice way to go as they say, he certainly knew nothing about it! I went home quite stunned – and had little or no sleep at all that day. I'd seen dead people before – during the war and a couple of times whilst I was in the army – but they hadn't just been in conversation with me! I can picture that moment yet – crystal clear – nearly three and a half decades later as I write.

But life goes on, and we settled back to the task. Christmas came and went, Easter likewise, then suddenly our wedding day was almost upon us. We were still searching for a place in which to set up home – few could afford to buy a house of their own then – not *before* their marriage that is. You usually spent the first two or three years of married life both working and saving hard for a deposit – then you went in search of a mortgage. And these weren't so easy to obtain then either, unlike the following couple of decades or so, when they were practically thrown at you.

I was on the forecourt of Hadlow Garage one day, filling the tank on our Vespa and pondering the approach of 'the big day' – just seven weeks away. Where on earth were we going to live – our searching so far had been fruitless. Just then Mrs Hawkins (the boss' wife) appeared and made her way over to me. 'Are you still looking for new digs?' she asked, knowing this had been the case a while previously. 'Only I'm looking for someone I know I can trust!' Through his job – away from the garage – it was soon to become necessary for Mr Hawkins to go abroad quite often, and that dear lady was rather nervous at the prospect of spending nights with only herself and her daughter Valerie in the house. David and Polly had taken possession of a bungalow about half a mile away – close – but not close enough for the comfort of Mrs H.

'What a shame' I replied, and told her of our impending marriage. Then the thought struck me. 'Now if it was a *flat* you were offering' I ventured, 'I'd have been *more* than interested, and that's a fact!' She pondered this a moment then said – 'That's a thought – leave it with me and I'll talk to my husband about it. Come and see me again tomorrow.' I was really excited as I related this little interlude that evening. 'But what about your job?' asked Margaret, 'when you're on night shift!' 'Oh well,' I responded, 'we'll worry about that when we come to it. Let's see if we get the flat first!'

I called to see Mrs Hawkins next day, full of apprehension. It seemed ages since we'd spoken about it and I wondered how Mr Hawkins had reacted. Happily, my fears were groundless. 'We'll have to call in a plumber so that we can convert one of the bedrooms into a kitchen for you' she said kindly. I could have hugged her. She showed me the rest of the rooms we'd be having, and I was like a dog with two tails. Terms and things were settled, but there remained the question of my job. 'Oh, don't worry about that' I assured her – 'jobs are much easier to acquire than flats – I'll soon find something else!' How times change.

Having secured accommodation seven weeks in advance of our actual moving in, I was able to do all the decorating in plenty of time, and even make a cupboard and shelving as well. Margaret and I then went choosing furniture and carpets and things, and arranging delivery and fitting. The upshot of which was that we returned from our honeymoon in Cornwall and moved straight in – Margaret's dear mother having supervised the delivery and installation of everything in our absence. It was great, and a welcome compensation for us two – it having rained all day and every day throughout our honeymoon! In fact it was several days before either of us could stop waddling.

I carried on at The Distillers for a few weeks, Mr Hawkins being still at home at the time, then set about securing a new job – a job that didn't involve nightwork. And that was when I became a 'Tally Man'. Or to use the correct title – a Credit Salesman.

This got off to a rather dubious start too – although the incident to which I am about to refer occurred before I'd even got the job. In fact, I'd not even set foot on the company's premises then – nor had I met any member of its staff. I was on my way up to London to attend the initial interview, and I'd borrowed Margaret's father's car

– he now being my father-in-law of course. We had no car of our own yet, and I felt that turning up on our scooter mightn't be quite the thing. I poodled confidently up the A20 – these were pre-motorway times remember – in my smart charcoal-grey suit, the one I'd just recently bought to get married in, and my dazzling white shirt, smart tie and nicely polished shoes. As I travelled I wondered what being a Credit Salesman involved.

Suddenly the engine began to cough and splutter rather ominously, and feeling it was just about to conk out altogether, I quickly steered her on to the grass verge out of the way. I lifted the bonnet and peered in. Nothing obvious – but hang on a minute – what was this strong smell of petrol, and why was the outside of the carburetter damp? I felt around a bit with my bare hands – not having any tools with me – but succeeded only in coating them liberally in black sludgy stuff, which also managed to find its way under my nicely scrubbed finger-nails. Nice, I thought, *that* should help.

I remembered passing an RAC patrol van, parked in a lay-by about a mile back. So I looked around Dad's car in the hope of finding the appropriate membership badge. Ah – what's this lovely bright badge on the front grille? Damn and blast – AA rather than RAC! And no sign of the AA anywhere right then. So I hoofed it back to the lay-by – trying to keep my filthy hands wide of my almost new suit – in the hope that I might appeal to the better side of the RAC man and enlist his help. 'After all' – I assured him – 'Had it been *my* car I'd have been in the RAC – not that other lot!' Whether or not he believed me, he came up trumps and drove me back to my sad looking little chariot.

Having all the necessary tools on board, he was soon able to rectify the fault, which I could easily have done myself if *I'd* had any. It was only a jet which had worked loose in the carburettor, then slowly unscrewed itself, allowing too much fuel to pass – causing it to flood. I thanked this good Samaritan – who was pleased anyway to have been of such timely help – and tried to do something with my hands. I found a grubby looking piece of rag in the boot, and gave them a jolly good rub. Unfortunately, this took very little off – but did manage to spread it around more evenly. If I'd wiped it around my face as well, I could quite easily have auditioned for the 'Black and White Minstrel Show' I should think. Might even have been rich and famous by now! I rather doubt that though – I can't sing a note.

I backed off the verge and resumed my journey, knowing full well that I'd had it anyway. After all, I was an hour adrift already and I'd a way to go yet. And look at the state of me! But how wrong can you be? Mr Phillips – the Sales-manager – welcomed me with outstretched hand. I offered mine, then hesitated when I caught sight of the mess it was in, but he took it anyway. He listened to my explanation as to why I was so late, then, glancing at his own hand, accepted it with a grin. Two good Samaritans in one day! And as you'll have gathered – I got the job.

And I'd not had one like this before. After collecting my vehicle on day one – a smart little Austin A35 – it was loaded with three hundred poundsworth of goods, under the guidance of Mr Phillips, who knew what I was likely to need. Thirty-odd years later, you can see that £300 was a fair amount then, something like about seven thousand quids-worth I reckon. The necessary paraphernalia was popped into my brief-case – order forms, sales-sheets, price-lists, bank paying-in book etc., and some 'Day Books' (ledgers) were placed aboard somewhere.

The beauty of this job was that I only had to call in at the main office and showroom, in London, once a week. All the local reps – of whom there were about thirty-five, I think, and whose areas were relatively close to the office – had to go in every day, but the four 'country' reps, of which I was now one, would have lost too much time to-ing and fro-ing. So I was my own man for most of the time. But Thursday, my day in London, was always extremely hectic and I couldn't wait to get back home and unwind. How those locals put up with it every day I couldn't imagine, for several of them were ladies, and mighty smart and attractive they were too, but they all got the rough edge of the Sales Manager's tongue as he bawled them out quite regularly.

I inherited an established route – the previous guy having received the order of the boot – for some or other inadequacy or indiscretion, and I had a fair amount of 'cleaning up' to do. By which I mean the withholding of goods that certain of my clients longed to get their hands on – whilst I concentrated on collecting some of the very considerable arrears. This had to be done in a most tactful manner, which wasn't always easy with some of them, who could become quite aggressive.

The system operated thus. A 'canvasser' would open up a new area, tempting the housewives with a 'one-off' sale. This could be one of several things; a set of the latest saucepans for example, or a handsome colour portrait of the children – where appropriate. 'And it'll only cost you half a crown a week!, – was their main sales pitch. It was all right for them – they had the easy bit – they only had to persuade the client to accept this offer and sign on the dotted line, then they were gone – off to some other area. The client took possession of these goods – for a mere half-crown – and was generally quite happy. Until the following week. For that was when we came into the picture, intent mainly on collecting the next half-crown, but also to assess the prospects of further business.

And I must say, I surprised myself here, for I very quickly became quite wily. Without the client realising it, we had to 'pump' away, in an effort to build up a complete picture of the family. How many children, their ages, how many of them were working, what jobs they did, how much they earned, what their interests were. One tack might be...... 'Wilson?' – pause and frown – 'Wilson! *I* know a Wilson – Arthur Wilson, drives a Green Line bus! That wouldn't be him would it?' 'No,' – would come the reply – 'my husband's name's Fred, and he works at the gasworks. And he couldn't drive a bloody bus anyway – it's as much as he can do to handle his old Ford Prefect!'

'Oh well, my mistake' you'd say – hastily entering on your note pad – 'Boiler-suits, sturdy Work-Shirts, pair of Wing-mirrors, Footpump, Picnic set, Roofrack. For we sold practically everything on that job, from watches to washing machines, lingerie to carpets and furniture, cycles to lawn-mowers, children's toys to the most up-to-date cameras. The complete range of ladies' and gents' fashion wear, made-to-measure suits, shoes, bedding – the lot! And all good stuff – Axminster, Wilton, G-Plan, Hornby, Meccano, Raleigh, Pedigree, Slumberland, Dunlopillo etc. So you can see how tempting it was to some folk, when they saw the stock we carried, and glanced through the catalogues covering the larger items. You can see also just how much there was for me to acquaint myself with in a very short time, for the training period was one week.

Anyway, off I set on that first day, glad that Mr Phillips was in the seat beside me, for I felt a bit like 'Flash Gordon' – heading into the unknown. Supposing I couldn't sell? I know I'd had no trouble selling the cigarettes and confectionery – three or four years before – but I didn't actually have to *sell* that stuff, I really only had to do little more than take their orders. Neither did I have to collect any cash. On this job, whilst it was very important to achieve maximum sales – exploring the full potential of the area – by golly, you had to be sure to collect everything that was due as well. Selling,in fact, was as easy as falling off a log in many cases, particularly to those on low income, who'd have cleared you out on the spot. But trying to collect the cash afterwards – that was a totally different kettle of fish!!!

I became known to my customers as the 'Tuesday man', or 'Friday man' – or whichever day of the week I happened to call on them. But never of course, was I the 'Thursday man' – for that was my day up in the 'metrolops'. Ugh! I had some very good customers – eventually – who bought lots of things from me and paid on the nail, without any trouble at all. Which, needless to say, was a most enjoyable situation all round – they were happy, I was happy, and there was no bawling out for me on Thursdays. But in those early weeks I was led a fair old dance by those 'less-desirables', and would have loved to have got my hands on the canvasser who'd lumbered us with them in the first place. Preferably in the area of the throat!

But looking back, I can see the humour of those little battles I had, trying to prise the money out of the D.S.s. 'D.S.', by the way, was what appeared – in large red letters – at the head of those sheets in the sales ledger relating to those people we were trying to weed out. They simply meant DON'T SERVE! But in no way were we to let them become aware of our tactics, which were to sell them absolutely nothing – without actually saying *no* to them – and continue collecting, in dribs and drabs usually, the money they owed – until their account was clear. Then it was 'tatty-bye' and good riddance.

Occasionally somebody would submit to the pressure and actually sell something to a D.S. And boy, didn't they cop it when Mr Phillips got hold of them – which was usually on a Thursday with about forty of us looking on. Rather reminiscent of bath-time in The Homes, when we were all compelled to witness the punishment of poor old John Wakeman. For it was Mr Phillips himself who entered all these special instructions in our ledgers, and *he* wasn't fooling around!

Some used to give you all sorts of excuses as to why they couldn't pay you that week. 'My mother's been very ill and I've spent it all on bus fares visiting her,' they'd say. 'But don't worry – I'll pay double next week!' So you'd enter 2 WNW, – in the space where you should have been entering the half-crown or whatever it was that they should have paid. You couldn't be too hard on them, for after all – how could you be certain they weren't telling the truth? You just hoped Mr Phillips would go along with it too. And that particular entry by the way – if you haven't already guessed – meant two weeks next week.

I've seen me finish the bulk of my calls for the day, go home to Hadlow, then later in the evening – after a nice meal – drive out maybe fifteen or twenty miles to a call where they'd been out when I'd called earlier on, in the hope of collecting two or three shillings! But my persistence paid off in the end, for I did indeed finish up with the optimum route – fairly high sales and no dodgy payers.

But it was still a fairly demanding business, for you were constantly expected to improve on your sales. To which end we'd have pretty regular promotions, as an encouragement. It might be a promotion on soft furnishings, or carpets, or maybe bedroom suites. Probably anything we may be overloaded with at the time. There was nothing in it for the customers mind, they paid the full price and there were no give-aways. But the prizes offered to the top salesman – or woman – were generally well worth going for. This might be a record player (music-centres weren't here then), or a smart camera, or a quality wristwatch maybe. I didn't do too badly I suppose, I once won some books of Green Shield Trading Stamps, which were well worth having, and I remember winning a portable radio, which wasn't. Worth having I mean – it was without question a portable radio – but too tinny for my ear I'm afraid.

The first few weeks were the worst, for I'd not only to win the confidence of the worthwhile customers, I'd also to match the wiles and guiles of the others. I'd pull up right outside the house, walk down the path and knock at the front door. Nothing – absolutely deserted. I'd try again later and get the same result. It could be quite demoralising when you got several on the trot like this, especially as Thursday approached!

Then one day, just as I was about to drive dejectedly off after one such call, I saw a slight movement of the front room curtain. 'Crafty blighters!' I thought – or words to that effect – and decided to drive around the block and come back again. Only this time I stopped quite a bit short of the house – in the tuck of a slight bend. I walked from here to the house, hugging the hedges and things of the gardens I was passing, then finally nipped quietly down the path and knocked at the door. I could hear voices from within, relaxed now in the knowledge that the danger had passed for another week. The look of astonishment and guilt was something to behold as the woman calmly opened the door, then realised who I was. But it was too late now, and after a few moans and groans she'd cough up!

On other occasions I'd leave my vehicle similarly parked, then leg it to the house, knock at the front door and instantly dash round the side and crouch low outside the kitchen door at the back. I could imagine their reaction upon hearing my knock, for they'd realise it was the Tuesday Man or whatever – then with hushed voices they'd tip-toe quickly to the back of the house and hide in the kitchen till they thought I'd gone. Then, as their chatter resumed I'd knock on the back door. Gotcha!

As I say, I became quite wily through this sort of thing – proper cat and mouse it was – and Margaret noticed this change in me. But I'd taken this job on, and by Jiminy I was going to do it. But I must say, I find it quite incredible now, when I recall the lengths to which I'd go to collect those half-crowns. Tenacity I guess you'd call it – part of the make-up of the old 'Bulldog Breed'!

Eventually I succeeded in cleaning up the route, but it was still not really my kind of job and I wasn't happy at it. I guess my nervous system or something reflected this feeling, for after some months my hair – normally thick and wavy – went dead straight. It was still thick, but straight and lank. So I decided to discard the title of 'Tally-man' and seek pastures new.

Usually, I'd fix my next job up before severing myself from the current one, but so anxious was I to get away that the next time I saw Mr Phillips, I handed him my resignation. He was visibly shaken by this action, and bade me sit down for a moment to talk things over. 'After all' he said, 'our 'country reps' have to be something of a *special* breed – being on their own most of the time – people we know we can trust, and rely upon. And your route is now one of the cleanest of the lot, with good sales figures too!' I tried to explain how I felt, but he managed to put up a much stronger argument than I could, and finally persuaded me to carry on. 'You've *done* all the hard work' he pointed out in conclusion, 'it can only get *better* now!'

But it didn't, although I *was* trying to see it in a different light now. So two or three weeks later, there we sat once again – either side of his desk – as I tried valiantly to make him see it my way. But again he out-talked me and slid my envelope back across the desk.

It was said at the time – by various friends and acquaintances – that I had the 'gift of the gab'. Well, this was quite true to a point, I had to admit – particularly since I'd been in this job. But he was much higher up the ladder than I was, so it was quite obvious that his gift was that much stronger than mine. The 'gift of the gob' most probably.

I left his office and drove home, quite disappointed at my failure to do what I knew I should have to do quite soon now. It was only a question of time. And I kept looking at my hair. 'I think it's beginning to fall out now,' I groaned to Margaret one morning – 'if it isn't I think it jolly soon will be!' I'd never ever seen it looking like this – it was as though I was looking at somebody else through a window rather than at my own reflection in the shaving mirror. But, she assured me it wasn't, so I donned the harness again and trotted off to see my customers, who by now had indeed been pruned down to the best of them. Which helped quite a bit of course, but didn't alter the fact. Go I must.

Before I move on from this episode, I must say how nice it was at Christmas on that job. There were lots of children, of all ages, in the families on whom I called. And we did everything in the way of toys and gifts. From Hornby train-sets and accessories, and Meccano in all grades, both mentioned previously, to cricket and football gear. Oh, and 'Scalectrix' or whatever it was called, was 'in' at the time. Then there were lovely dolls prams and pushchairs for the girls, and the most beautiful dolls that did almost everything. Teddy bears, scooters, and super bicycles and tricycles – including the old favourite 'Mickey Mouse' trike – and those smart little pedal cars that used to smash into everyone's ankles. Building bricks and things for the toddlers, roller-skates, jigsaw puzzles, paintboxes. And we could cater just as fully for every other age group too – short of a full-size car or yacht! The excitement and anticipation of those kids was quite infectious as Christmas Eve drew nearer and nearer, and I began to get some idea of how old Santa must have felt as he edged his way carefully down the chimneys. I don't know how *he* gets on nowadays come to think of it, with all this central heating.

But troughs follow peaks, and after Christmas it was quite hard-going initially, with fairly low sales. Maybe a bit of winter clothing, the odd electric blanket, or if there was snow about, possibly a toboggan or two. But little else for a while, so – back to the gloom.

I found myself driving past the Turf Company one morning, (miles off my route) in the Spring of '62. I was a bit cheesed off, so I tarried awhile and let my thoughts wander, as I took in the old familiar scene. I really had enjoyed my spell on there a couple of years back, and was certainly a lot happier then. 'Ah well' I thought aloud to myself, as I slipped the gear lever into first, then, just as I was about to move off, who should suddenly appear close by but Harold! He spotted me instantly and came over. I got out of the vehicle and we shook hands. I think this was our first encounter since I'd left in the late summer of 1960. We stood chatting and swapping pleasantries. 'My secretary left you know' he suddenly informed me, though I can't remember now whether he gave a reason for her departure. 'And I've got a foreman now who comes from Gravesend. But he's no bloody good, and I think his days are numbered!' Apparently none of the lads could get along with this chap at all – and some really despised him.

'Don't suppose you'd consider joining us again would you?' he asked, and somehow I just knew that question would come. The gloom began to lift quickly from me, and I felt a nice kind of stirring inside. 'Could be' – I tried to sound as casual as my excitement would allow – 'let's talk about it'. Mind you, it didn't matter what we might say now; I knew I was going back! We strolled across and looked at the comparatively new office – small and cosy but quite adequate. The rest of the building programme had also been completed, more or less. There were still a good many apple trees to be grubbed out though, for that was a fill-in job when things were quiet on the main work-front – mainly during high summer.

So once more our eyes met across Mr Phillip's desk up in London, and back went my envelope again. But this time I was very much more determined about it and he sensed this right away, putting up practically no resistance at all. So it was third time lucky for me, although luck didn't really come into it, for I was going anyway. 'Shame' he said, as we eventually shook hands again at the door of his office – and I thought back to the state my hand was in the last time he'd taken it – 'good country reps aren't easy to come by, and you've done a really good job on that route!' I thanked him for his kind words. 'If ever you change your mind......' he concluded. Then I was gone.

There is another memory from that era – which very nearly escaped me in fact – although when I read back through this I'm sure I'll think of a good many that did!

It was company policy on the Credit Sales job that all our vehicles be fitted with burglar alarms – obviously a stipulation imposed by the Insurance Company – and the last thing we all had to do on our Thursday trip to the main office and showrooms was to have our alarm tested. Which must, in retrospect, have been rather a noisy affair I should think, with about forty of them all sounding off at once. With a few strings for accompaniment, I think we might even have taken a shot at the finale of Mozart's Horn Concerto No. 4 – although I'm pretty certain the English Chamber Orchestra's version would have been infinitely less cacophonous!

Whenever we left our vehicle unattended – even if only for a few seconds – we had to set the alarm by inserting a key into a 'Yale' type lock situated immediately behind the driver's door on the outside of the vehicle, and turning it a quarter turn. Much as we do to actuate the car door lock nowadays. To unset – or disarm it you simply turned the key back again.

Alarms were not I believe, so much a part of the everyday scene in those days – well over thirty years ago – as they are today. Neither I suspect, were they as sophisticated, although the latter of these observations is more speculative. With *our* alarms, which would have been most up-to-date at the time, the circuit was made the instant a door, the bonnet, or the boot-lid was opened – even a fraction. This immediately set the horn blaring, and the only way to stop it was with the key. One's instinct – on setting it off inadvertently – would be to quickly slam the door or bonnet shut again. No joy I'm afraid – you had to have the key!

Living in the flat at the garage as we were then, I used to park my vehicle overnight, full of stock, on a piece of waste ground immediately behind the garage itself, where some of their own vehicles generally stood. It was handy there, at the same time out of the way, yet still well within view of our kitchen window.

On this occasion Mr Hawkins was abroad somewhere, so Mrs H was alone in their part of the accommodation, although I've a feeling daughter Valerie might well have been there too. Whichever, we all went to our beds at the end of the day, the sandman came, and off we went to dreamland.

At about 0130 I was yanked from a lovely deep sleep into full consciousness, when this terrible blaring noise suddenly pierced the deep-purple peacefulness of the night. I shook my head, wriggled my fingers in my ears, but no.....it was still there! 'What on earth's *that*?' asked Margaret sleepily, just as the penny had dropped and I was leaping out of bed for all I was worth. 'It's that blasted burglar alarm on my motor' I thundered, grabbing for my socks in the dark; 'something's triggered it off!'

I dashed into our sitting room in the dark (I'd decided for some reason to leave all the lights off) to collect my car-keys from their usual resting place on the sideboard. Thus armed, and clad only in pyjamas and slippers, I descended the stairs in about two jumps, then shot through the front door and out on to the somewhat pot-holed forecourt – due any day now for resurfacing.

It was raining – isn't it always on such occasions? – and I had to run the full one-

hundred-or-so-feet length of the forecourt, then up the side of the garage itself to
reach the source of this really appalling racket. And of course, in the pitch-dark – and
by the law of Sod – I must have found every one of those mini-craters as I splashed
my way hurriedly along this course. I got soaked! But so anxious was I to kill the
noise that I didn't notice it too much at the time. I could imagine bedroom lights
coming on one after the other in the immediate neighbourhood, and a few polite
requests pouring lustily from angrily flung windows.

After what seemed an age, but could only have been a minute or so, I reached my
vehicle. The place appeared to be deserted, so I figured it must have been a short in
the circuit, although I must say, I was giving little real thought to the possibility of
prowlers right then. I offered the keys to the lock, and fumbled like a cow with a
musket as I tried to find the right one. If only I'd had time to grab a torch! 'Come on,
come *on*!' I cursed as I fumbled on, the noise now deafeningly close to my ear. Then
it dawned on me; in my haste – and in the dark – I'd grabbed Margaret's keys by
mistake!

Dogs were beginning to bark and I fancied I heard Mabel's parrot giving it some
as I hop-scotched my way back along the forecourt – the horn blasting merrily away.
I would probably have *missed* more of the craters had I paid less heed to them,
instead of which I retraced every damned splosh!! I kicked off my carpet sponges at
the door, and rushed barefoot up the stairs to grab the right keys. And *this* time, a
torch! Back along the now illuminated forecourt I dashed, unable to believe I'd
found quite so many pot-holes on the two previous laps – for it wasn't really *that*
bad. I duly disarmed the little peace-breaker, then after a quick look round, now
aided by the beam of the torch, made my way calmly – if a bit breathlessly – back to
the house. It was so quiet now it was eerie. And – panic over and torch in hand – my
feet found unbroken ground with every step. A classic example of 'more haste, less
speed'!

'Gosh!' said dear Mrs H as we re-grouped on the landing afterwards, 'I think you
were *ever* so brave – rushing out there like that.' I looked at her quizzically. 'Well
just think' she continued – '*anything* could have been lying in wait for you out there
in the dark......and you in only your pyjamas!'

And she was right too, as it happened – about the danger I mean – for we learned
from our village Bobby next morning (was it Frank Lomax – or had he retired by
then and passed the cuffs and truncheon on to Sergeant Eldrett?) that two prisoners
had in fact escaped from Borstal that night – about twelve to fifteen miles from us –
and were known to have headed in our direction!

'Probably wanted to swap their getaway car' he suggested – as we related our
little incident – 'in order to throw us off the scent!' But by all accounts they'd had

their collars felt again by now and were safely re-incarcerated. 'So there's no need to worry now' he assured us, as he pocketed his notebook and made his departure.

To tell the truth, I don't know *what* was in my mind as I leapt from my bed and hurtled off – other than a most urgent desire to stop the infernal racket those two desperados had set off when they'd managed to prise open my bonnet a crack. But the alarm proved its worth; it must have frightened 'em very near to death I should think, for they took to their heels the moment it went off and were nowhere to be seen when I blundered on to the scene moments later. I've often wondered though as to the outcome of this little incident – had they still been there when my soggy, pyjama clad figure burst in on them. Brandishing no more than a bunch of keys at that!

I must say, it felt great swapping the suit and tie for jeans and casual shirt as I returned to the turfing scene, although in truth I was equally at home in either. It was just that I knew where I was going......all that lovely fresh air and sunshine. Certainly, there'd be frozen hands, rain-sodden clothing, and all the hazards of winter too – but that was yonks away – there was all the Spring, all the Summer, and all of Autumn to come first. And I stepped right back in as though I'd never left.

Sure enough, the guy from Gravesend wasn't long in leaving, at which point I was appointed foreman, and it was almost as though we'd gone back in time to where Harold had offered me this position in the first place. The things we do! Still, I'd had a couple of experiences I might otherwise have missed. *And* learned a bit.

Of all the jobs I've had – both before and since those times – people find it hard to understand why I look back on that one with such fondness. A fondness shared I'm sure, by several of the others who were on there at the time. Bob Fairweather, his younger brother Bunt, Harold's son Dave, John Sands, Doug (Doogal) Jenner, Brian Stanley, old Uncle Tom Cob...... no, hang on, he was with another lot wasn't he? Then there were the three Peters – Cheddar, Cookie and Pheasant – names I'd given them so they'd know who I was calling, and which I'd derived from their surnames which were Cheeseman, Cook and Peacock respectively. For as I've said earlier, it could be a real b------ of a job in winter. But as I've also said earlier, there was this really close comradeship, when we needed to pull hard together to get out of a particularly tight spot for example, or even play hard together in high summer when both the demand for turf and the prosect of cutting it were fairly minimal. *Then* we'd have some sport in the turf-field I can tell you – having first justified our being there of course.

But hardship first. Well – one at least. It wasn't in winter as it happens, but conditions were rather wet and boggy, which was the main drawback. But it's funny how one thing can trigger off another.

We were cutting at a farm in Withyham, just over the Sussex border I believe. It was a Saturday, and as I left for work Margaret asked, as she usually would, 'What time do you think you'll be home?' 'Oh – somewhere around the middle of the day I should think' I replied. We weren't excessively busy, and normal finishing time on Saturdays was twelve noon. 'So what time shall I have dinner ready then – about one?' 'That sounds fine' I answered, 'I'll be well home by then!'

The farm was well in off the public highway, but there was a hard road all the way to it, so that was fine. And to reach the field we were cutting that day we had to drive through the farmyard, down a tree-lined track, then across a couple of ploughed fields, and there we were. When I say *across* the ploughed fields, I mean sticking to the headlands of course, where the ground is firm and uncultivated! We'd taken three lorries that day, which we would load up ready for Monday's deliveries.

We made our way down to the field in question without incident, then we mowed and we cut and we stacked and we loaded, all in good heart, with a whole week-end to ourselves at the end of it. We laughed and joked as we worked, and discussed our plans for the week-end. Eventually the last lorry was loaded and roped on, so we secured all the field equipment (which always stayed in the field) for the weekend, and began the long-ish haul up to the road.

The first lorry set off and entered the first of the ploughed fields, keeping strictly to the headlands, then into the second – same again – then it entered this track, after which it would be easy going with hard road all the way out. The track, by the way, was a rather attractive feature, for the trees that lined each side arched over at the top, forming something of a long bower. As I've indicated, it was on a slight gradient, say, one in eight, running down from the farmyard. But it was well made up with hardcore, so we didn't expect problems here.

How wrong can you be?! About a third of the way up the track the gremlins struck, and what a different complexion *that* put on the scene! Wheel-spin had developed, making progress extremely slow and difficult, and prolonged attempts to make it only succeeded in causing the hardcore to spew up out of the tracks, eventually jamming tightly against the differential housing and spare wheel carrier, which had already sunk to surface level anyway. At length we gave up trying. She was well and truly stuck, and it would take a good deal of effort and sweat to extricate her now. And both the other lorries were on the wrong side of her, which was really bad news, for they were all we had to travel home in, having left the vans back in our yard.

We considered the options, the best of which was to tow her out. Our fork-lift tractor was – fortunately – up in the farmyard – *ahead* of her. The only trouble was, we usually needed to have a loaded pallet on the forks – which were rear-mounted – to improve her grip. And all the pallets were back in the turf field. But we decided to give it a try and hope for the best – after all, the trees were too close to the sides of the lorry to do much else – like off-loading and taking her up empty.

The stout wire hawser was set in place, the strain taken up, then, with our shoulders all thrust into the back of the lorry, up went the shout 'Come on lads – go for it!' But try as we might – with practically no room to manoeuvre – she refused to budge. The unladen tractor, which wasn't even equipped with differential-lock, just stood and spun, as did the lorry – plastering us lot with mud into the bargain!

Faces dropped as we fell back on option two, which was for some of us to trudge all the way back for some pallet boards – which were very heavy to carry, being of stout construction – and the rest to start off-loading about three hundred turves to the rear, and manhandle another hundred or so to the ground in front of the lorry so that we could stack them on to a pallet to ballast the tractor. With no room to move round the sides of the wagon this was no easy task. But we made it with a fair bit of sweating and swearing, and an air of confidence returned, lifting slightly the glum expressions on some of our faces. Mind you, even if we were successful in this attempt to get her out, we'd still to retrieve the off-loaded turf and re-load it on to the lorry up in the farmyard. We'd also to make good the track, in readiness for the other two waiting lorries.

Well, with a supreme effort, we finally managed to draw that wagon up and into the farmyard. 'Hooray' whooped 'Pheasant' – 'looks like I'll make it to the flicks tonight after all!' The hawser was removed, and the tractor made towards the track to collect the off-loaded turves, which had now been stacked on pallets.

And would you believe it – that damned tractor, normally so reliable, decided that this might be a good time to break down. And break down it did!

Down went the faces again, as we reassessed the situation. Two loaded lorries down in the field, their only way out blocked by three pallets of turf, the means with which to remove this obstacle standing knackered up in the farmyard, and the only wagon that was high and dry now sporting only two thirds of a load! We could hardly take her home like that – the sum total of a whole day's graft – by about seven or eight of us!

The time now was mid- to late afternoon, and I'd not had the opportunity to let Margaret know that I'd be '*a bit late*'. I wondered how my dinner was looking now, sitting on the 'top' keeping warm. We'd none of us any food left, what little we'd taken – being Saturday – had all been polished off by mid-morning – after all, we'd be home by midday anyway. Cigarette packets and tobacco tins were all dangerously low now too – you tend to smoke more under situations of stress. I thought about my dinner again, and decided I could sit and eat it right this minute, *whatever* it looked like! And I'm sure everyone else had similar thoughts.

'Well I reckon there's only one thing for it now' said Harold – 'we'll have to carry those turves up to the top in armloads!' What a thought!! They weighed all of twenty pounds each and were quite muddy. If you took say five at a time – held in front of you – by the time you'd stumbled up that rough track and reached the top they'd feel more like a ton than a hundredweight. But there was no alternative, so we buckled to, and I'll tell you this – nobody managed five at a time – not after the initial trip. More like two I should think. But we none the less made it, then set about repairing the track.

It was mid-evening before we'd finished this operation, and quite dark. Pheasant's chances of snuggling up in the back row were no more than a memory now. Still – if we could get *home* that'd be something! We were all quite knackered, dirty, and starving hungry, and down to a few manky-looking dog-ends between us. But our spirits lifted a little when we heard the distant sound of the second lorry making its way towards the bottom of the track. The drone of the engine got a little louder, then louder still as it neared the track, and there we all stood – with bated breath. 'Come on, come *on*'. We were all willing it on. Then suddenly all went quiet. The cab door slammed shut. 'Oh *no*!' we all groaned in unison – 'not something else!'

We started down the track to see what had happened, and met Bob I think it was, on his way up. 'Soddin' half-shaft's gone I think' – he said in a tone that fully reflected his utter despondency – 'I can't get her to move at all!'

So – there wasn't a celluloid cat in hell's chance of moving *her* for a few days – not with that sort of problem, and she was now blocking the path of the third lorry. We re-grouped up at the top again and considered our prospects once more.

It was pitch dark now, and we were all but dead. Well, it felt as though we were anyway. 'Stupid bloody tractor!' growled Dougal, swinging a kick at one of its back wheels. Then – 'Ouch!' as his foot bounced back – the heel digging into the shin of his other leg! We were all fully in accord with his sentiments of course, for if ever there was a time for her to break down........!

Then amongst the mumbling and grumbling, somebody suddenly piped up – 'Listen. *Listen*!' We all fell silent and cocked an ear. Sure enough – there it was – the distant drone of an engine. It gradually grew louder as the vehicle left the furthest of the ploughed fields and entered the next. 'What the hell....?' began Harold incredulously, knowing the situation regarding Bob's lorry. On it came, a steady, fairly high-pitched even tone. We all looked at each other – in total disbelief – yet secretly hopeful.

And then it happened. The tone suddenly changed to one of urgency and franticness (there *is* such a word) – and we knew only too well what that meant! Down the track we trudged again, quite dispirited now and fully resigned to what we knew – without any shadow of doubt – awaited us. (Sounds a bit like Gerard Hoffner and the barrel of bricks – all this up-ing and down-ing!) And sure enough – the last straw had indeed hit the camel's back. I can't remember now just who was driving the third lorry, but he'd decided to try and make it by rushing past Bob's stricken lorry as fast as he could – in the hope that he could get through that bit of ploughed ground and back onto the headland in front of it – then on and up to the track. But he'd succeeded only in going from bad to worse, for with ten tons of turf aboard there was no chance. As soon as he left the headland – down he went – right up to his axles.

So that was it. We were forced to abandon two out of the three lorries for the time being. And the tractor sat there like a stuffed shirt. Several bothers and blasts were uttered as we dragged ourselves back up that track, where we completed the load on the first lorry and roped it on, all in the pitch dark. Then somehow the whole lot of us clambered aboard – some on top of the load I guess – and finally set course for Hadlow.

'Hallo' I said to Margaret, as I arrived home one hour before midnight. 'I expect my dinner's had it – hasn't it?' What an understatement! Poor Margaret was totally fed up, and had been worried too of course, with me not keeping her informed. But could she have been as fed up as we all were?

We gathered in the 'yard' as usual on the Monday morning, all fully recovered now, and had a damned good laugh about it all. At least we'd made it home, and nobody had come off any worse – or better – than anyone else. 'I'd already seen that picture anyway!' said Pete (Pheasant), although we all knew he wouldn't have seen much of it in any case, even if he had been home in time. Not in the back row he wouldn't!

I went into some detail over that particular incident to give a bit of an idea of how involved things could get now and then. There were countless others like it – over the years I spent at it – and all just as trying, though some to a maybe lesser degree regarding the duration. So I won't bother to enlarge on any more of them at this point.

Instead I'll switch to the lighter side I think. Like the fun we'd have in the turf field in high Summer. Being lads – for the most part – we were always wrestling and tussling with each other, like a bunch of tiger-cubs I suppose, and that was mostly quite enjoyable. But occasionally we'd compete with each other in other ways. Such as selecting a nice hazel-wand each from the hedgerow or a nearby nut-plat, then rolling a lump of sticky mud into a pellet – like a piece of plasticine – and sticking it on the tip. You'd all stand in line, then, lifting your wand up and behind you you'd bring it swiftly forward like a whip. Your pellet would fly off the end at great velocity – if you were lucky – and the object of course was to see who could get furthest. If this went on for any length of time there'd be a certain penalty to pay, for you'd have a mighty stiff old arm and shoulder next morning!

Then, if we could find anything resembling a discus we'd thrash away at that until an overall champion had been established. More aching arms! One day there was a shout from Bob. 'Look what I've found' he whooped, 'this'll be good!' The rest of us moseyed over to see what marvel he'd unearthed, and were quite astonished to see that he was holding – cupped in both hands – what appeared to be an outsize cannon-ball. What it was or where it had come from goodness only knows, unless it was part of an old leg-restraint from medieval times – the old ball and chain job! Mind you, it was so heavy that I should think if anyone *had* tried to run off with that attached to their ankle – they'd have left their whole leg behind. But we never found any leg bones, so I don't know what it could have been.

We all realised the potential of this particular find, although I think some were regarding it's size and weight with a certain amount of trepidation. Nevertheless, a line was drawn on the ground, and so began the Shot-Putting contest. 'Me first,' said Bob – 'finder's privilege!' With these words he raised it and held it tucked between chin and shoulder, knees buckling a wee bit as he did so, and prepared to set the standard. We didn't bother with all that twirling on the spot business – like whirling Dervishes – I think we'd have probably knocked ourselves out if we had. We simply toed the line, summoned all our strength, then hurled it forward as hard as we could.

'Clear the way' called Bob as he prepared to send it hurtling on it's way, and we all stood back. We needn't have bothered – for although Bob was a good strong 20 year-old, and very competitive – the thing landed with a thud no more than a yard ahead of him. We all fell about at this, but really the laugh was on us, for although we went on for a good-ish time – well into the afternoon – nobody could match Bob's first attempt, including Bob himself. My that thing was heavy, and strive as we might, the contest ended with Bob as undisputed champion. We couldn't have gone on much longer anyway, for safety's sake – for as our arms grew weaker and weaker the thing was landing so short that you had to pull your feet back quickly for fear of getting your toes crushed! And I reckon a tidy few worms would have gone home that day with a jolly fine headache too!

Well, if we thought throwing the javelin – which we also fitted in at times – and the discus was an arm-aching business, we were in for a shock next morning. We all looked at each other as we grouped in the yard, desperately trying not to move even the fingers of our throwing arms – they ached so. Well it wasn't so much that they ached, they were *so* stiff that any slight movement sent the most awful pain searing through them. Just like the jabs those sadistic blighters had administered to us in the army! And we had a whole day's work ahead of us yet.

But we managed it of course – with a good many oooh's and aaah's – and when the stiffness had gone, some days later, off we went again. Occasionally we'd play football for a change. But I must repeat, we fitted all this kind of activity around the work, when we weren't too busy. Most times of year it was backs bent and hard at it! I can't remember how we passed quiet times in mid-winter – I think we were always busy doing maintenance or repair work in the yard, and looking after the stock. For we had at one time 1500 laying hens, 150 geese, and about a hundred rabbits. Then there were umpteen pallet boards to repair and things like that.

There was another pastime in which we'd indulge ourselves at times, although I cannot now remember the objective of this one. It would involve a good-sized tree right on the river bank, for there was usually a river running through or around the turf field. A long, stout rope would be attached to the back of one of the tractors, the other end slung over a limb of the tree. The limb always had to be one that stretched right out and over the river. The tractor was moved slowly forwards or backwards, with somebody clutching the rope and dangling over the river – and there we are – I just cannot remember the rest! But wait a minute........ it's coming back........! Yes – I've got it.

As the tractor moved slowly away from the river bank – with you standing near the edge, holding t'other end of the rope – the point would come when all the slack had been taken up and you began to swing out. The tractor would stop at the very moment your feet left the ground, and unless you shinned up that rope pretty damn quick, you were in trouble. For as you struggled upwards for all you were worth the tractor started reversing towards the bank again, giving you a sensation similar to that of running the wrong way on an escalator!

Your aim was to reach the limb of the tree without getting wet, then climb back down to safety. That of the tractor driver was to see that you didn't! But everybody had a turn on the tractor so we all had equal chance – you just hoped that when it was you holding the rope – the driver wasn't too skilful with his gear change. Of course, the success rate wasn't always 100%, which meant a jolly good dunking for somebody, but it was all good fun and we never lost anybody. At least I don't think we did – although come to think of it – I haven't seen young Nigel Leftley since those times!!

I should imagine 'Cheddar' would have had the record number of dunkings at that particular game, for he really was a bit of a nut, and got up to some crazy things. He was also rather accident prone, for if adversity was going to strike it was mostly him that it homed in on. For instance, we were mowing and raking off in the field, at the height – and the heat – of Summer. We were all stripped off as usual, and looking like chunks of mahogany. Cheddar was raking ,with the usual long-handled grass rake, and he suddenly turned it upside down and started using it as a vaulting pole.

He was only hopping across the rows of hay – but in his usual clumsy manner. 'Bet you couldn't clear that quickthorn!' said somebody. Cheddar eyed the hedge, which wasn't that tall. 'Who couldn't?' he replied, chuffed at the challenge. 'Watch this!'

He took a run at it and at the right moment dug the end of his 'pole' into the ground and began to hurl himself up. Almost instantly – but not before he'd committed himself – the rake handle snapped and down came Cheddar, slap-bang on top of the hedge. 'Yeoooow!' he hollered, as countless long, sharp needles pierced his near-naked body. He was in great agony of course, but we couldn't help laughing our socks off as we went to his aid. We extricated him – with some difficulty – and laid him on the grass. 'Stupid bloody rakes!' he cursed, 'Why the heck can't they make stronger handles?' – completely overlooking the fact that pole-vaulting would have been the last thing in the mind of the designer when that aspect of a grass rake was determined.

On another occasion we were unloading turf at a site somewhere up in London. The whole load of 1000 had to come off, and there were three or four of us at it. You normally took as many as you felt comfortable with and carried them the short distance to the stack – maybe three or four generally. There was a bus stop right next to where the lorry stood, and the people queuing there watched us – enjoying the diversion. As is the case with lads, a bit of showmanship crept in and armfuls began to get bigger and bigger. Five. Six. Seven! It was summer and the turves weren't heavy, in fact they could sometimes be less than half their winter weight. Somebody puffed past Cheddar with eight in his arms. Cheddar watched him, then looked at the people in the bus queue. An imp-ish, not-to-be-outdone grin came to his face as he eyed up the stacks on the lorry – which were in fourteens. He summoned all his strength and began to drag a whole stack to the side of the lorry. One last look at the open-mouthed expressions in the bus queue, then – with one almighty effort – the whole fourteen were off the lorry and in his arms! The rest of us were back at the lorry by now and began to chivvy him a bit, egging him on. He staggered and swayed under the weight as he slowly turned and went to move away, and just at that moment a dog decided to cross his path. He couldn't see it of course, with this mountain of turf in front of his face, and – well – you can imagine the rest. He came a real purler – turf everywhere, dog yelping like a stuck-pig. And us and the people in the bus queue absolutely doubled up!

We had a turf field at Shoreham – the one near Otford in Kent – not the Shoreham in West Sussex. To get to our field we had to drive across a shallow stream – not over it, for there was no bridge – but through it. It was only a few inches deep and never normally presented any problems. You just needed to hit it at a speed sufficient to get you through it and up the shallow sloping bank on the other side. So when you were crossing it empty, it was a bit of a bouncy business.

On the occasion I am about to recall, there were two or three of our lads riding on the back of my lorry, which was a platform type with no sides, and one of them was Cheddar. Need I go on? Well, I shall anyway. 'Hang on!' I shouted through the open window as I prepared to cross. I climbed the shallow bank on the far side, and happened to glance in my driving mirror. And there he was – flailing around in midstream like a half-drowned rat! Unlike the others – who had held on to the headboard immediately behind the cab – he'd sat with his legs dangling over the back end! He was a Cheddar, he was. I reckon I could almost fill a book with his antics alone – but that isn't what I set out to do, so I'll resist the temptation.

Going back to old George – George Chapman, that is – he was a rum sort as I've said. He'd say things like: 'In all this time I've given you nothing, yet *still* you ask for more!' Or – 'I'd sooner go without than not have any!' There were many more, and he'd obviously picked them up from others the same as I was picking them up from him. But I love all those daft old sayings, and have a great capacity for storing them up in my head. As he obviously did too. Describing somebody he regarded as stupid he'd say – 'He'd skin a rabbit for fourpence, and bugger up a shilling knife doing it!' No wonder I didn't mind working with the old devil – and unlike the others on the firm – I soon developed a sneaking admiration for him.

At one time he lived in accommodation that was part of 'Nash the Butchers' premises in our village – either above or behind the shop. He didn't drive, so I picked him up in the firm's van each morning. One morning when I called for him he was actually in the shop, buying something for his 'tea' that night. 'I'll have half a pound of those sausages' he was saying, and as Geoff cut them off and weighed them up, George spotted me waiting at the open door. 'Oh – and I'll have a sheep's head too' he continued – 'but be sure to leave the eyes in – so that it'll see me through the week!' Bloody fool!

I tendered for a job at Tovil, near Maidstone, for Richard Hearne – the famous 'Mr Pastry' on children's television. He'd bought this pair of semi-detached farm cottages, which although 'period', were rather run-down – presumably because they'd stood empty and neglected for some time. The pair formed one building of course, and were a few centuries old I believe, and from the point of view of restoration, presented bags of potential. None of this was anything to do with us of course – our interest lay mainly in the outside. The grounds in which the building stood were quite nominal really, considering the times in which it had been built, but by today's standards would be viewed as of goodly size. My tender was accepted and we made a start.

The main part of the job was to transform a 'bullock-yard', of about 50' x 50' proportions, into a large fish-pond of about 30' x 20', with grassed and paved areas surrounding. There was other work too – 'dry' walls, where one level gave way to another for instance – and small lawns. But as I say, this pond was to be the main feature, and the amount of graft that was involved in that was nobody's business!!

Immediately below the surface of the entire bullock-yard was all this Kentish Ragstone – indigenous to the county, as the name implies – and ideal for supporting all those hefty bullocks. And this was the material we were to use for the construction of the pond and dry walling. 'And I want you to be extremely careful when you're digging the stone out' instructed Mr Pastry, as I discussed the project with him on day one. 'I want every piece to remain intact, irrespective of size!'

Dave was with me on that first day, and although we normally 'worked on' – whatever the weather – it rained so hard and so persistently that day that we 'stood up' for the afternoon. There was a largish black shed on the edge of the yard, which bore evidence of being home to a bunch of wild farm cats at the time. But they were out right then, so we took refuge in there. We stood yarning and watching the stair-rods bouncing off the craggy surface outside, and no doubt considering the possibilities of converting our van to some sort of boat for the journey home!

'Here – look at this' said Dave suddenly, as he picked up an old knife from a ledge. It was long and black and had a pretty good point on it, so it wasn't long before we'd set a target on the end wall of the shed, and embarked on a knife-throwing contest. Which, although it didn't go on as long as the monsoon outside, did take us nicely up to knocking off time! I must say, we had a jolly nice afternoon – under the circumstances – but the next morning Dave looked at me with a frown. 'How's your shoulder?' he inquired. 'Don't ask!' I winced.

But soon Dave was off on to something else, probably down in the turf field I suppose, and from then on it was mostly just George and me. We had no mechanical means of attacking these submerged boulders, just a couple of picks and spades, and a bodge-bar! But we found things lying around, and were able to use the fulcrum and lever approach where necessary. And did we sweat?! And George was *never* seen without his jacket on – waistcoat and trilby hat too in fact!!

We struggled and struggled with one particularly large blighter, and were just about to 'accidentally' break it – to make things a little easier – when up turned Mr Pastry. 'That looks like a lovely one' he beamed, as George and I resumed our struggle. 'I'd like to know just how big that one is once it's out. Be sure not to break it!' So we had to forget all about the little accident we'd planned – and would have *had* if he'd come a little later – and slog on.

When finally it lay at our feet – but above ground now – we put the tape to it. Five by three by two – *feet* that is. 'Soddin' great thing!' said George, as he lifted his trilby to release some steam and mop his brow.

We carried on for several days unearthing all these boulders, though the majority of them were, thank goodness, of a more reasonable size. We were getting a fair stock-pile of them now, in readiness for the more constructive side of the job, which, whilst it would till be very heavy work, would be much more interesting.

'I've got the *Kent Messenger* people coming out later today' Mr P informed us one morning, 'and I want the photos to look good. So I'd certainly like *that* little beauty in the foreground' he said – nodding toward the miniature Mount Everest that had almost seen us two off. When they arrived, he showed them around, then came over to George and me. 'I want you chaps in the picture too' he said, and indicated where we should position ourselves. The scene was set, and the cameras clicked.

Back at the yard the chaps were quite impressed when we informed them we'd be appearing in the *Kent Messenger* the following week. They sniggered when it came out and they saw the photograph. There, right in the foreground, was Mr Pastry, pick in hand and one foot resting on the boulder – just like a big game-hunter with his kill – and George and I merged so completely into the background that you had to really strain your eyes to see much more than a trilby hat! And *we*'d done all the work so far. But, to give him his due, he did help us a bit here and there – in between T.V. appearances.

That pond looked great when finally we'd finished it. We spaced four 'pockets' around the outside for marsh-plants – each about bath-size and built right into the main wall of the pond – with a connecting pipe at the bottom for water supply. Big *old* London paving slabs – dark grey, well trodden, and of irregular size, were set around the top at the edge, and a plinth for a statue set right on the floor of the pond. We soiled and levelled the surrounding area ready for turfing, and the turf arrived just as we were about to pack for up the two or three days off we had at Christmas.

And on that Boxing Day, in 1962 I think it was, the snow came – thick and fast – followed by one of the longest freeze-ups I can remember, other than that of 1947. Everything stopped, and we were yard-bound for thirteen solid weeks! Another winter to remember – and no mistake.

By the end of that winter of 62/63, we were all just about at the end of our tethers, and I marvelled that we'd all stuck it out. Tempers had become a little frayed now and again, for although there were things to do in the yard, they were mostly quite boring and totally devoid of the kind of action and challenge we'd come to thrive on. I think that was one of the main attractions of that job really – the challenge. Then the great sense of satisfaction and achievement as the challenge was met. Never overlooking of course, the wonderful working environment we enjoyed for the 'biggest half' of the year.

Spring 1963 came – and not a moment too soon. We began to shed some of our outer layers of clothing – so vital to us during that prolonged freeze-up – starting of course with the string. A piece of string tied around your waist, outside all your clothing, worked wonders, and was generally regarded as the equivalent of another overcoat – but without further restriction to movement – for it prevented the cold air coming up inside and around your back. A piece below each knee would have served equal purpose – protecting various other regions – but we were all too young and proud I guess, to come down to that level. As the clothes were shed, the smiles were donned; and we awaited the word.

The thaw came to an end, and the subsequent surface water began to soak in or drain away, and we'd watch Harold's reaction as he met us in the yard each morning. He'd sniff the air, study the sky, and stomp the earth in two or three places. Then one morning he'd say the magic words. 'I reckon we could load up the gear and go down and try it – what d'you think?' A totally unnecessary question as far as we were concerned – we'd got the message before it had even been uttered and were already loading the 'Sod Cutter', mowers, cans of fuel and oil, pallets etc, and roping down. Drivers were assigned to the tractors for the journey down and very soon the yard was silent – for the first time in three months – as we drove off, full of anticipation and excitement, into the start of the new season. Hardship, hazard and all.

The winter weeks *were* useful of course, for they gave us the opportunity to put everything back into good order. Servicing and repair work was carried out on field equipment, tractors were seen to, lorries had wheel or tyre changes, brakes adjusted, faulty light-bulbs and things replaced, and things generally underwent tidying up and tightening up all round. And of course, antifreeze was inserted as and where necessary.

And there were other things besides the equipment. That particular winter there were hundreds of tree roots to dig out of the frozen ground, that had clung defiantly in when the orchard was being grubbed. I should think that was one of the worst jobs of all – digging out tree roots! Pallet boards needed to be repaired – as did fencing. Then there were rabbit-hutches to make, for we kept up to a hundred of those pretty, inoffensive little creatures – eventually! Needless to say, we'd started off with a number considerably lower.

The Field – or 'orchard', as we still called it for years afterwards – was eventually cleared of all roots etc, then ploughed, cultivated, and planted up with seven thousand blackcurrant bushes – half 'Wellingtons' and half 'Baldwins'. Why I should remember those quantities and varieties I can't say; but I do. Various other soft fruits and market-garden crops were experimented with – raspberries, strawberries, gooseberries, loganberries (I think), runner-beans, peas etc – but we finally came down to just blackcurrants and raspberries, which covered just half the field. The other half was grassed down – and so began the build-up of our chicken flocks, and a little later – geese. Which gave us something else with which to occupy ourselves in subsequent winter slack periods.

Where Margaret and I live now, immediately overlooking that field, we are almost surrounded by sheep, with cattle just beyond those in front of us, rolling hills beyond them, and it's lovely. We've been here close on thirty years now, too. So every spring we have the sheer delight of watching the new-born lambs frolicking and frisking – which we can see from our sitting room – just yards away. We get an even better view from our front bedroom, immediately above, and one year, when we had my brother George and sister-in-law Vera to stay, we gave them our bedroom as usual. In the morning I took them up a cup of tea, and drew the curtains back for them. And when they came down to breakfast, Vera was full of it. 'I couldn't *believe* it!' – she said incredulously – 'I could sit there drinking my tea and watching those lambs... *in bed*!!'

And as for us two, well, you'd think we'd be oblivious to it after all these years, but every Spring we find ourselves riveted to the spot again, spending a good many hours in all just watching and marvelling at the lambs. They are so fascinating. And yet, to me, the creature that epitomises country life more than any other is the humble chicken. I say humble – yet in no way does such a description apply to some of the roosters we've had in these parts over the years. I love the soft, relaxing gurgling and clucking of the hens – but that wonderful 'cock-a-doodle-doing' – well, that really sends shivers up and down my spine.

Maybe it goes right back to my days at Ma and Pop's during the war, when, as a youngster, I used to watch those beautiful, fluffy day-old chicks in their incubator on our front room table, become first pullets, then full-grown hens, laying all those beautiful eggs, so lovely and warm when I collected them from their nest boxes each day. I can't believe that was half a century ago!

A few years back we had roosters on three sides of us. One belonged to Harold, which was to our front, one was George's – who has a ten-acre field behind the nut-plat that our back garden adjoins – and one was to our side. I think actually that last one was George's as well, but he always called from some distance more to the west of us. They formed something of a triangle.

The first and third of these three were good old fashioned roosters with proud, lusty calls, but that other one – well, I used to roar with laughter at him. I don't know whether there'd been a cuckoo mixed up somewhere in his ancestry, but he seemed a little unsure of himself, for his call was undoubtedly a cross between the two. 'Cock-a-doodle-*cuck*oo! – he'd call!

At first I thought I'd imagined it, but I listened again and again, and there was no mistaking it. 'Cock-a-doodle-*cuck*oo!' – plain as a pikestaff. First Harold's would call from the front of us, then the one to our rear, then – 'Cock-a-doodle-*cuck*oo'. He seems to have gone now, this Chickoo as I called him, for it's a year or so since we heard that very distinctive call. Unless of course, George was giving him the wrong 'Rooster-Booster', and has since discovered and rectified the error, for we still hear the normal rooster calls.

But I really do love chickens, butterflies and dragonflies too, all supreme reminders of Summer in the countryside to me. Although we don't see too many of the latter these days I must say. 'Civilisation' marching on I suppose – crushing anything that gets in it's path!

As Harold's chicken flocks grew, we erected more large chicken houses to accommodate them, although they were all free-range, and eventually they totalled something like fifteen hundred as I say. And there was never any difficulty selling their eggs – well, none that I can remember. But of course their food-hoppers within the houses attracted the rats, and although we saw nothing of them, we knew their numbers were growing. Like a silent army. Something would have to be done about them, before the cost of the feedstuff outstripped the returns on the eggs. So a rat-hunt was arranged. Well – hardly a hunt really – for we knew exactly where they were. But you know what I mean.

Much against my nature, I took part. I am a respecter of *all* forms of life, and hate the thought of anything being killed, but although I may be many things, I am a realist, and I could see the necessity for this event. Just as long as the killing was quick and positive!

The roosts – which ran right down one side of each building – were above what we called 'dung-alleys', and were of course where the hens got their 'heads down' for the night. There were sides to these alleys, boxing them in like large compost heaps, and they all adjoined one to the other. Over a period of time the manure would naturally build up and up, and would have engulfed the perches and all if allowed to. And under all this lot lived the rats!

So on this day, we closed all windows and doors – us ratcatchers – shutting ourselves in with them. We split into two groups, one group digging out the dung and carting it off, the other group standing poised and alert with their various weapons in readiness for our friends – when they began to move. Brian held a spade, Dave one of his highly-prized guns, someone else a pickaxe handle and so on.

Our strategy was to clear the middle alley, then make a small hole at the bottom of each of its side partitions, connecting it to its neighbours. Then we'd take each of the side alleys in turn. Little or nothing happened during the clearing of the middle alley, then, part way down the next – they began to appear. Talk about a sinking ship – they were darting around everywhere in their – alas – futile attempts to escape. Spades and pickaxe handles flailed and thudded, and the lads wielding them had to go very carefully, for the darned things were running up our legs and everywhere. Poor old Dave – so thick and fast were they appearing at one point that he didn't have time to re-load his gun – so he reverted to using it as a club. And smashed it!

And our strategy worked – for as they felt us closing in on them with our digging out tools, they made their way down before us – eventually finding a convenient 'way out' in the form of the hole we'd made at the bottom of the dividing partition. And as they came through into the cleared middle section – one at a time – it was relatively easy for the annihilation group. Bop-bop-bop! When the first of the side sections had been cleared, the hole at the bottom was sealed and work began on the next.

At the end of it all we rounded up the dead bodies and carted them off for disposal – and I counted all those from one house as they were put into the wheelbarrow. *Eighty-seven!* And there were either two or three houses to go yet. Some of the lads really enjoyed that afternoon, but here's one that didn't! It wasn't my scene at all, and I never got involved in such activity again. And never shall.

The flock of geese was steadily increasing too as Harold bought a few more every now and again. One day, two ganders were delivered. They came by van and were full grown, and for some reason had to be carried the considerable distance across to the goose hut. Dave took one and I the other. There is a proper way to carry geese of course, which we knew – and adopted. Even so, it took all our strength to contain those blighters as we carried them across, they were so strong and struggled like billy-o. But we made it – just!

I'm blessed if they didn't give us a laugh or two as well – those geese. Every morning a huge flock of wild Canada Geese used to pass over, then later on – late afternoon – they'd pass over again on their way back. They still do for that matter. So regular was this practice that our lot took not the slightest bit of notice as they grazed contentedly beneath them.

Then one day, on the return flight, the wild geese decided to come down into our field, – right amongst ours – goodness knows why. As you might imagine, this caused a bit of a shemozzle for a while, but they soon settled back to the business of feeding their faces. In due course the wild ones decided it was time to mosey on home, and took off – en masse. Our lot looked on in wonder and disbelief! They looked at each other, and you could almost hear them thinking – 'Cor – *that* looked good – I wonder if *we* can do it?'

So they flapped their wings about a bit, took a bit of a run, and discovered that they could. And did! Up and away they went – every man-jack of 'em. We couldn't believe our eyes. 'Come back, come back!' wailed Harold, as they circled above him – 'what am I going to say to my regulars when they come in for their eggs?' Of course they ignored his pleas, they were enjoying themselves far too much even to hear, but unused as they were to flying they soon tired, and after another thoroughly unco-ordinated, scrappy looking circuit or two, came in to land. Well – crash-land in most cases.

Relief spread instantly across Harold's face, huge grins across ours, and something pretty close to sheer ecstasy on those of the geese – as they no doubt looked eagerly ahead to having another go tomorrow.

But – disappointment was to be theirs I'm afraid, for early on next morning, long before the wild geese were due, they were herded inside pretty smartish for a wing-clipping session! This only involved 'tipping' the end feathers of one wing – just enough to unbalance them when they tried it on again. Poor little devils, you had to feel sorry for them as they lurched and tripped over everywhere in their attempts to improve upon yesterday. And when the Canada geese passed over a little later, it was a toss-up as to which were the wildest – them or ours! But the Canada geese never landed in our field again, and our lot settled down and forgot all their lofty ideas of flying. But it certainly was a good laugh for us lot, excluding Harold of course – although even he had a good chuckle afterwards.

We were yard-bound again for a short spell one winter, the one following the arrival of the two ganders it was. We topped their drinking troughs up each morning from a forty-gallon drum positioned just outside the hut, filled their feed troughs, and collected the eggs. Just as we did the chickens. Their number (the geese) peaked at 150, so there were a tidy few eggs to collect each day.

This particular winter this chore fell to me. Easy enough I thought as I wandered across to their hut on the first occasion. I withdrew the latch-pin from the door of the hut, and was nearly flattened as they all came galloping out – squawking and thrashing their wings about. They pestered me a little as I attended to their troughs, but I managed to fight them off. But when I went into the hut for the eggs, well – that was something altogether different.

Those two old ganders spotted me going in and must have realised my intention, for they came charging across at me – heads down – like a couple of wild boars. I saw them coming and quickly shut the door – I didn't want *my* arms or legs broken by their powerful wings. I gathered the eggs into the bucket, the two of them prowling outside as I did – then had to wait my chance to slip out and clear the wire fence that ran immediately down one side of the hut – bucket and all – whilst they weren't looking.

I was glad that little episode was over, and determined to work out a different approach the next time, which was of course the following morning. But this time I dealt with the troughs first, leaving the egg-collecting for the time being, then hopped back over the fence, from where it was just possible to reach the latch-pin. I placed the bucket out of sight – toward the back end of the hut – then leaned across for the pin. As soon as it was clear the door burst open and out they charged – but just as quickly – I*'d* nipped back the other way and joined that bucket. I peeped round the corner of the hut, and there was no mistaking the venom in the eyes of those two as they sought me out. But I stood fast, and after a while they gave up and joined the others at the troughs, and when I could see the moment was right I nipped carefully back over the fence and sneaked in. Minutes later – mission completed – I snuck back out again and over the fence to safety, but that pair had me in their sights as I went, firmly gripping that bucket of eggs. I just hoped they weren't too quick tumbling me.

Another thing we did during the 62/63 freeze-up was to make concrete blocks. Harold had a block-making machine, though where it had come from I cannot now recall. I say 'machine' because that was how it was generally referred to, but a more appropriate word would be apparatus I guess, for it wasn't mechanised in any way. It was more like a moulding press. You lifted the lid, inserted a block-sized pallet, then shovelled in some mix and pulled the lid down. The lid was lifted straight up again and there was your block – all compressed and formed to shape and size. You lifted it carefully out on it's pallet, and stood it down to set alongside all the others. When fully set they were stacked up in the yard.

As it was so bitterly cold at the time, with the temperature below freezing all day, it was decided we'd set ourselves up inside the tractor shed, alongside the office. We had a cement mixer, and when the sand/ballast aggregate arrived we had it shot right inside the shed. Left outside it would have frozen solid over-night and been impossible to work with.

We set to, making several mixings, and by the end of the day had produced a fair number of blocks. The work wasn't exactly stimulating, and little skill was required, but it kept us moving and gave us a sense of purpose. And it was a darned sight better than digging out roots. We went home that night with a certain feeling of fulfilment, and looked forward to the next day with considerably less apathy than had been the 'norm' of late.

We opened the big door next morning – all keen and raring to go – only to find that the frost had got in and had penetrated quite deeply the heap of ballast. Once in, there was no way it would go – not in those perpetually sub-zero temperatures – without the application of some heat. So we set up a brazier right close to the heap, and as it thawed, so we fed it into the mixer.

The whole shed began to warm a little as the fire got going, and we all thought what a nice change it made – not to be working out there in the bitter cold. But as the temperature began to rise – towards zero – so a screen of smoke began to appear too. We were burning wood, anything we could lay our hand to I guess, and some of it would have had mud or roofing felt and suchlike frozen hard on to it, and as it thawed it started to smoke. But we had to have heat for the sake of the work, and there was no alternative supply, so that was that!

Visibility worsened as the fog thickened, and every now and then the door would fly open as somebody came staggering out, coughing and spluttering and rubbing at his streaming eyes. It got that bad at times that we were operating on only two of our senses – touch and hearing – for we could see no further than about two feet at the most, and both taste and smell were totally overladen with smoke. Yet – I'm certain that each of us would have agreed that this particular job was preferable to some of those we'd been engaged upon so far that winter. And it was nice sitting up close to the brazier at lunchtime, brewing up and toasting our sandwiches.

One day I found a piece of strong steel mesh which, placed across the top of the brazier, formed an ideal base for a frying pan. So eggs, bacon, sausages etc. became part of our daily menu – lovely hot soup too. And fortunately, we could taste them well enough to identify and enjoy them – in spite of the smoke – so life wasn't so bad. But I can still see that door bursting, and hear the coughing and spluttering that followed.

Another break from being yard-bound that winter was the transporting of about fifty tons of pig-manure, from a farm at Four Elms to one in Cuckoo Lane, Hadlow. It felt great leaving the yard in a couple of the lorries – which themselves must have wondered what was happening – after their prolonged idleness. About four of us went on that little job – the others having been deployed elsewhere – and it was still bitterly cold, with the temperature well below zero all day. And driving conditions were still pretty hazardous too. But we were *out* – and seeing some action! We managed the journey over reasonably well, it's only about twelve miles anyway, but slithered all over the frozen farmyard when we got there, as we tried to position the first lorry by the dung-heap for loading. But of course, we made it eventually.

The heating in the lorries was well short of adequate – if in fact such facility existed at all – so we were all well 'snatched' by the time we got there. We stomped our feet, and thrashed our arms across our bodies, trying to warm ourselves into action, but all rather ineffective, alas.

'Ah well, let's get stuck in,' I said as I doled out the dung-forks, 'Perhaps that'll warm us up a bit.' And that was an understatement if ever there was one! We stood atop that dung-heap and began forking it on – and in no time at all we were all as warm as toast – sweating, even! The warming-up process began at our feet, for the dung into which we'd sunk, nigh to the tops of our wellies, was lovely and warm below the surface, and the bodily movements did the rest. Some of us even shed a coat or two I believe, and that's saying something for *that* winter. That job lasted a couple of days I think, for ours were not tipper lorries, so it was forked both on and off. We stank to high heaven of course, but were as happy as the proverbial pigs – for not only were we nice and warm for the duration of the job – our appetites were sharpened enormously.

As turf stripping was completed at one farm, we'd load up all the gear for moving on and setting in at the next, perhaps thirty or forty miles away. We were always in Kent or Sussex somewhere – all good sheep country – and it was quite pleasant getting to know practically every road, lane, track, town, village, hamlet and farm in your own area, plus a good bit beyond, for we went considerably further afield when we were delivering or landscaping.

We set in at a new location one morning, at a place in our own area called 'Oxenhoath', with which I believe Lord Baden-Powell, the founder of the Boy Scout movement had connections at one time. Within the grounds of Oxenhoath – which incidentally forms part of the frontal view from our cottage – is a stretch of water called 'The Banyard' which was most popular with the local fishing fraternity. Fishing clubs from other areas too for that matter. It's many years since the time I am about to recall, but I think it is rather like a small, tree-lined lake.

We unloaded all the gear and soon got under way, setting in just below The Banyard itself to start with. Bob's younger brother Bunt hadn't turned up for work that day, having sent word that he was sick, and far too poorly to venture out. He and Bob lived at Adamswell Farm, no more than about two miles from Oxenhoath as it happened. But George Chapman *was* with us, which was something of a rarity really for he was normally involved only in landscaping.

We'd not been long at it before little whisperings and chucklings began to develop amongst some of the lads, and there was clearly something afoot, outside of the norm. And it turned out that Bunt – 'too ill for work' – had decided a spot of fishing would suit him better than working that day, and was in fact, right here in The Banyard! Of course, he hadn't known we were about to set in at Oxenhoath, and on peering between the trees to see what all the kerfuffle was about, was absolutely horrified – on *two* counts. For not only had he to dodge Harold – who'd come with us to see us started – he'd to dodge George as well. For Bunt you see, had no fishing licence, and George...... yep, *he* was the Water Bailiff at the time! What a day to go sick. And what a place to spend it in!

I can't remember now just how long Bunt – who was only a couple of miles away

from home remember – was imprisoned in The Banyard, for although Harold left us
to it after a couple of hours, George would have stayed a good deal longer! We kept
sniggering and tittering amongst ourselves all morning, and George – totally unaware
of the situation – thought we were all mad. 'Daft buggers' he kept saying. Proper
spoilt Bunt's day that did, he'd set off that morning in high hopes of catching
something – and spent practically the whole day trying to avoid being caught
himself.

Those years – right through the sixties – must definitely have been the 'boom'
time in the turfing business. So much building was going on then, lots of modern
houses, blocks of flats, business complexes etc. And suddenly, large grassed areas
were all the fashion. We were kept very busy, and increased our number accordingly
– equipment too. Many others decided to 'get in on the action' of course, so there
was no shortage of competition. But there seemed to be plenty to go round, and we
all got along well enough together.

And on the landscaping side there was the satisfaction of seeing the transformation
you'd made, sometimes on a site little better than a wilderness to start with. And you
met lots of different people, and travelled new ground quite often. Yep – all in all a
good life, though I suspect the shine might wear off with age. Mind you, we paid for
it at times as I've said in the Winter. Like on those days when it rained non-stop,
start to finish, day after day. You'd turn up for work all dry, warm and comfortable,
and in no time at all you'd be soaked right through to the skin. And thus you'd stay –
all day. There'd be times when you'd seem always to have clothes stretched out or
hanging up to dry at home. T'was a job to keep up with it then. Or you could pick up
a spade or suchlike on a very frosty morning, and it would stick to your hand. Try
releasing it too quickly – which we mostly did – and it would take some of your skin
with it. And turf cutting at coastal locations – Lydd for instance, or Leysdown on the
Isle of Sheppey – could be particularly uncomfortable when sleet or snow came at
you horizontally in the very strong winds. Then there was all that digging out of
bogged-down vehicles, and running repairs.

More than once I've slithered under a lorry – stuck in the mud somewhere – and
had to remove the differential assembly. This would be following a broken half-
shaft, whose sheared end had dropped into the diff before you could poke it through
from t'other side. All the oil would have to be drained first of course, and with
insufficient room to place a receptacle for the catching of same, I just had to let it go
and soak into the ground, covering the area with straw afterwards so that I could
carry out the job.

Those 'diffs' weighed enough when you were *standing* with one in your arms, so
you can imagine the difficulty of handling them lying down. But somehow I'd

manage to lift it out of its casing, remove the offending article and get it back into position, then tighten up all the nuts, replenish the lost oil and re-connect the 'prop' shaft. And of course, because of the restricted working space it had to be a one-man operation. So you can image the tremendous satisfaction when, new half-shaft fitted and everything else restored, that vehicle was started up and moved out. Or can you? I doubt it! But it was well worth all the muck, sweat and struggle to me. Even so, I don't think I'd relish having to tackle it now!

And what with dried-up dinners, split fingers, finger nails being prised from their beds et cetera, you wondered at times why on earth you did it. And then Spring would come, and all those hardships would be forgotten in its promise. Lambs everywhere, and all the daffodils, crocus, polyanthus and the like. Not forgetting the lovely wild flowers – daisies, celandine, henbit, cowslip. Then later the meadow buttercup and clover, and later still the poppies. None of which, I ought to add, would have been present in the turf we were cutting, bar perhaps the odd bit of clover.

We're all gullible to some degree I guess, giving others a laugh at our own expense. I'm remembering the lady who approached us on a job one day. 'I'm being plagued by moles' she complained, 'and my lawn is becoming a right mess. What can I do?' We all looked at each other, and a twinkle came to Dave's eye. 'The best thing you can do' he answered – with a half-wink in our direction – 'is to catch the little blighters, then bury 'em alive. That'll do it!' Most grateful for this little snippet of inside information, she scurried happily off home to tell her husband!

And so the years went, one season following another, the complexion of the job changing with them. Joy would give way to despair, but return quickly enough to make it all worth while. And the despair was always well outweighed by the pleasures – well in my case certainly. Then one day one of the younger lads declared that he was leaving. It was boom time all around then and opportunities were springing up everywhere, with big earnings to be had. He duly left, and Harold decided not to replace him – the peak of our boom having already been reached by then.

We soldiered on, then somebody else left – then another – and our number dwindled as they too were not replaced. The market-garden side of the business was settling down quite nicely now and presented far fewer problems than the turfing side – once regular outlets for the produce had been secured. So the one business gradually eased down as the other became more established, and suddenly there were but four of us left.

So – love it though I did, I had to face the inevitability of it's eventual demise and seek an alternative occupation. But though I've had something like nine or ten jobs since, with a fair bit of variation between them, I've never found anything to come near that particular kind of life. It certainly was one on it's own – for me at any rate.

Before I leave it completely there is one incident I often smile over when I think back to it, although it concerned just me. And you wouldn't have seen me smiling at the time.

We were grassing at the new Sewage Works in Sissinghurst. The weather was particularly hot at the time – scorching in fact. The soil we were levelling was clay, and although it was of such a consistency as to be quite workable, it was very pale in colour – almost white in fact in the sun's glare. The stonework around the tops of the sewage beds was very pale grey and that too reflected the glare. It was June if I remember correctly, and as the sun reached its zenith around noon it was directly above us and there was nowhere to find a bit of shady relief from its relentless heat and glare.

You could well have imagined a troop of the Foreign Legion appearing at any moment – a camel or two at least! Brother, was that hot. We were stripped to just jeans and footwear, and I clearly remember Dave laying his legs – one at a time – on this grey stonework whilst one of us chopped through the seams of his jeans with a half-mattock so that he could convert them to shorts. Others followed his example – to blazes with the expense – after all, who could imagine it ever being wet or cold again?!

We sweltered on through the day, preparing the ground for the seed and turf that would follow, then – blessed relief – finishing time came at last. We clambered gratefully aboard our pick-up truck for the nice cool ride home, each of us no doubt, holding mental pictures of pints of lovely cold shandy at the end of it as we popped into the 'Three Squirrels' on our way home from the yard.

But that was when I had my first sign of the agony I would experience over the next forty-eight hours. This sign was, in itself, innocuous enough, just a little itch in my armpit. I scratched, but back it came. I scratched again, but still it persisted – and not only that, another one appeared. Then another, and another, and by the time we arrived back at the yard all thoughts of refreshing glasses of shandy had been knocked into oblivion by a desperate urge to get home to our flat and plunge into the bath!

I emerged from the bath feeling clean and fresh, but was most relieved to have got rid of that blasted irritation. But, wait a minute – *had* it gone? Itch! Itch! No it damned well hadn't. But scratching seemed only to succeed in making it worse, so I resisted this temptation as much as I could all through dinner and the rest of the evening. Which was anything but easy I can tell you, for I could feel it springing up everywhere.

I had certain misgivings about going to bed, for warmth and touch seemed to be the main irritants. And I was right. Within twenty minutes I'd leapt from my bed and was beside myself with the intense irritation. I didn't wish to spoil Margaret's sleep, so I slipped quietly into the sitting room, switching the light on as I did. And what a revelation. I was covered from head to toe – *literally* – in huge blisters, rather like a giant-size nettle-rash. I doubt whether more than one square centimetre of my entire body was clear of them and it felt as though I was being eaten alive by zillions of very vicious ants.

I wondered what I could do – this late in the day – for I couldn't bear a stitch of clothing near me. Then I remembered we had some Calamine Lotion somewhere, so I tracked this down and smeared it over my entire body. I placed a cloth on the seat of a chair, then sat – stark naked – on the very edge of it, so that I made minimum contact – and prepared myself for a long night.

For a while I felt a modicum of relief, then, as the lotion dried it seemed to tighten on me – like another skin. I was going mad now and doing everything I could to stop myself scratching. Eventually of course, I could resist no longer, and had just a teeny scratch at my knee. Well, that was like opening the floodgates, for in no time at all I was scratching myself all over, like a thing demented. Which, come to think of it, is exactly what I was. The more I tore into myself, the more I wanted to. And that's how I spent the whole night!

When Margaret found me in the morning I was just about all-in, and not a pretty sight at all. I'd torn at myself so violently that I looked as though I'd been doing battle with a tiger and been lucky to escape with my life. I was deeply scratched all over – and I *mean* all over – and was covered in blood. And you should have seen the furniture – it, and the entire room was covered in a blanket of white powdery dust, where I'd ripped through the Calamine Lotion.

How I managed to bear the clothes on myself I don't know, but I dressed and went to see the doctor as soon as I could – stripping myself naked again before I'd reached the top of the stairs on my return! And as you may well have guessed – it was 'Prickly Heat'! But that condition can hit you in various degrees, from a few irritating little 'heat bumps' – which we called them as kids, and which is all most people get – through to the intensity that I was experiencing, which was Prickly Heat at its very worst. Trust me, never do things by half! As it happened, my doctor was subject to this very same problem – and to the same degree – so I had his complete and heartfelt sympathy.

Apparently, having got so hot at work that day, and not being able to cool myself in any way, my blood had 'boiled', causing my skin to erupt in that way. Evidently I was – and still am for that matter – prone to this kind of malady. Something to do

with the sweat glands, according to my doctor. 'Whenever you feel you are getting a
bit hot' he advised, 'stand in front of a fan – or take a cool shower!' All very well if
circumstances permit – but they seldom if every did in our kind of business. I could
have kept jumping in the river I suppose, as was no doubt suggested from time to
time.

I fell victim to this condition just twice more after that, but not quite so severely
thank heavens, and I *did* know by then that it would begin to recede after forty-eight
hours anyway. But that first time – it felt more like forty-eight days!

On one of those later occasions I tried to forestall it by sitting in the bath – in *cold*
water – with Margaret jugging the water continuously over my head. We kept this up
till I'd gone blue with cold and was shivering quite violently. I then went outside
naked – it being dark at the time – where I stayed for quite some time, then spent the
rest of the evening sitting naked on a stool in our kitchen, with my feet on the cold
floor.

I don't think I've ever felt as cold as that, for as long as that, and I certainly
shivered some that evening. Yet *still* it got to me – and I had another ripping time. I
just hadn't caught it early enough.

On the subject of sewage works, there was another incident worthy of mention.
Well, that isn't exactly true I suppose, for there *was* no incident actually. But there so
easily could have been, and had that been the case it would certainly have put every
other incident recorded on these pages well into the shade.

Dave and I had a job to do at another smallish sewage works, deep in the Kentish
countryside. Like the Sissinghurst one it was undergoing improvement and updating.
But *unlike* the latter – which was finished prior to us being called in – work on this
one had barely begun. I expect now it looks fine, but at that time it was quite, quite
grotty.

Picture the scenario if you can. Centre-stage was this largish open tank, though I
can't remember now whether it was a clinker-bed or not – or whether it was at
ground level or a little above. Whichever, it was full, and I will describe the contents
as simply rather unpleasant – though believe me, I could elaborate on this quite a bit
and still remain well within the bounds of truth.

Around the edge of the tank was a footpath, either concrete or slabbed,
approximately three feet in width. And from the outer edge of this path were the areas
we had to turf. 'So where's the problem?' you ask. Well – I'll tell you. Those areas
were not flat, very much to the contrary in fact, for they weren't too many degrees
short of the vertical!

We'd had steep banks to turf before – you simply worked from the bottom
upwards – 'nailing' the turves into position using hardwood pegs, which could be

removed later once the turves had become well rooted and knit together.

We laid the bottom row of turf, long-ways up, inserting the nails as we went. This covered a strip three feet high – the length of a turf. Then on to the second row. Great – we'd now made six feet, but it was more than clear that we'd not reach to nail the next row – and there were at least two more rows above that. We found a short ladder and managed one more row, then we were stumped. 'There's nothing for it' I said to Dave – after we'd mulled it over a bit – 'we'll just have to lay them from above – off the top of the bank!' And that's just what we did.

We transferred turf and tools to the top, then looked down. And as my memory clears I can confirm that it was not a clinker-bed – it was a tank of – well – 'liquor', though I wouldn't know how deep. What a prospect! 'More of a job for Sir Edmund Hilary and Sherpa Tensing I should think' suggested Dave. 'Well.... yes' I replied, 'but only then if they were wearing diving suits and snorkels!' I peered again into those unsavoury depths below. 'Oh well – faint heart ne'er won fair lady' I said, with a good deal more courage than I'm sure either of us *felt* – 'let's get at it!'

So we did 'turn-about' on those slopes, the one lying face down on the flat surface above, grasping the other by the ankles as he lay head-first down the bank, hammering (though not too merrily) away at the pegs. It was quite a strenuous business, whichever part you were playing, but more so I should say for the one dangling almost immediately above that tank!! So we had to swop over fairly frequently. 'I hope your grip's good and strong' I said to Dave as I inched into the upside down for my first stint on the 'wall of death' – quite confident of course that it was. Well...... *fairly* confident! 'Yes' he came back, 'and I bloody well hope yours is too!' Talk about 'your life in their hands'.

We finished the job – without incident as I say – but I must say, I kept wondering as the blood flowed down to my scalp, whether I might have done anything lately to upset him – just enough to tempt the 'evil' side of his nature. 'I was thinking exactly the same' chuckled Dave, when I confessed to these misgivings later. 'It's a good job we're mates isn't it?'

And it certainly was, for you can imagine the outcome (or should that be in-going) had there been just one moment's lack of concentration. I've heard of being dropped in it, but I don't think the originator of that saying would have had *quite* that in mind.

We had a largish job to do at Brentwood in Essex, for the Ford Motor Company. This involved the carting and spreading of many loads of topsoil, and the supply and laying of umpteen thousand turves, so we were up there quite a while.

Being one who's always set himself a target to work to, I'd say to the lads first thing – 'Right, we'll steam along and lay 400 (say) without stopping, then we'll stop and have a decent smoke!' It could of course be three hundred, or maybe six hundred

– depending upon how many we were. Then we'd get stuck in again, refreshed after our 'blow', and aim to get the next batch down. And so on.

We set to the target one morning, and after a while I looked at my watch to see how we were doing. 'Strewth!' I said, 'it's taking us a time to get *these* down, we should have been having our smoke by now!' So we shifted into overdrive and completed the batch – then stopped. Break over, we attacked the next lot. 'I don't know how we managed to get behind like that' I said to the others, as we got back into the swing, 'for we weren't late starting! Still, maybe we can catch up again'. At which we all stepped up the pace a little.

But we didn't seem to be catching up, so up went the pace even further. We stopped for lunch, then had to go absolutely flat out all afternoon to get the day's quota down by knocking-off time. 'Bloody hard-going today wasn't it?' said Cheddar, as we gathered our tools together afterwards. 'I should think that *was*' I agreed, 'come on – let's get loaded and off home!' The journey usually took about one and a half hours, and it was five o'clock then.

This was long before the advent of the M25 – most of the other Motorways too in fact. And the Dartford Tunnel hadn't long been in operation either – the *first* tunnel that is! So off we set on our winding journey, all grateful for the rest after the gruelling day. We emerged from the tunnel and I turned off the A2 for Longfield.

We suddenly became aware that there were very many schoolchildren afoot, all with books, satchels etc. 'I wonder what's going on here' I said – 'they're usually home long before this!' I looked at my watch...... just coming up to six. 'Perhaps they've had something special on at school today.'

A mile or so short of Longfield, Eddie Browning, who occupied the passenger seat next to me, suddenly threw up his hands. 'Stop, *stop*!' he yelled excitedly, as if some dreadful thought had just occurred to him, then wriggled agitatedly as I slowed to a gentle stop – after all, there was no emergency that I could see. 'Come on, come *on*!' he pleaded, and even before I'd stopped he'd flung open the door, leapt out, and was off down the road like a long-dog.

Which was saying something for Eddie, for he was built for comfort rather than speed, being almost as wide as he was high. We waited as he panted his way back to the van, grinning from ear to ear. 'So – what was all *that* about?' I asked, 'and what's so funny anyway?'

'This!' he beamed, and brought his hand from behind him, revealing three crisp one pound notes. 'I spotted them in that farm gateway – lying there in the grass!' What a find – three pounds was a goodly sum then, nearly a third of a week's pay in fact. And how had he managed to pick out the green notes in the grass as we sped past at about 45mph?!

'You must have eyes like a bloody hawk' offered somebody. 'Yes, and that's not all' he chuckled gleefully, 'I asked one of those kids why they're all so late going home from school today, and guess what – they're not late at all – it's only about four o'clock. It's your watch that's wrong!' I couldn't believe it at first, then I remembered how we'd had to pull out all the stops to get the day's work done. Further inquiries soon confirmed the truth. My watch – normally so reliable – had gained approximately two hours over the course of the day. No wonder we'd had to thrash along so!

We all had a good laugh as the relief spread through us, then somebody said what a pity it was that I was the only one wearing a watch. 'Ah yes' I countered, 'but if we'd knocked off two hours later – like we should have done – I'll lay that money wouldn't still have been there!' 'True' chortled Eddie, face still beaming, 'I vote we make for the café, where it'll be tea and cakes all round – on me!' So, with nobody in opposition, the motion was carried, and that's just what we did. And I reckon Eddie still had a couple of those greenbacks left over afterwards.

But – true to the saying, – all good things come to an end, and with only four of us left the writing on the wall was clear enough. So off I went in search once more – late 1969 I think it was – yet I knew somehow that the best of my working career was behind me now. Maybe it was just to do with getting older – I don't know – for I still had an open mind and was eager as ever for challenges new.

And challenge I had, sure enough in the ensuing quarter century, but interesting and diverse as these ten or so jobs were, they were mostly of a technical nature, and there seems little worthy of mention now. But perhaps it is presumptuous of me to think there might have been anything of interest thus far in these ramblings anyway – to anyone other than myself! Although *I* like listening to the memories of others, so perhaps there are more of the same ilk. Or – maybe if I were to bury this lot now, how might it read in say...two centuries time? (Still a load o' rubbish I expect!)

But though these later challenges lacked the fun and adventure of the others – just a means to an end for the most part – perhaps I should make brief mention here and there, if only to complete the picture.

The first of them was as a Heavy Goods Vehicle driver (HGV) for a firm of General Carriers. I think there were something like a hundred and three vehicles at our Aylesford depot – most of which were assigned to regular routes throughout the south of England – but there was a small float of 'spare' vehicles and drivers to cover emergencies and holidays.

I was taken on as a spare driver, which was a bit more of a challenge than the lot of a 'regular' driver – which most of them seemed to prefer – for you never knew where you'd be going until you booked in at 0600 on the day. *Or* what type of vehicle you'd be driving. And even when you *reached* your designated area, you still had to find somewhere in the region of sixty to eighty premises – of various descriptions – for we delivered anything, anywhere. I even went to a Nudist Camp one day, but all I saw was a pair of dirty great......wait for it......gates, very securely locked, with a large box alongside for deliveries. I'm not sure what was in my parcel – tennis balls I think!

Of course, it helped enormously when you knew your route – as in the case of the regular-route guys – for you could load all your deliveries on in the correct order, thus minimising the effort required at t'other end. These were all 'box' vans, with a translucent centre section to the roof for light.Heat too unfortunately on warm sunny days! My goodness you could sweat some in there as you clambered over your load hunting our your deliveries. Especially on a day such as when I had two full pallets of paper right at the very back, for what we happened to know would be my first call. When I arrived I found the place closed for the annual fortnight's holiday, which of course a regular driver would have known about.

What should I do – head back to the depot and lift them off – or carry on and work round them? When I say round I really mean over, for the only way past them was over the top, where there was a gap of about two feet.

But the depot was at least thirty miles back, and I had a fair stretch of uncharted waters ahead of me, well – uncharted as far as I was concerned. So I opted for the latter and pressed on. And didn't I suffer, for it developed into a very warm and sunny day, so not only was I tackling something akin to an assault course all day long, it was inside a blessed oven. I must've lost *pounds* that day

But again, as a spare driver you were always in different areas, which made it a bit more interesting, and your salary was slightly enhanced over that of the regulars anyway, to off-set this hardship. So it was swings and roundabouts as far as I was concerned really.

But there was little or no excitement in this job – that's all it was really, a job – and no sparkle at all. And back at the depot there could be a fair bit of hassle at times, with everyone anxious to get loaded and away. And old 'Adolph' from Canterbury had his disciples amongst the growing ranks of Traffic Wardens throughout the land, although thankfully they constituted only a small percentage of the whole force I must say. Even so, it could mar your day sometimes, and what with the lack of challenge, and one thing and another......

So I turned the page again, and now found myself working for another small but enterprising local firm which specialised in Agricultural Haulage, as a driver. HGV again of course. We dealt mainly in hay, straw, animal feedstuffs, and bulk corn (wheat, barley, oats), but there were other sides to it as well – fertilisers, seed-potatoes – things like that. For hard work this job was about the equal of the turfing business, as indeed it was for the predominantly rural and rustic nature of its environment too – which suited me down to the ground of course. Figuratively speaking that is, for quite often I'd be atop a great haystack, or high in a Dutch-barn somewhere as we brought in and stacked the last of the summer's hay or straw.

But nice though it was, it was a young man's job really, for it was all graft – unless you were driving a bulk corn lorry where the simple flick of a lever tipped your load off for you. I was still in my prime at the time, and really thrived on all this hard physical effort, but I couldn't see me lugging eighteen-stone (2¼ cwt) sacks of corn about for instance, when I was old and grey. The driving part was fine, and the wagons were excellent – right up to date and beautifully maintained. The lads too were a decent bunch, and small in number, although somehow I could never quite get that same feeling of camaraderie that had been so strong on the turfing firm. Nor indeed was there a fraction of the fun.

After two years another opportunity came to my attention. This was even *more* local to me – within spitting distance in fact – and sounded particularly interesting. It was both clean and challenging, and I felt tailor-made for it. For I held an HGV licence, knew my way around pretty well, and was well-used to dealing with people, and could look quite smart when so called upon. And I have a great love of plants.

After two interviews, one at a local hotel in town and one a week or so later in Lincolnshire, I was offered the position of Van Salesman – which was nothing at all to do with the selling of vans – but *was* all about selling houseplants and things *from* a van. A large van, that is – of HGV proportions – that was shelved throughout and fitted out as a mobile shop. The interview in Lincolnshire took the whole day, after an early start from home in Kent, although a fair proportion of the time was spent strolling through the acres and acres of glass where all those beautiful plants were grown, and I'd never in all my life seen such variety and colour. They were truly gorgeous, and quite, quite fascinating.

I had one week's training for the job, which took place in the lovely Yorkshire Dales and Derbyshire Peak District, then headed south to develop the first of five new territories in London and Home Counties, which I think was about the only area in England not yet developed by that particular company.

And whereas the week's training up north had been quite relaxed and enjoyable – for me at least – this was quite different to start with though still very enjoyable. Up there, those routes were well-established and the salesmen fully accepted – welcomed with open arms in many instances. All my calls had to be found, the territory formed, and the customers convinced – which I think was the hardest part really, for there was considerable 'opposition' already well in place everywhere. Every plant had to be learned – that is – instantly recognised and identified by both its Latin name – in full – *and* its common name or names, for some plants have more than one common name, its cultural requirements learned by heart, its price memorised. And there were scores and scores of different species, and varieties in most of these too!

To the customer we spoke in common names – for example Grape Ivy, Shrimp Plant, Sweetheart Vine, Stag Horn Fern – but on all our paperwork every entry had to be written in Latin, as in this example – Rhoicissus Rhomboidea, Beloperone Guttata, Philodendron Scandens, Platycerium Bifercatum. So it was like speaking two different languages all the time. Which in fact it was. And just at this very time we were swinging over to this horrible decimal currency and everything too, which complicated things even further. Not only did I have to remember that a Chrysanthemum for example was five shillings and sevenpence, I had to very quickly convert it and enter it as 28p. So again, whilst we were all still thinking and talking pounds, shillings and pence – the latter of the 'd' kind – we were doing all our paperwork and banking in pence – of the 'p' kind.

I say 'horrible' decimal currency, as I for one regret bitterly the transition from the good old ha'pennies, pennies, threepenny bits, (and silver joeys) tanners, shillings, (bobs), florins, half-crowns, ten-bob notes etc, that we'd all known and loved all our lives – and our parents before us – to this cheap and cheerful looking foreign muck. Well, foreign influenced anyway – just 'cos they can only calculate in *tens*! Damned liberty I call it – as indeed I do this blasted Channel Tunnel – which in my *honest* opinion will bring nowt but trouble once the initial excitement's worn off. But there you are – you can't tell 'em, can you? – and maybe it won't happen in my time anyway. The *trouble* I mean.

I'm one who's always been very proud of his heritage. In fact on 'Empire Day' at school, which was May 24th (Queen Victoria's birthday), I used to very nearly drool with envy as I watched all the other kids strutting around in their smart uniforms – Wolf-Cubs, Boy-Scouts, Boys Brigade, Church Lads Brigade, Sea-Scouts, Girl-Guides, Brownies etc – (well, not so much those last two I guess) for I never had the opportunity to join anything myself!

But I think I'd have to confess to the odd dent or two beginning to appear in this pride, for we must surely be something of a laughing stock now in the eyes of many other nations, with our lowering of standards – particularly educational in my view – the amount of bungling we accept from some of those elected to supposedly safeguard our general interests – and the rising tide of pussy-footers in the ranks of those charged with the setting out of punishments where called for. It seems now that the most heinous of crimes can attract the most ludicrous 'punishment'.

Like a fabulous holiday abroad – of several weeks duration and at a cost of many thousands of pounds – with the threat that unless the miscreant's ways are changed there's every probability they'll have to suffer a repeat! Makes my blood boil, especially when I know that I'm one of those having to foot the bill. I'd like to foot something else! This may be a rather extreme example I guess, but life itself most definitely seems to carry a very much lower value these days, well in the eyes of the law at any rate – for I wouldn't necessarily say the same of some Insurance Companies! And they say crime doesn't pay? All I can say is, if that's where *crime* gets you, lead on Macduff – lead on. Unless of course somebody has totally re-defined the word. And that wouldn't surprise me either! But I become cynical.......

But we are, I think in danger of losing our identity, which in my view would be absolute sacrilege!! Although I mustn't become political either, for I was never that kind of animal anyway. Just common-sense and logic – that's me. I hope? But I really do feel very strongly about this – particularly the Europe thing – and am further saddened by the certain knowledge that we'll never be able to put things back again, however bad they get. Like lemmings – ever onward, regardless! Or gamblers, steadfastly pursuing a vain hope that things *must* come right in the end. But how often do they? Have *you* seen any hard-up bookies? And when did you last see a lemming? Well......there you are then!

Anyway, back to the plants. Within a few weeks I had set up my territory in the south-east corner of England's green and pleasant, forming five different routes – one for each day – covering the coastline from the Isle of Sheppey to Brighton, and all the areas inland of that line – Canterbury, Faversham, The Medway Towns, Maidstone etc. Some of my calls were a bit off the beaten track, so I pretty well combed the area.

I eventually won the confidence of my customers, calling regularly and punctually – the sure way – and at Christmas I sent them all a card, personally. Which amounted to something like three hundred cards, but was well worth it, for they all responded beautifully once the season got under way again. And I soon mastered the learning of the plants, which I'm certain was helped immensely by my natural love of them.

But it was a business of high-pressure, as is the way with most selling jobs. No matter how well you were doing, the Sales Manager's whip cracked relentlessly on, and I hated passing this pressure on to my customers, who were really more like friends for the most part.

After a couple of years I bought and fitted out my own vehicle, and went it alone for a while. The other four salesmen hadn't been doing at all well, in most cases going from bad to almost zero with their sales – despite the much higher degree of affluence in their areas over mine. Especially Surrey, Berkshire, London etc. They weren't mostly cabbage and 'tater' growers up *there*. Oh no – more your stock-broker chappies in those parts. Yet it seemed that *my* route was supporting the whole depot almost. So off I went. But the pressure remained – to some degree – so I opted out once more.

One incident still draws a chuckle from me, from that era, although it didn't directly concern me and I didn't witness the actual event. I, and most other delivery people for that matter, had been on the receiving end of a bit too much hassle in the case of one particular Traffic Warden in Canterbury. I got along well with Traffic Wardens on the whole, after all, they were only doing their job, which was hard enough I guess, with them still being relatively new to the scene then. But this particular guy was trying to form the 'Fourth Reich' I should think, and he hounded us mercilessly. So I gave up on that part of my route that came under his jurisdiction, and developed some new calls further out to compensate. And it was so nice to get him off my back!

Then one day some time later, I was in the back of my vehicle doing business with a client outside his shop, in a little seaside town whose name I'd best not divulge. I was parked on the inevitable double-yellow line – which was permissible for up to twenty minutes anyway – and after about ten minutes there was a heavy pounding on my back door. I opened it, and my heart sank. It was him – bloody Adolph! Well, that was the popular name for him, if popular be the right adjective.

What the heck was *he* doing here? I thought I'd left him and his dictatorial ways back in Canterbury. He did his usual bit of mouthing off, then moved on to lay into the next guy. 'Svinehund!' I called after him – making sure he was out of earshot first – then voiced my great disappointment at his presence in this area to my client. 'You and practically everyone else in town' he replied. 'He's done just about *all* of us for parking outside our own shops whilst we load up our deliveries. He did the baker just before you arrived!' The baker's shop was right next door and I could see the baker still fuming and hopping about inside. 'I reckon there'll be a list of court cases as long as your arm' he continued, 'and he's only been in this town a week!' Evidently they'd had more than enough of him in Canterbury, and he'd been transferred here as a result.

A couple of weeks later I drew up at the same call and my client came aboard. I checked my watch and looked around for Adolph. 'If you're looking for the Fuehrer, don't bother' he said reassuringly, 'you won't be seeing him again. Well not in these parts anyway!' Then grinning from ear to ear he went on to tell me what had happened. The townsfolk had become so fed up and exasperated with his obnoxiousness that they'd decided, finally, to teach him a lesson. Well – I don't suppose the vast majority of them had any physical part in it, nor in fact any pre-knowledge of it. But the whole town rejoiced when they heard about it afterwards. One hundred per cent they did!

Apparently, three or four of them had waylaid him late-ish one evening. They'd taken him to a quieter part of town – right by the sea front – and lashed him to a lamp-post. They pulled his peaked cap right down over his eyes, then cleared off and left him there. Rumour had it that he was there all night, but somehow I doubt the truth of that bit!

It doesn't amount to much I know; you were probably expecting to read that he'd been tarred and feathered or something – debagged at least – and are suffering something of an anti-climax. But it was such an indignity and embarrassment to him – little big-shot that he was, that it sufficed as far as everyone else was concerned. He was never seen again in *that* town, nor in fact did I ever see him anywhere else after that. And it kept that little town a-buzz for a while!

But as I say, I really didn't like the pressure side of the job, and it was at this point that I did a bit of soul-searching and made the decision to return to the field of engineering, and see if I couldn't now settle to being enclosed by walls all day. It was time I settled down and looked to the future – after all – I'd had a full twenty years of chop and change since my demob from the army. That isn't to say of course that I didn't enjoy this interlude, quite the reverse in most cases, for it was spiced with a fair bit of fun and adventure. And I came into contact with so many people, from so many different walks of life.

My new job – number seventeen I think – was quite interesting, but rather wide-ranging and involved, which meant it took a lot of learning – especially in view of my extra long lay-off from engineering. But I stuck to the task and progressed quite well, and within a year took control of my department. This was against my wishes initially, and followed a week-long refresher course up in Filey. Funny how I kept finding myself back up in Yorkshire. But my predecessor had left very suddenly, and the void had to be filled – so it fell to me.

I got to grips with it, and felt after a while that I was indeed now ready to shake the wanderlust from my boots and settle down to this job for the remainder of my working life. But this wasn't to be it seemed, for after about six years the recession that has plagued the last quarter of this twentieth century began to edge in. Gently at first, but enough alas to cause the downfall of that particular firm, after having thrived a good many decades up to then. So, it was back on to life's roundabout for me again, and the rest of the staff – some of whom had been there forty years and more.

In truth I'd seen this disaster coming, and did in fact leave and install myself elsewhere just ahead of the event. Travelling was becoming difficult for me anyway at the time – I'd decided to give up motor cycling the eleven-mile cross-country journey to work, having just had my third spill on the bike. I'd suffered no more than

bad bruising to myself, but my clothing and the bike had fared rather less well. And
we didn't want the drag of another car just then. So I'd looked closer to home.

My new job was on a par with the old one regarding interest and variety, although
I was now involved with precision instruments rather than engines and machines.
Not that there isn't a high degree of precision involved in the latter, but it's quite
different. So I had lots to learn again, for our products were quite diverse in size,
construction and function. But pay and conditions were considerably better, particularly
the latter, and although it was a much bigger firm than ever I'd worked in before –
there was a staff of one hundred and forty – I fitted in well and was quite happy. And
it was only about four miles from home so I bought myself another pushbike –
Margaret needing the car for *her* daily doings – and what with pushing those old
pedals round again for forty miles each week, giving up smoking, and the job itself, I
was better off all round. And definitely ready to settle here!

But......eight years on and whammo! – it was 'everybody out' again as the
recessionary axe found it's mark once more. And this firm had prospered for more
than a hundred years up till then! There was a great deal of shock, and a good many
tears that day I can tell you, as people walked off – stupefied – into the unknown.
Again, there were many whose service with the company spanned several decades –
right from school in some cases. And friendships were many and strong – we felt on
the whole like one big happy family. Bar the inevitable one or two that is. So you can
imagine......

But such is life. You can only progress *so* far into a wood before progress
becomes retreat, and we've been pushing it for close on two thousand years now.
There's a certain inevitability about it all as I see it, but then – who am I?

Anyway, this was the pattern from here on; I found another nice, interesting little
job in the same area, despite my now advancing years. But within three years that
damned axeman was back. Amazingly enough I managed to secure another, even
better job instantly, although I was now on the threshold of my seventh decade, and
people from all age groups were frantically seeking to re-install themselves somewhere.
Anywhere in the majority of cases, as the situation continued to deteriorate. The
scarcer jobs became, the more people there were chasing them, and of course, you
still can't get a quart into a pint pot – as far as I know – although I say that tongue-
in-cheek, for whilst pigs have yet to master the art of flying, man *has* landed on the
moon!

Sadly, after two years this job followed in the wake of the rest. As did the next.
And the next! It was indeed a very, very insecure world now, as far as employment
was concerned. And what with the slump in the property market in the South East,
people were getting into all sorts of trouble. Some were fortunate enough to be

untouched by it, and of course, that 'charmed' few floated blissfully above it all as ever.

I am now in a state of semi-retirement, although not by choice I might add, for there's too much meat left on the soles of my boots yet to hang them up for good! But it does give me time to catch up on a few other things that normally get pushed aside. Such as *this* for instance; it's a few years now since I first decided I *would* have a shot at logging this......er......call it what you will. It's been picked up, put down, picked up, put down; so many times – I'm amazed I've got this far. But I'm so glad that I have, for although it might not be everybody's cup of tea, I am without any shadow of doubt a creature of the past, and I hold these memories most dear – with the odd exception or two of course – and I expect to refer to them often as my ageing memory fades.

I sometimes wonder though, where and what I might be now, had my childhood been more conventional, like sharing my own home with my own mother and father, and my two brothers. I used to look upon it as a sad loss – which indeed it was – but I'm sure I've gained lots in other ways. And I place a very high value on most things in life – and I don't mean things material – and take very little for granted.

And would I have experienced the thrill of Northampton and all its freedom, the wonderful and most pleasurable experiences – some endearingly quaint – of Yorkshire, or the lovely time I had living with Ma and Pop in London – blitz, doodlebugs and all? And would I have met my wonderful Margaret, who'll chide me for describing her thus, but God knows it's true! There have been hard times too, times of much despair in fact, but most of us have our share I guess.

But I have no regrets, and if I could see that old tiger's eye glinting at me now – up there in that dark and spooky old attic of my early childhood, I'd wink right back.